Jean

Best Wishes

I Rebecca Propst

PSYCHOTHERAPY IN A RELIGIOUS FRAMEWORK

PSYCHOTHERAPY IN A RELIGIOUS FRAMEWORK
Spirituality in the Emotional Healing Process

L. Rebecca Propst, Ph.D.
Graduate School of Professional Studies
Lewis & Clark College
Portland, Oregon

HUMAN SCIENCES PRESS, INC.
72 FIFTH AVENUE,
NEW YORK, N.Y. 10011

To DOUGLAS G. CAMPBELL,
my husband and best friend

Library of Congress Cataloging-in-Publication Data
Propst, L. Rebecca.
  Psychotherapy in a religious framework.

  Includes index.
  1. Pastoral counseling.   2. Pastoral psychology.
3. Psychotherapy.   4. Cognitive therapy.
5. Behavior therapy.   I. Title.
BV4012.2.P66   1987   253.5   86-27582
ISBN 0-89885-350-8

CONTENTS

ACKNOWLEDGMENTS

Many people have contributed to the making of this book. The counseling psychology graduate students and clergy in my summer pastoral counseling courses served as one of the first audiences for these materials. Their comments and enthusiastic support were much appreciated.

My own patients have continually challenged and inspired me as they have struggled to become whole, often in the face of difficult, and sometimes overwhelming circumstances.

I owe much to numerous researchers in psychotherapy who have given us hope that indeed it is possible to have an impact on the emotional ills that beset us.

Mike Stark, my departmental chairman, aided my writing by his tireless efforts spent in keeping an academic department running in the face of the ever present campus politics. Kay Conroy, my secretary, has worked beyond the call of duty not only in her efforts in preparing the final copy of the manuscript but in her continued helpful supporting efforts throughout the course of the writing. Her conscientiousness is much appreciated.

Numerous individuals have made comments on earlier drafts of this work, including the Rev. Claudia Johnson Bown, Presbyterian pastor; Katrina van der Horst; Dr. Karen Bates Smith, practicing clinical psychologist; and Dr. Mark Valeri, assistant professor of religious studies, Lewis and Clark College.

My husband Douglas Campbell provided much help in reading many early drafts of the materials. He has also done the drawings for the book. Finally, he provided the much needed emotional support and spiritual example for my own spiritual pilgrimage.

PUBLISHER ACKNOWLEDGMENTS

Excerpt from *The Velveteen Rabbit* by Margery Williams. Used by permission of Doubleday & Company, Inc.

Excerpts from *Revelations of Divine Love: Juliana of Norwich,* translated by M. L. del Mastro. Copyright © 1977 by M. L. del Mastro. Reprinted by permission of Doubleday & Company, Inc.

Scripture references in the present volume are from the Revised Standard Version, unless otherwise indicated.

Chapter 1

INTRODUCTION

This book has been written for two audiences. First, it is intended as a useful manual for self-growth for Christian laity. Christians seeking guidance should find some clearly defined steps for applying the latest psychological techniques in stress and depression reduction in their life. Additionally, however, they will find that the emotional maturity advocated in those steps is founded on a bedrock of spirituality. It is hoped that that individual who struggles to cope with life's uncertainties, disappointments, and conflicts will find that Christian spirituality can make some psychological sense.

Many of the approaches advocated in the book can be profitably tried by any Christian picking up this book. Do not feel, however, that you must try every technique. We all have different spiritual journeys, and the role that Christ plays in your life must be sensitively discerned. Some approaches may be less understandable or relevant for you in your present journey. It may also be that previous wounds may prevent you from appropriating Christ in some of the ways suggested in this book. If such is the case, be gentle with yourself. The different direction of your own journey from that advocated in this volume does not imply an inferior journey. Rather, this difference is an indication of the richness of diversity that God has granted to followers of the way.

Also, you must realize that most of the exercises presented in this book require you to draw upon your own past. They require you to draw upon a faith and a relationship with Christ that already has been developing. Just as it is hard for an individual to imagine a quiet relaxing scene if he has never allowed himself to be in such a situation, so it is difficult for an individual to imagine a healing compassionate Christ if Christ has never been an active part of his experience or religious understanding. This does not mean that this book is out of your reach. Rather, it means that for you it may be necessary to cultivate such a relationship with the accepting Christ. You may need to nurture such a friendship as you would a tender young plant.

The second purpose of this volume is to provide a counseling guide for clergy, pastoral counselors, and psychotherapists. For the counseling professional it is hoped that this book will promote the serious inclusion of the patients' Christian spirituality in the core and fiber of the counseling and psychotherapy process.

The need for a spiritually grounded counseling guide for pastors and clergy can be clearly seen. Pastors and clergy do an immense amount of counseling. Between 42 percent and 60 percent of people who have emotional problems turn first to clergy for counsel (Kaseman & Anderson, 1977). Frequently these clergy are called upon to deal with serious emotional problems. Furthermore, there is often the expectation that these problems will be dealt with in a religious context. Unfortunately, this is not always the case. Even though the counseling session itself may open and close with prayer, the discussion of the patient's problem may leave theology behind. Those individual pastors who do attempt to consider theology, on the other hand, may short-circuit the psychological and interpersonal aspects of the problem.

Clergy are not the only focus of this book, however. Increasingly, many psychotherapists and general counselors are being asked to deal with their patients' religious beliefs in counseling. More than 50 percent of Americans say their religious beliefs are very important to them, while only 15 percent say their religious beliefs are of little or no importance. Many of these individuals either request a religious psychotherapist or communicate to their nonreligious therapists that they wish their religious values to be taken seriously.

The present book in pastoral counseling is unique in the field in at least three respects. First, the book aims to provide a very practical step-by-step guide. Perhaps because of their emphasis on harder-to-define theological or religious concepts, pastoral counseling books often tend to be more vague regarding the counseling process than general counseling guides. This is unfortunate, because pastors who are often less experienced and well trained than other counselors, generally need more, not less specific guidance. To meet this problem, this book will follow the increasingly popular format to be found in general psychotherapy books. An easy to follow step-by-step sequencing of the counseling will be presented.

The second unique focus of the book is its emphasis on those psychotherapy techniques that the psychotherapy research literature suggests are effective treatments. The past 15 years have seen very rapid advancement in our understanding of the cause and treatment of depression and anxiety. By and large, most of this advancement has focused on a cognitive-behavioral understanding and treatment of these disorders. This approach emphasizes that the individual's thoughts and assumptions play an important role in his difficulties. The individual must learn to challenge and control these maladaptive assumptions. Additionally, the individual may need to learn new interpersonal skills. I have drawn on this rapidly growing body of knowledge and thus have focused on the cognitive-behavioral treatment of anxieties and affective disorders.

A final unique feature of this book is its active use of both theology and psychology in the counseling process. All too often, Christian spirituality has not been emphasized in pastoral counseling. The present book attempts to provide a broad-based approach to Christian spirituality that should appeal to both religious and nonreligious counselors who work with Christian patients. In this regard, the present volume is also ideally suited for seminary courses in pastoral counseling.

The spiritual focus of this book is Christian. Beyond that, however, it will be difficult for the reader to discern any strong theological bias. My intention has been to mine the riches from many of the different traditions within the Christian faith.

Even the frequent references to Barth are not meant to imply a necessarily Barthian position. It should be carefully noted that most of my references to Barth are limited to his *Church Dogmatics* volume on the creature (Vol. III, Part 2).

I have drawn from both Roman Catholic and Protestant traditions. In addition, the *Jesus Prayer* (Brianchaninov, 1860/1952) comes from Eastern Orthodox Christendom. Within Protestantism, I have quoted a variety of viewpoints ranging from the classical reformed thought of Calvin or Luther to contemporary Liberation theology. The central framework of this work is not a particular theological system. I shall leave such system-building to the theologians. They are better at it than I. I hope, however, that the reader will be able to discern a central role for the figure of Jesus. Indeed, it is my intention that Jesus the Christ represent the backbone of the counseling relationship. This centrality of Jesus Christ reflects my assumptions that it is ultimately to Jesus Christ that we turn for healing.

An elderly man, dying of cancer, came to the same conclusion. Just prior to his death, he had a period of confusion and semiconsciousness. He later became lucid again in the last few days of his life. He reported to his friends and family that during his semiconscious state he felt himself going down into a deep abyss. He felt comforted, however, by the presence of Jesus and the sense of Jesus' acceptance even while experiencing the darkness and confusion of the abyss. That experience led him later to remark to his friends that ultimately the presence of Jesus with him in the abyss was all that mattered. "Correct" theological opinions are much less important.

So it is with the counselor who is confronted with the hurt and wounded seeker. The figure of Jesus works in a multitude of ways. The presence of Christ can bring needed clarity into the darkness of emotional pain. The presence of Christ can also be the model of appropriate behavior in a confusing environment. Finally, the presence of Christ can be an assurance of acceptance in the midst of both our own and others' condemning voices. I hope, through what follows, to add to the reader's skills, knowledge, and confidence in including Christ in the emotional healing process.

All names used in examples in the text are fictitious in order to protect the identity of the original patient.

Every effort has also been made to avoid sexist language. This has generally been done by using both female and male pronouns when discussing examples. However, quotes that used "he" or "man" to express general humanity were not modified out of respect for the original authors, most of whom were writing prior to our present sensitivity to gender issues.

Finally, I have also tried to put somewhat more technical material and explanations in footnotes for the benefit of my nonpsychologist readers.

Format of Book

The discussion of each of the techniques in this volume will include some pointers that the individual using this book for personal growth may find helpful. Sometimes, I will also suggest those techniques that are probably more effectively used with a guide or counselor. However, in general, it should be noted that any technique can be tried alone if the process will help you feel better about yourself. If, however, the process seems complicated or frustrating to you, and leads you to become frustrated with yourself, that procedure is probably better done with a guide.

Counselors, clergy, and psychotherapists should also find a useful manual in this volume which will give them step-by-step procedures for teaching cognitive-behavioral techniques to their Christian patients in the context of the patients' spirituality.

Chapter 10 is a technical key to the rest of the book provided for the counselor. This chapter explains the overall outline of the procedures and refers the counselor to the relevant chapters in the remainder of the book. This chapter may be skipped by those individuals who are not primarily interested in counseling procedures.

Chapter 2 presents a brief history of this subject, as well as the reason for using cognitive behavioral therapy. Chapters 3 through 9 focus on specific aspects of emotional healing. These chapters should be of interest to the general reader as well as the counselor. Chapter 3 focuses on the nature of a healing relationship and the way in which cognitive therapy may be seen to be part of the spiritual growth process.

Chapter 4 discusses the idea and processes of self-examination. Chapters 5, 6, and 7 offer suggestions on how our pain might be transformed and examined in the light of our spirituality. Finally, Chapters 8 and 9 show by reason and example that neither emotional healing nor healthy spirituality can be theoretical. Any increase in health only becomes real when it is incarnated by actions and translated into deeds. This is the behavioral part of our transformation.

Chapter 2

BEYOND COUNSELING

Some Background Issues

The divine art of miracle is not an art of suspending the pattern
to which events conform but of feeding new events into that pattern.—C. S. Lewis, 1947, p. 61

Background Thoughts

Emotional pain is a part of life. Healing that pain is both a complex
scientific undertaking and a sacred religious task. Recently the psychological and biological sciences have been contributing intriguing
and immensely helpful pieces to the puzzle of emotional pain.

Emotional pain, however, must be touched by something deeper
than mere biology, or neural processes. Most counselors who sit face
to face with a person in the midst of a crisis, are only too aware that
there is something that they must reach in that individual before there
will be change. This "something" is just as indispensable for the behaviorist who speaks in stimulus-response terms as it is for the existentialist or humanist who speaks in terms of meaning. Mere counseling techniques, proven though they may be, will fail absolutely if
the woman or man facing us has deep despair. This individual will
wall out our techniques. Another ingredient must be added to the
process.

Jerome Franks (1982), a prominent psychotherapy researcher,

has suggested what this ingredient might be in a recent summary of counseling and psychotherapy research. He feels that successful counseling results from such factors as the somewhat undefinable healing powers of the therapist and the remoralization of the patient. We as therapists and counselors must be able to give that individual sitting in front of us hope.

There are to be found increasing numbers of writers, both theologians and psychologists who are eager to talk about this special ingredient which seems to be so necessary in counseling. Some call it placebo (cf. Prioleau, Murdock, & Brody, 1983) and others call it positive expectations (Wilkins, 1979). Still others, primarily theologians and humanistic psychologists, call this ingredient spirit. Christian writers may call this spirit *Spirit*, meaning the spirit of the transcendent God, present in Christ.

Hope, positive expectations, placebo, spirit—perhaps all of these terms are attempting to define that seemingly undefinable ingredient that needs to be present in the moments of emotional healing. We grasp for something more than mere procedures or techniques, when confronted with emotional pain.

This thirst for something deeper to touch our emotional pain is a thirst for the ultimate fulfillment of our desires, which is God. Christians experiencing grief are not content with a narrow view of themselves and their universe. They feel boxed in. They struggle for a broader perspective that would enable them to transcend, and yes, even laugh at their emotional pain. The recent popularity of the book, *The Road Less Traveled* by M. Scott Peck (1978), among nonreligious as well as religious individuals, is one example of this struggle for a larger perspective.

Anyone who observes emotional pain sees an individual struggling to make sense of her experiences. These individuals strive to step outside their experiences and see them from a different angle. They seek a way to transcend their chaotic confusion. They grope for an ultimate vantage point that will allow their predicament to be seen in a different light. Christian faith teaches that the ultimate transcendent perspective is to be found in God, as revealed in Jesus Christ.

This book is an attempt to consider seriously the role of the individual's Christian spirituality in the counseling process. It has in common with a number of other writers, (for example, Adrian Van Kaam, 1976; Thomas Merton, 1961; and Thomas Oden, 1967) a serious commitment to a spiritual dimension that cannot be completely reduced to or explained by the psychological.

A commitment to the spiritual does not deny a commitment to the scientific. One does not replace the other. Rather, the spiritual may be seen to complement and extend the scientific.

The current work will use some concepts from the cognitive-behavioral psychotherapy model which has been shown to be very effective in treating depression and anxiety. This model is based on two primary components, as its name implies. First, the model asserts that the cognitions, or thoughts, ideas, and assumptions of an individual are an important determiner of that person's emotional state. (See Figure 2-1.) These thoughts influence emotions and behaviors, which in turn influence other thoughts.

These thoughts and assumptions must be modified for health to be regained. The behavioral component of this term implies that the individual must be taught new behaviors.

Although techniques that have been labeled "behavioral" will play an important role in this book, merely using them does not make one a philosophical behaviorist. It has been repeatedly emphasized in the psychotherapy field that theoretical beliefs and specific intervention techniques are not necessarily connected. Knowledge gained from scientific observation may be interpreted differently in different philosophical systems.

For example, setting specific concrete limits for children has been observed to be helpful for children's self-esteem. Both radical behaviorists and Christians assert that these rules are helpful and beneficial for the children. However, they may give alternative and, indeed, vastly different philosophical reasons for the validity of these rules. They interpret the same observation differently within their alternative systems. Thus, procedures are applied in the present volume if psychotherapy research and observation has found them to be valid and effective. The rationale for their effectiveness can be presented at many different levels.

A final note about my choice of terminology in this work is due at this point. The individual sitting in front of us in the counseling session has usually been referred to as either the client or the patient. Both of these terms have limitations. *Client* refers to one who pays for services, and a *patient* is one who is ill and is healed by another. Neither of these terms adequately communicate the idea of a dynamic relationship of mutuality which should be the norm of counseling.

The Christian tradition provides alternative terms for the counselor such as comforter, advocate, helper, or supporter. As counselors we model the activities of one such as Jesus or the Holy Spirit. In the

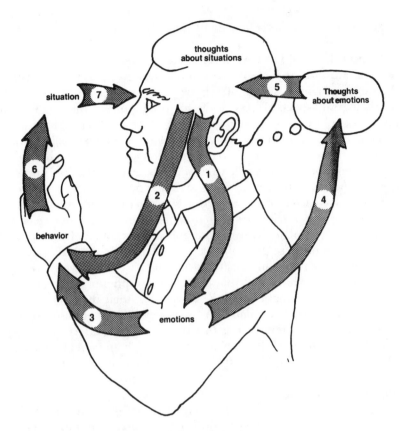

Figure 2-1

The relationships between an individual's thoughts, emotions, and behaviors. Thoughts influence emotions (1) and behaviors (2). Emotions influence behaviors (3) and our thoughts about our emotions (4). Our thoughts about our emotions, in turn, influence our thoughts about situations (5).

Finally, our behaviors influence the situation (6), and the situation influences our thoughts about a situation (7).

Johannine writings, these helping activities were referred to as the activities of the Paraclete (Behm, 1967, pp. 800–814). Unfortunately, however, no alternative terms for the one being helped are readily suggested by our tradition. Therefore, *patient* will be used when one word is necessary. Effort will be made, however, to expand the sense of this term beyond its traditional meaning.

Brief History of Psychotherapy and Religion

Recently there has been a renewed interest in the psychology of religion. Most of the focus of this interest, however, has been on either the developmental aspects of religion (e.g., Fowler, 1981), its social psychological aspects (Dittes, 1969), or the nature of the religious or mystical experience itself (e.g., Hood & Morris, 1981). Religion as a psychotherapeutic modality has received little attention. Spilka, Hood, and Gorsuch (1985), in their recent psychology of religion text, only lightly touch on the possibility that religious experience itself may be therapeutic. They briefly mention several types of religious phenomena which have been discussed with respect to their therapeutic value.

Among the possibilities that they mention are intense religious experience, glossolalia, conversion, and prayer (pp. 301–305). Most of the studies of these phenomena concentrated on analyzing the nature of the experience in question. In each case there have been some studies that have indicated that each of these phenomena may have some therapeutic benefits. Definite answers on their therapeutic value, however, are not yet available. An overview of the question of psychotherapy and religion reveals that the therapeutic effects of religion have been examined only as correlates of the phenomena in question. There have been few if any attempts actively to use religious activities or phenomena as treatments for emotional problems in controlled clinical trial studies.

Meadow and Kahoe (1984) also mention religious healing in their text and briefly discuss the parallels between psychotherapy and conversion and repentance. Generally, both practices involve, first, a realization that one's present life is unsound and, then, an attempt to change that life. Extensive research in this area, however, does not yet exist.

Early in our history, psychotherapy and religious healing were synonymous. Calestro (1972) contends that psychotherapy is actually the "bastard progeny" of a long tradition of neoreligious and magical practices that have been part of all cultures. He suggests that both primitive healing and contemporary psychotherapy depend primarily upon suggestibility, trust, and hope for the source of their therapeutic effects. These factors influence the individual's expectations that, indeed, something will happen. Emotional symptoms found throughout the world are generally shaped by the local beliefs, norms, and general patterns of living in a particular culture. Native Americans, for example, have described more than 20 different kinds of depression.

(Shore & Manson, 1981). Therefore, it is important that the healing methods also conform to the beliefs of the culture. In many primitive cultures, the religious shaman held an important role as both a physical and psychological healer. He or she healed by using the local religious beliefs of the culture and the heightened emotions of the patient to create a sacred atmosphere (Calestro, 1972). The healing act itself was part of a religious ritual, and the healer was perceived as receiving power from the supernatural. Healing generally involved both emotional release and guilt reduction, but this could only occur when the patient shared the beliefs and values of the healer and of their community.

These early links between psychological healing and religion were carried into Christianity with the advent of pastoral care and counseling. Faith healing, meditation, and confession all played psychological as well as spiritual roles in the individual's life. (See *Pastoral Care in Historical Perspective* by Jaeckel & Clebsch, 1964).

Both Calestro (1972) and Prince (1973) have suggested that a closer examination of the role of healer among primitive peoples, and in religious contexts, may help us to understand more fully the psychological healing process. Indeed, aspects of primitive healing such as positive expectations of help, specific mysterious techniques which the patient does not clearly understand, heightened emotions and a shared belief system between patient and therapists, all seem to be part of modern psychotherapy. (The modern belief system which the patient and therapist share is a belief in the validity and wonder of science.)

In contrast to all previous periods of history, the twentieth century has seen a split between the arena of emotional healing and spirituality. Freud considered religion a neurotic attempt to remain a dependent child with God as a parent. He noted that there was a close resemblance between religious ritual and compulsions, and considered religious training responsible for much neurotic misery. For Freud, religion induced illness because the demands of religion, and early religious influences, caused us to repress certain impulses. In fact, in his early work, Freud (1911/1958) stated that this denial of certain aspects of ourselves, which he labeled repression, was the chief cause of mental illness, because the denied aspects of ourselves later become symptoms.[1]

After Freud opened the twentieth century with his hostile volleys toward religion, his younger contemporary, Jung, followed with a completely different point of view. Carl Jung has made some of the most historically significant contributions in this century to our thinking on the interrelationship of psychotherapy and religion. Jung extended Freud's concept of a personal unconscious (consisting of repressed earlier experiences) to include a universal or collective unconscious. The collective unconscious includes universal ideas that typically have a large emotional component, and thus provoke strong emotions in the individual. These ideas (called archetypes) are often expressed as religious symbols in any culture. Jung thus provided a dynamic model for the role and source of religion in the individual's life. A wider consciousness and the experience and expression of these "religious" ideas or archetypes are part of the goals of Jungian analysis (Jung, 1954/1959).

After 80 years of animosity between the theory and practice of psychotherapy and religion (significantly interrupted only by Jung), the pendulum has swung the other way. Recent psychotherapy research has again begun to consider religious or semireligious themes in its compass. At least two streams of current or recent developments relevant to both religious themes and psychotherapy exist: work on meditation and on the placebo response.

The study of meditation has figured prominently in the current relationship between emotional healing and psychotherapy and spirituality.

Shapiro (1980) defines meditation as a conscious attempt to focus attention in a nonanalytic way. It is an attempt not to dwell on discursive ruminative thought. There are two broad categories of meditation. In concentrative meditation one learns to focus one's attention imperturbably on a specific object, such as one's breath, an emotion, an idea, or an external object (Walsh, 1983). In mindful meditation, however, the individual is open to everything, focusing on whatever passes through one's field of awareness. Delmonte (Delmonte & Kenney, 1985) states that the goal of mindful meditation is to come to know one's own mental processes and thus to begin to have the power to change or control those processes. In both types of meditation one merely observes one's thoughts, rather than entering into dialogue with them. Thoughts are allowed to come and go. Regardless of what comes into awareness, the individual maintains a relaxed neutral attitude (Shapiro, 1980).

Clinical research has suggested that meditation is very similar to other self-regulation strategies that have come out of the cognitive-behavioral research paradigm, such as learning to monitor and modify one's thoughts (Shapiro, 1980; Zuroff & Schwartz, 1978). The crucial components of any meditation, whether it be TM, a simple focusing on breathing, or focusing on a religious object, appear to be positive expectations, increased self-observation, an ability to focus thoughts in an unperturbed manner, and a relaxation response that results in decreased oxygen use.

More recently, meditative states have been likened to the cognitive therapy process of becoming aware of how one views one's world. Indeed the capacity to "let go," which is often associated with meditation, has been seen as necessary before one can integrate new elements into one's view of the world (cf. Delmonte & Kenny, 1985). Shapiro (Shapiro & Zifferblatt, 1976) describes the meditative process as a cognitive process in which the individual watches his thoughts and gradually becomes desensitized to them. As he watches his thoughts, he changes his mind about them. The neutral observation of thoughts coming and going results in the set that such thoughts are acceptable. Shapiro compares this process to a process of systematic desensitization, in which we become desensitized to a negative object or situation by learning to stay relaxed as we gradually approach it. We are still thinking. Our attitude is changed, however. These disturbing thoughts are no longer defined as disturbing. Shapiro feels that this role of meta-cognitions (thoughts about thoughts) is insufficiently acknowledged in the Eastern tradition, in its claims of emptying the mind. The individual is still thinking; he is merely thinking only about what thoughts are in the mind.

The recent attention give to meditation in clinical research is notable. It signals the possibility that the therapeutic effects of processes associated with some religious practices may be more closely examined.

Recent research into the nature and impact of placebos on clinical change is the second type of research that may build more bridges between psychotherapy and religion.

Prioleau, Murdock, and Brody (1983) state that a definition of a placebo is an effective treatment that does not contain any therapeutic components. The problem, however, is that we do not know, at present, enough about psychotherapy to be sure that the placebo in question actually does *not* have any therapeutic components. Indeed, Wilkins (1983) contends that some treatments may be effective simply because they engender a type of placebo process. Kazdin (in Wilkins, 1979) feels that nonspecific placebo factors are part of all effective treatments. The goal is not to demonstrate that our treatments are free of nonspecific placebo factors, but that they go *beyond* those factors.

Ross and Olson (1981) go further, and propose that the placebo—changing our expectations and thoughts about our world—*is* actually the *treatment*. These changed expectations in turn may lead to greater compliance with instructions, changed attributions regarding the cause of a problem, or even a greater tendency to interpret ambiguous sensations or situations positively. It is possible that a more positive set, or expectations, may also trigger the release of endorphines, which are naturally occurring relaxants produced by the body. Because expectations are strongly influenced by our beliefs and values, the most effective way to enhance those expectations and the effectiveness of the treatment is to frame the treatment in the language of the belief system of the patient, such as was done in primitive psychotherapy. One study by the author (Propst, 1980) found that the use of the patient's religious values does indeed enhance treatment efficacy.

The recent attention given to the role of placebo in psychotherapy, especially within the cognitive-behavioral paradigm, may be setting the stage for a return to procedures similar to the early relationship between religion and psychotherapy.

Why Cognitive Therapy and Not Jung?

We previously noted that the one exception to the animosity between psychotherapy and religion since Freud has been the work of Carl Jung. It is important, therefore, to point out the similarities and differences between Jung's approach and that of the present work.

Jung asserts that woman and man must be transformed into wholeness. The problem, according to Jung, is that the typical individual has cut off from himself much of his being and awareness (Jung 1957/1970). The healthy individual, however, is able to recognize all sides of himself, including opposites, such as selfishness and altruism. Jungian analysis provides an opportunity for the individual to explore the unknown or dark sides of themselves with someone else.

Symbols, including religious symbols, are the real integrators in this exploration process. All of the conflicting ideas and chaos that an individual may experience become organized around a certain idea or symbol derived from the individual's collective unconscious. The clue to putting both sides together for the individual comes from the individual's dreams. In Jungian analysis, however, this integration of the opposites and the many aspects of the self into a meaningful whole is usually not, according to Jung, actively pursued by thinking or understanding. Rather, the path toward unification of the opposites in the individual's personality is directed by that person's unconscious.

Teleology is the driving force in Jung. For Jung, this means that life does not proceed randomly. It is purposive, or teleological, and shaped by beckoning goals. There is always a force within us that is pushing us towards wholeness, and we attain harmony when we are in tune with that force. In some sense we must wait for the unconscious to give us direction. Both the patient and the therapist sit back and watch the unconscious work. The goal of the Jungian is not to become open only to the unconscious, but to this directive force within the psyche that unifies the opposites (Jocabi, 1973).

Jung has been an important figure in religious psychotherapy because of his contention that it is religious symbols arising from the unconscious that perform an integrating function in our lives. According to Jung, these symbols are reflected in all of the religions of the world. Jung has reawakened us to the value of religion in our emotional lives and he has provided a psychological explanation for the value of religion that has helped some people believe again. His use of symbols has drawn a dynamic connection between emotional healing and spirituality. However, his model has limitations. Therefore, while recognizing the immense value of Jung's work as an explanation of the importance of religion in the personality, we will add more directive elements to the role of religious faith in psychotherapy that are not present in some forms of traditional Jungian analysis.

Currently, cognitive therapy has several advantages over Jungian analysis. First of all, we have some evidence that it "works." A clinical technique must be clinically powerful enough to justify its use. It must provide sufficient relief of suffering and enhanced ability to cope with life's tragedies to make it worth the time and effort to learn and use it. Most of the clinical procedures of cognitive therapy have been widely researched, and the results are encouraging. Jungian analysis, thus far, has not received that kind of scrutiny. For example, The *Handbook of Psychotherapy and Behavior Change*, (Garfield & Bergin, 1978), a standard reference that summarizes the research support for the effectiveness of various treatments, makes only one reference to brief Jungian therapy, and that reference showed brief Jungian therapy to be no more effective than a control group with no therapy. Thus, though that volume contained numerous references to research on behavior therapies, cognitive therapies, various types of group therapies, marital and family therapies, and psychoanalytic therapy, indicating substantial examination of the effectiveness of those treatments, Jungian therapy cannot claim the same statistics.

Cognitive therapy may have a second psychological advantage over Jungian analysis. The teleological basis of Jungian analysis may encourage a passive waiting on direction from the unconscious, as was noted above. Recent research, however, suggests that it is usually more effective to encourage an individual suffering from depression or anxiety to take an active approach to problems. Jung emphasizes that our integration comes not by means of thinking, understanding, or explaining our life. Rather, both the patient and the therapist sit back and watch the unconscious bring about that integration. An active coping style, however, is advocated for those with affective disorders, or anxiety. (See Woolfolk & Lehrer, 1984.) Both Jungian analysis and cognitive therapy stress the development of a broader, more inclusive and adaptive perspective. In cognitive therapy, however, this perspective is pursued in a more active manner, as this volume will demonstrate.

A third and related point is that Jungian analysis emphasizes only increased awareness of self. Cognitive therapy, while advocating such an awareness, goes further to emphasize that the individual must actively transform that awareness via cognitive restructuring. For example, contrary to popular misconception, dream analysis can also play an important role in cognitive therapy. According to the cognitive therapy model, the dream dramatizes an individual's self-image and world-view. Dreams are a clue to the individual's underlying automatic thoughts or assumptions. In contrast to Jung's approach, however, in cognitive therapy, the individual can deliberately change the content of the dream images and does not have to wait for the dream to change itself (Beck & Emery, 1979, pp. 75–76).

Finally, since the techniques of cognitive therapy are more clearly specified, they are more easily learned than are dynamic procedures by pastors and pastoral counselors engaged in emotional healing via the individual's spirituality.

Jungian analysis must also be evaluated from the standpoint of Christian spirituality as well as from that of psychotherapy research. This context raises several concerns.

First, although we learn as Christians that true spirituality and emotional healing are expressed in community, the formative and redemptive role of our relations with others is not emphasized in Jung. In Christianity, one responds to the other as a true other, not merely as a projection of oneself. Jung is not clear on this distinction.

Secondly, Jung assumes that *knowledge* of wider consciousness leads to a more authentic existence. Christian spirituality, on the other hand, emphasizes that the infusion of an enabling *grace* leads to such an existence. Grace comes from our focus on God rather than ourselves. For Jung, the integrating symbol of one's existence is not necessarily the transcendent God. Integration might come in either direction, either towards or away from God. True Christian spirituality, however, is to meet Jesus, crucified and risen, and thereby to face ourselves. We face our dark areas and our shadow side even while in the presence of the risen Christ.

In summary, the difference between cognitive therapy and Jungian analysis is one of emphasis. In both cases there is emphasis on increased awareness of the unknown parts of ourselves, and an integration of those parts into a fuller self. Cognitive therapy suggests a more active pursuit of these goals. In both cases, the religious thoughts and assumptions of the individual can be an important part of therapy. Cognitive therapy, itself, however, unlike Jungian analysis, does not propose a religious reason to account for the importance of these values. Christian spirituality is freer to provide its own reasons within the context of cognitive therapy.

Chapter 3

THE HEALING PARTNERSHIP

Inward Examination and Outward Relationships

A man who confesses his sins in the presence of a brother knows
that he is no longer alone with himself; he experiences the presence of God in the reality of the other person.
—Dietrich Bonhoeffer, 1954, p. 116

A Healing Partnership

Emotional healing is craved by all persons. Life's experiences too
often leave us bruised and fractured. We feel the accumulated stresses
and ravages on our egos and emotions. Each day brings with it new
onslaughts, new persons to impress, new circumstances to outmaneu-
ver, and new thoughts to subdue. Ultimately life takes its toll on us.

We want to clean out the residues, and heal the wounds. We want
to let down, to relax, to become as a little child.

We search for sources of healing by seeking out relationships.
Some of us mentally go through our address book ostensively looking
for someone to spend an afternoon with, play tennis with, or eat dinner
with. What we really want is a healer, a relationship where we can feel
acceptance, a relationship where we can get rid of the residues. For
many of us, there are moments of despair when we realize that there
are very few of those relationships in our lives.

There are also those individuals among us who contend that

relationships will always disappoint. They may label themselves as contemplatives, or individualists. Healing comes from within, they say. They claim that they are not interested in the approval of others, but must find themselves. These people may avoid others. They may wall themselves off from either the support or scrutiny of others. Sometimes they may use others as only an extension of themselves.

Neither the avoider nor the seeker of relationships will find healing, for true healing does not come totally from our relationships with others, nor totally apart from our relationships with them.

Mardi Horowitz (1978), a psychodynamic psychiatrist, contends that there are two components of any effective healing situation. First, healing happens in the context of relationships which, in the counseling situation, means the relationship between the therapist and the patient. In everyday life this means the relationship between the individual and his friends, spouse, or family. The relationship allows us to check out our inner feelings and thoughts with someone else, with reality. We need to ask our spouse what he thinks of our anger at our neighbor; we ask our best friend what he thinks of our work; we may break into tears, perhaps secretly hoping the one we are with will put his or her arm around us, or say they understand. We must feel validated. We need room to relive our negative relationships from the past. We need room to try out new ideas and this time to receive a positive response from others. Some psychologists call the reliving of relationships from the past *transference,* meaning that we transfer our feelings and thoughts about past relationships to our present relationships.

If we have some reasonably good supportive relationships, we *risk.* We risk trying out new behaviors, sharing our emotions. We risk sharing our inner thoughts. We risk examining ourselves.

This inner examination is the second necessary ingredient of emotional healing. Mardi Horowitz calls this process "working through." Healing will not come without the repeated review of ideas and feelings, in order to see them from another perspective. We must examine the way we think about ourselves and our current struggles and emotional pains. This means examining our memories, our internal images, and our thoughts and actions, to understand what they are. Ultimately, we must struggle to change those images and thoughts. They must be seen in a more positive light.

The healing relationship and the healing self-examination are the subjects of this chapter.

The Therapeutic Relationship

Our relationship with others.   A healthy therapeutic relationship with another human being must have several ingredients. First, psychoanalysts such as Horowitz (1978) emphasize that a therapeutic relationship must provide one with *a safe place*. Ordinarily we are fearful, and this fear makes us move away from others. We keep a "safe" distance. We fear lest the person we perceive ourselves to be is found wanting, yet we still desire a safe intimate relationship. We do not want to be alone. It is this relationship that allows us to display ourselves, our ideas, our feelings, and our passions, without fear that such displays will be trampled beneath others' judgments, or quenched by others' disregard, or their indifference. Safety is thus one primary ingredient of a therapeutic relationship.

In cognitive psychotherapy the healer must provide a healing relationship, a relationship of trust. The relationship itself may not be the primary instrument of change, but without the healer's genuine interest and regard, the techniques are useless (Beck, Rush, Shaw, & Emery, 1979). The healer must provide some gentle encouragement for the hurting person to examine his thoughts and feelings. All of the patient's views are heard. Some views are given alternatives. The patient need not fear that the guide will show lack of interest, disapproval, disappointment, or impatience at his attempts to gain autonomy. In this way, cognitive therapy provides a haven, which allows one to *risk* again in the outside world.

Autonomy is strengthened and encouraged in any good cognitive therapy. In fact, the encouragement of independence is one of the prime contributors of the cognitive therapy model to our understanding of healing relationships. Both the therapist and the patient work together to help the patient find new ways to think about and react to his world. The patient accepts the challenge of finding a new way to live and a new self-image. Ultimately, both counselor and patient establish a collaborative covenant of mutual acting. Directions and models for transforming thoughts are provided by the therapist, but the patient is ultimately the captain who makes the final choices and tests the new models. Autonomy and the encouragement of independence rather than dependence is one of the prime contributions of cognitive therapy to the notion of a healthy relationship. Sometimes, in the past, psychoanalysis has been guilty of encouraging too much dependence in the patient on the therapy; so the encouragement of autonomy must remain a very important ingredient in a good therapeutic relationship.

Gradually the patient is able to trust the counselor as a source of both benevolent care and wise guidance. The patient also becomes more vulnerable by ceasing to analyze everything that happens in the relationship. The relationship becomes *experienced*, not just analyzed. In this process, the patient ceases looking at the relationship and the counselor, and begins to examine himself. He is unafraid to reveal himself to the other.

The cognitive-behavioral therapist takes a somewhat more active role in the healing relationship than the analyst. She may actively direct, exhort, compliment, support, or challenge. At times, she exhibits some vulnerability by modeling responses. The psychoanalytic therapist maintains more neutrality, and is less likely to suggest responses. Both allow the individual freedom to explore all possibilities in a collaborative fashion. An individual must be given intimacy, direction, and support. The closeness that develops must not, however, obliterate differences. The individual must ultimately have freedom to develop himself in his own way.

Psychotherapists, regardless of their orientation, consider healthy human relationships to be indispensable for wholeness. Christian theologians have also talked about the health that is inherent in our relationships with others. Our true humanness is best exemplified by Jesus. He was "a man for others" (Karl Barth, 1960, p. 203). He placed himself in solidarity with others. He joined his emotions and feelings to the pain and emotions of others. Several times in the New Testament, the writer comments that Jesus had *pity* on those he was with. Barth (p. 211) notes that this pity of Jesus is often described by a Greek verb which in the New Testament is applied only to Jesus himself. This verb implies that the suffering and sin of the other went right into the heart of Jesus, so that their plight was his own. The word denotes a movement in the "bowels" or the innermost parts, and is an intense form of compassion. For example, in Matthew 9:56, Jesus experienced this emotion toward the crowds who had no shepherd. If you have ever seen someone else in pain and felt an ache in your stomach for that person, you can understand some of this compassion. If you have lain awake at night searching for a way to ease that other's pain, you know something of the tenderness of Jesus.

Jesus did not merely help others from a safe distance, he put himself in their place. He died for others (John 3:16). He gave his body for others (John 6:51). He *was for others*. Indeed, the meaning of his existence and his identity is to be found in his relationship with others.

Psychological science has documented the importance of our relationships with others for our own self-identities. In fact, most schools have asserted that we gain self-definition only as we study how others react to us. "We see ourselves as we see other people seeing us" (George Herbert Mead, 1934). Our identity comes to reflect the views of those around us, like a looking-glass. We gain our self-definitions from our parents and significant others (cf. Gergen, 1971), who serve as a mirror.

Karl Barth (1960) has captured this mirror phenomenon in theological terms. He has said that we are only an "I" in relationship to others. We can only have an "I" if there is a "thou." He considers that the minimum definition of humanity is being in encounter (p. 247ff). The really uniquely human thing that we do is not eating, or sleeping, or even thinking: it is being human with another person. This being human with another is not a superficial presence. Humanness involves actions. It is modeling the humanness of Jesus.

First, being human with another is looking them in the eye. To look one in the eye is to allow oneself to be seen and to see the other; then we allow ourselves to be known by the other. Karl Barth has remarked that, "true humanity consists of mutual speech and hearing" (p. 252). We listen to the other and their understanding of themselves as we share our own understanding of ourselves. We must accept that our understanding of each other is incomplete, and we must dialogue, to gain a greater understanding of the other.

Finally, according to Barth, true humanity consists of rendering mutual assistance to each other gladly. We must place ourselves at the service of others. In all of these actions we are following the model of Jesus.

The encounter described above must not be something that is prescribed from outside. It is something chosen freely by the participants. We are together by inner, not outer necessity.

To this picture of mutual assistance, however, Barth adds two caveats. First, one should not lose oneself in the other. No person can forget her own life, tasks, and responsibilities. One individual is not a copy of another individual. We do not copy the other, but instead seek our own vocation. Secondly, one should not seek to control the other, to use the other merely as an extension of one's own being. We are not with the other, merely to find ourselves in the other. Rather, we encounter and respect the other as an independent human being. Basic humanity is free association. Each individual is given the freedom to be herself in the relationship.

A true healing relationship is also one in which the healer and patient "look each other in the eye." This is certainly true for the patient. The patient must feel that she or he is truly known by the other, in order to be open to suggestions for change from the other. The healer must also allow herself to be seen, or to be known. This may not mean that the healer shares as much detail as the patient. What is shared, however, must be genuine. In cognitive therapy, the healer shares by modeling whole behavior for the other, by being genuine with the other. The healer is not for herself but for the other. What is shared is for the other. Self-disclosure of the healer is and must always be offered with the patient's welfare in mind.

The whole counseling relationship is a process of mutual speech and hearing. The first task of any counselor is listening. ". .Everyone should be quick to listen, slow to speak, and slow to become angry" (James 1:19). Healing in any relationship depends upon each person being heard by the other. The patient must feel that he has been heard and understood; so the good healer must develop observational skills. When teaching counseling to students, I usually have them spend hours listening to videotapes of individuals for whom they have no background data. They are often surprised to learn that they can obtain much information and understanding merely by hearing and watching. Of course, true healing will only come when the patient also has been able to hear and understand the healer.

Giving mutual assistance gladly is a capstone of the counseling relationship. First, and most obviously, the counselor must really care for the patient, and be eager to give help. Any indication of resistance to dealing with the patient will be perceived by that individual, and the relationship will not develop as it should.

I recall during my training period in graduate school having difficulty with one particular patient. This particular individual would not respond to anything I tried. Finally, my supervisor commented, "On a scale of 1 to 10, how much do you like this person?" When I did not answer the question directly, my supervisor repeated it. I realized then that only my *glad and freely given* assistance would have any impact. If I did not like the individual, I should not be working with him. The counselor renders a great deal of sacred assistance. When we express acceptance to that individual sitting in front of us we become a mediator of divine grace to that person. We take the patient's chaos and confusion and emotional suffering into ourselves, and we give them a corrective emotional experience by helping them to sort through and relabel their thoughts and feelings. They use not only their experience with us to aid this process, but their experiences with others in their present environment. Thus, our service to others cannot be motivated by guilt, or it will be given and perceived as involuntary. Our service to others is truly whole only when it is motivated by love.

I believe the therapeutic relationship is one of *mutual* assistance because the patient must also give to the one seeking to help. The strength of cognitive therapy is that the patient is challenged to autonomy. The patient must risk new behaviors in the environment, and actively try on new ways of thinking. Only when the one seeking help makes the active choices, and recognizes that the helping process has been mutual and collaborative, will healing occur. The healer is not a doctor who does things to the patient, but a coach who helps the patient to do things for herself. This mutuality is needed to allow the patient to maintain a sense of identity. Dependence upon the therapist is neither necessary nor desired.

The importance of fostering self-autonomy in counseling cannot be overemphasized. Neither can the temptation to take it away. Unfortunately, many patients will also try to please the therapist by giving away their autonomy.

A young woman who had a history of depression and emotional abuse by her siblings had signed up for one of my workshops which was oriented not only towards professional counselors, but clergy and laity. One day, during the course of the workshop, she shared with the entire group her frustrations over her younger brother (age twelve) who continually insulted and belittled her. She was twenty-nine, and, due to her depression, was living at home. All of the members of the group, without exception, began to give her advice about the problem. Most were professional counselors. She listened to each politely and tried to understand how she could implement their suggestions. I stopped the process with my comment:

"What do *you* want?"

She was puzzled, and asked, "What do you mean?"

I repeated, "What do *you* want from your family?"

She remained confused, and said, "I am not sure what you mean."

"What do *you* want?

"I am not sure."

"What do you want to do?—*you* have to decide."

"I want to hit my brother."

"What do you really want from your family?" As I said this, I sat up straighter in the chair and looked straight at her.

She looked back at me and said again, "I am not sure."

"What do *you want?* It is your choice."

She paused, looked at me intensely, and then looked as if she was going to cry. Finally, she sat up straighter and said; "I want some respect."

"How do *you* want to get it?" I repeated.

She paused, and said, "I don't know."

At that point, I dropped the interaction, and told her that it was certainly her choice.

She commented, "You know, I really felt empowered when we talked. I had never realized before that it was up to me."

Any relationship that fosters healing has the characteristics of acceptance, and respect for autonomy.

Our relationship with God.   Prince (1973) has said that a good therapeutic relationship is not unlike one's relationship with God. In both, the person develops a healthy dependence upon another, and has a measure of unreasoned belief in that other's abilities. In both cases the seeker is willing to try new experiences, to probe new questions, and to risk new adventures. All of these actions are undertaken, even though the person is fearful, uncertain of the outcome, and often unsure as to the next step. In giving the counselor some benevolent authority over oneself, one often finds oneself on a faith journey into a new and more adaptive, personally satisfying manner of living. The counselor is not given authority merely because she is perceived to be benevolent and caring. She is not given authority merely because she is perceived to be a wise guide. Rather, the counselor is given some authority and attention because she is perceived to understand the other's pain.

Christian spirituality is similar. We have a caring God made real in our experiences through Jesus Christ. The Christian mystics such as Juliana of Norwich (1392/1977) have emphasized Jesus's tender care for us. Juliana reminds us that Christ looks at us with love. She also reminds us that Jesus delights to dwell with us and would not choose to dwell in any other place (cf. p. 186). We have a wise God who is ruler of the universe. Ultimately, however, God's love is most therapeutic because it is empathetic. Hebrews 4:15 states . . . "For we have not a high priest that cannot empathize with the feelings of our infirmities, but one that has been in all points tempted like as we are, yet without sin." The Greek word, *empatheo*, (empathize) is closest to our word empathy, the primary activity of the therapist.

My patients have often remarked that learning to empathize with Jesus and understand that he felt great desolation and abandonment in his Passion gave new meaning to their own desolation. Merely reading the scripture as a doctrinal or religious exercise was not helpful. But seeing Jesus as a real human person, who also struggled, *was*.

A healing relationship with another and a healing relationship with God have some similarities, as we have noted. The differences are obvious. The human healer is finite in wisdom, caring, and empathy. Often we see that finiteness only too clearly. God is infinite in wisdom, caring, and empathy, but we are unable to see those qualities clearly in our present existence. " . . . Now we see but a poor reflection; then we shall see face to face. Now I know in part; then I shall know fully, even as I am fully known" (1 Cor. 13:12, NIV).

Our healing relationship with the infinite God is perfect but never seen clearly in this existence. Our healing relationships with finite others are imperfect, but these relationships are more clearly perceived by us. Both of these relationships are necessary. Indeed, without some form of healing from both of those directions in our life, we cease to be human.

Karl Barth (1960) notes that real humanness is being called by God (p. 150ff.). We are human as we are confronted by the divine other in Jesus. Barth notes further that to be human is to be with God. We must hear that we are beings derived, grounded, determined, and conditioned by God. To be human is to be called and summoned by God and to hear that call and respond to it. We then live our human lives as an answer to this call or summons of God. We come to God and are accepted and received.

To be told that we are human when we hear the call of God and respond to it seems irrelevant to our everyday experience.

What is relevant to our everyday experience is the sameness that we experience. Each morning seems remarkably like the previous morning. Each sleepy-eyed trek to the kitchen for our morning coffee seems reminiscent of something we did before. Each person we see in our office, or each package we send or deliver seems just like the package we delivered last year. Each day we leave the workplace, or take food out of the freezer for the evening meal, does not seem any more interesting than it did the day before. Some of us shut out the boredom by watching television. We then despair that the evening was wasted. At the same time we are relieved. At least we weren't bored that evening. At the same time we hope that eventually there will be something more. The popular song *Is That All There Is?* haunts even us Christians at times. Occasionally we think of our own death.

That thought causes a quiet crisis, and has even been labeled the mid-life crisis.

Usually, we are just part of the crowd. Sometimes that suits us fine. Sometimes blending in with others gives us a comfortable feeling of belonging, of anonymity. Nothing is expected. At other times we feel the loss of something. There must be something more. For some people, this feeling is subtle. For others, the summons to something else comes like an electric shock.

The character Mole in Kenneth Grahame's *Wind in the Willows* (1965), is one who experienced this shock. He and his friend Rat were trudging home on a late winter's evening, each of them thinking their own thoughts—about supper and a warm fire. Grahame writes:

> Suddenly. . . . it was one of those. . . . calls from out the void that suddenly reached Mole. . . . making him tingle through and through with its very familiar appeal, even while yet he could not clearly remember what it was. . . . He stopped dead in his tracks. . . his nose searching hither and thither in its efforts to recapture . . . the telegraphic current, that had so strongly moved him. . . . A moment, and he had caught it again. . . . Home! . . . . The call was clear, the summons was plain. He must obey it instantly. (pp. 78–79)

Despite the Rat's insistence and the approaching snow, Mole found it difficult, and indeed, impossible to go on in his usual way. His sobs soon convinced Rat that they had to go back. There really was no choice in the matter. And so they did. And so Mole found his lost home.

Mole's sudden sense of something added, of something different, of something familiar, but forgotten, changed his course. God's call to us is also that sense of something added, of something different, of something familiar but forgotten. At first it is unrecognizable. At first it is only a still small voice. Eventually, however, the voice pervades our existence, and the course of our life is changed. We find our home and the source of our humanness—God.

We are relieved to discover the call of God in our lives. We are relieved to be able to realize and believe that our existence is more than the temporariness of biology. This relief begins when we begin to view ourselves differently, because the call of God begins to compel us to honestly dialogue with ourselves. Indeed, it is only with this call or summons of God that we can even begin to transcend ourselves, and discover new meaning in our existence. We discover that there is something in us infinitely more valuable than our bones and sinews. We are significant persons.

This discovered significance has two ramifications. First, we cannot retreat from this knowledge of our significance. Indeed, we cannot retreat from this God who has called us, anymore than Mole could resist the scent of his old home. When the smell was recognized, it pervaded his entire existence, and when it appeared that he must go on as before and deny the call, it left him in a "paroxysm of grief." Likewise, , we are utterly reached by God (Karl Barth, p. 141ff.)—"O Lord, you have searched me. . . . Where can I go from your Spirit? Where can I flee from your presence? . . . . If I go up to the heavens, you are there; If I make my bed in the depths, you are there. . . ." (Psalms 139, NIV).

When God is present, our emotions, thoughts, and pains take on a new reality. They matter. They are significant to God.

A second ramification of being summoned by God is that we gain a new view of ourselves. We see ourselves in Christ as being accepted. Karl Barth (1955/1958) states that just as Jesus was the representative of all humanity in his suffering and humiliation, so he is the representative of all humanity in his exaltation. God has exalted and accepted him, and by virtue of our inclusion in the humanity of Jesus, we are also accepted. God demonstrates a great kindness towards humanity in Jesus. In our identity with that humanity of Jesus, we have simply to realize that we are also accepted. Jesus's story is our story. We can come to define ourselves in Christ. Thus, Jesus is not just a model out there whom we try to duplicate; rather he represents who we are as far as God is concerned. We are okay. We are accepted. Our views of ourselves are changed radically (pp. 3–154).

The third ramification of being summoned by God is that our knowledge of ourselves as uniquely human cannot remain merely theoretical. As we are summoned by God, we are summoned to responsibility before God. Knowledge is insight, not factual or philosophical. We gain some insight into our freedom, our responsibility to act (James 1:22–24). We may not merely listen to the word, we are to do what it says. After we have looked at ourselves in the mirror upon being confronted by God, we become responsible beings. We cannot merely go away and immediately forget what we look like. Whole humanness is action.

Some individuals, however, may protest that they do not feel called. In saying this they often express disappointment and a certain irritation at us. Both the irritation and disappointment come from a failure to understand. They seek for a call in terms that others have described. They fail to recognize that no two individuals have a similar experience. They should be challenged to look for a call in their own experiences, in their own daily life events. The disappointment they experience when others speak of their call may in fact be God's call in their life. Juliana of Norwich (1392/1977) described our desire for God as, in fact, the work of God in our lives. She asked in her prayers for the wound of longing for God. One's disappointment is indeed the inner longing and desire for God, which was put there by God. Who else could have put it there?

Being called by God is necessary for healing wholeness. Encountering other persons is also necessary. If God's call to us tells us that we are unique persons, the other person's relationship with us tells us in what *ways* we are unique.

The counselor must communicate the other's uniqueness. She must assume the frame of reference of the patient, and participate in his confusion and search. Only when we have joined with the person in front of us, can he look at himself clearly. Only when we have provided an accepting and objective mirror, can this person see beyond his present confusion. Likewise, only as Jesus Christ joined with us in his incarnation could he hope fully to take our pain and chaos and make it whole. He is the one who has told us, in his call to us in our darkness and confusion, that we are now acceptable to God.

The Working-through Process of Cognitive Therapy

A safe whole relationship is ultimately important because it facilitates the process of self-examination. We risk a clearer look at ourselves.

Cognitive-behavioral therapy emphasizes the self-examination of thoughts and the changing or restructuring of those thoughts. Early on, we learn to impose an order on our environment via our thoughts and assumptions. This order arises from our early interpersonal experiences. Therefore, it makes sense that *changed* thoughts and assumptions must also arise from interpersonal experiences. It is hard to change our assumptive worlds, because it is threatening when our filtering system for looking at the world is attacked. Only a non-threatening relationship will enable such a change. (Franks, 1982).

For example, when someone continually threatens, challenges, and belittles us for a point of view or set of assumptions we may hold, we feel hurt, and withdraw, as an animal withdraws from a flame. We certainly do not listen to the other's suggestions for changes in our point of view. Often, we loudly assert our own point of view in defense against the other's attacks. However, if someone accepts us, helps us to feel good about ourselves and our opinions, we do not withdraw from them. After a while, noticing that the other person holds a different point of view, we may begin mentally to compare our point of view with this new alternative. Such a mental dialogue inevitably results in some modification of our viewpoint.

The crucial ingredient in cognitive-behavioral therapy is the idea that our thoughts and beliefs largely determine our emotions and feelings. For example, if one individual's thinking is dominated by the idea, "Unless I do everything perfectly, I am a complete failure," he will react to situations in a certain manner. Any imperfections or difficulties encountered in the course of his life's tasks will be cause for frustrations, disgust, or anger at himself, and despondency.

Recent research into the relationship between cognitions (thoughts) and emotions indicates a close relationship between the two. Different theories give differing emphasis to the role of cognitions or the environment in creating emotions. In most theories, both the environment and cognitions are important. Just as individuals are not merely passive perceivers of their environment, neither do they totally create their own worlds. Most probably, they gather information from the environment by selectively perceiving what is there. The case of the depressed individual who perceives another's indifference as hostility or dislike is common. Such an individual will not notice those mannerisms common to indifference, but instead will see only those behaviors associated with hostility.

Cognitive theory (Kovacs & Beck, 1978) does not assume that well-adjusted people necessarily think more logically or perceive more accurately. Instead, it merely assumes that less adjusted individuals are stuck in certain idiosyncratic or maladaptive ways of looking at or thinking about their world. Symptoms are shaped by individuals' beliefs about their world and themselves.

The cognitive therapist, and indeed any psychotherapist, must take the beliefs and understandings of his patient and reinterpret them for the patient into a more adaptive framework. In order to help individuals see something in a different context, however, that context must be related to something already familiar to the patient (Goldfried, 1982).

I remember one man who found that learning to communicate

more clearly with his wife was embarrassing. It wasn't that he did not want to learn. Rather, he felt foolish saying all those new things to his wife in the counseling session. Because I asked him to practice listening, he felt it was artificial. That was the only label he could put on such an experience. I asked him if he had learned to drive on a stick shift. Indeed he had. I then asked him to remember how he very slowly and deliberately had to go through all of the steps in stopping the car. He had to put his foot on the brakes, and almost immediately put the clutch in, or the car would stall. And, after the clutch was in, he had to shift gears. He remembered the initial feeling of awkward-ness and his current experience of automatic reactions, while engaging in the same behavior. The analogy was extended to communication skills, which though initially awkward, later become automatic. The feelings and thoughts he experienced in the counseling sessions need-ed to be related to an earlier interpretive framework. Only then did the therapy begin to make sense. His expectations about therapy were changed and hope appeared.

The therapist should provide the patient with a larger interpretive framework that makes sense in terms of the individual's own expe-rience. A healthy framework should ultimately communicate two ideas. First, life is never perfect, and that is okay. Secondly, one can ultimately have some control over one's life. There are many types of irrational assumptions and distorted thoughts that may lead to negative emo-tions. These will be discussed in more detail in Chapter 6. However, all of these ideas can be seen as related in some manner to the two ideas discussed in this chapter. Good therapy must always lead to self-examination in light of these two ideas.

Life is never perfect.   The individual in pain must learn to un-derstand at a very deep level that life is full of problems. Life holds a tragic element. Never will everything be perfect. Never will everyone like us. Never will we always find a perfect solution to our problems. Rarely, can we, as the yuppie-oriented commercials proclaim, "have it all." The existence of problems does not single one out as a stig-matized victim.

Life has a dark side, and the emotionally healthy individual is only too aware of this darkness. Paradoxically, however, depressed and anxious individuals have difficulty accepting this truth.

The perfectionist is a classic example of the failure to confront this truth about life. Such an individual is highly vulnerable to depres-sion. The most common perfectionist is the one who insists on performing a task perfectly or not at all. Another type of perfectionism is present in the individual who tries to please everyone.

Elizabeth was a thirty-year-old single woman pastor. She sought my help for a mild depression, and general dissatisfaction and stress related to her work. She was pastoring a small church in a very small community in a rural part of the state. She drove into the city once a month to escape the pressures and boredom that she experienced. Her social life had ceased to exist. A more careful inspection of her life revealed that she spent almost all of her time in work related to the church. Because the parsonage was next door to the church, she typically had visitors at all hours.

In addition, she felt an obligation to keep the flower gardens surrounding the church and the parsonage in the lush state in which she found them when she arrived. This she undertook because several people in the church suggested very strongly that this was her job. She felt unable to say no. Her environment (often the typical world of a pastor) demanded of her that she be perfect at everything. She was trying to oblige. She was quite fearful of her parishioners' disapproval. The overcoming of this perfection trap (approval addiction, as David Burns, 1980, calls it) came with the realization that not even Jesus could please all religious people.

Judy was someone who had fallen into the trap of "religious perfectionism." Unlike Elizabeth, she was seriously depressed. Like Elizabeth, however, she also had no activities outside of her work, which was teaching third grade. Her few activities consisted of baby-sitting and being superintendent of the Sunday school. She had very little interaction with single people her own age. Initially, however, she denied her unhappiness. She suffered from a common religious perfectionism that insists that the good Christian always has 'The Joy of the Lord' and is always bright and sparkling.

Her comment to me early in her psychotherapy was, "I don't know why I am depressed. I have tried praising the Lord when I am down. However, it doesn't work and I've concluded that I don't have enough faith. I have tried very hard to be happy to others." This was certainly very true. Judy had a tendency to avoid tears with a nervous laugh.

I replied, "Have you ever heard of the dark night of the soul?" I began to explain that while she felt bad for not always being joyful, there might actually be a positive side to her depressed feelings. I mentioned the idea that some contemplatives such as St. John of the Cross actually felt that our sense of darkness or abandonment by God is one of the stages of faith. (See Chapter 6.)

When she returned to the next session, she related that it had been a difficult struggle the previous week coming to terms with the idea that darkness could somehow have a positive role in her life.

A few months later, Judy presented me with an essay on the experience of being down. She related that she had finally come to the understanding that positive emotion is not a thermometer of the Christian life. She related:

> Sometimes, in the middle of the bad times, I've had to shake myself and say "Jesus still loves you—just because you are feeling down doesn't change his love for you or your love for him." What a relief! It's nice to be free from that load of guilt. . . .
>
> Several times, we have talked about wanting to be flaming fires for God. We have talked about how the middle step between the chunk of wood and flame is a charred piece of wood. Negative emotions can be part of the process to work some very positive traits and attributes in a life. I have found this true. Through experiencing these emotions, rather than pretending they don't exist, I have become a more real, caring, and genuine person.
>
> An excerpt from Margery Williams's (1981) book, *The Velveteen Rabbit*, expresses it best for me:
>
> "The Skin Horse had lived longer in the nursery than any of the others. He was so old that his brown coat was bald in patches and showed the seams underneath, and most of the hairs in his tail had been pulled out to string bead necklaces. He was wise, for he had seen a long succession of mechanical toys arrive to boast and swagger, and by-and-by break their mainsprings and pass away, and he knew that they were only toys, and would never turn into anything else. For nursery magic is very strange and wonderful, and only those play-things that are old and wise and experienced like the Skin Horse understand all about it.
>
> 'What is REAL'? asked the Rabbit one day, when they were lying side by side near the nursery fender, before Nana came to tidy the room. 'Does it mean having things that buzz inside you and a stick-out-handle?'
>
> 'Real isn't how you are made,' said the Skin Horse, 'It's a thing that happens to you. When a child loves you for a long, long time, not just to play with, but REALLY loves you, then you become Real.'
>
> 'Does it hurt?' asked the Rabbit.
>
> 'Sometimes,' said the Skin Horse, for he was always truthful. 'When you are Real you don't mind being hurt.'
>
> 'Does it happen all at once, like being wound up,' he asked, 'or bit by bit?'

'It doesn't happen all at once,' said the Skin Horse, 'you become. It takes a long time. That's why it doesn't often happen to
people who break easily, or have sharp edges, or who have to be
carefully kept. Generally by the time you are Real most of your
hair has been loved off, and your eyes drop out and you get loose
in the joints and very shabby. But these things don't matter at all,
because once you are Real you can't be ugly, except to people who
don't understand.' "

Judy ended her letter by saying that her frequent times of
depression had made her more compassionate. She said that as a third-
grade teacher she realized that having a child with learning problems
is a frightening experience for many parents. "In sharing with them
(especially the negatives) I am more able to leave them with hope—
the same hope I cling to so desperately when I am down. I am more
able to minister to their feelings. Just as hope is so important to me
when I am down, so I can communicate to them hope and the prospect
that their child can change if we all work together."

Through therapy, Judy moved from a place where she could not
bear to experience any negative feelings, to a place where negative
feelings were seen as a part of a normal REAL life. She moved from
being a whining child to a mature adult.

Jesus is our model for understanding a fuller view of life. Indeed,
although Jesus was one declared good by God, he suffered much.
According to the New Testament, the main purpose of his life was to
suffer for our redemption. As Christians, we do not have a safe comfortable God, but rather, we have, as Jürgen Moltmann has said, "A
crucified God." Jesus's very unpleasant death gave new dignity to pain,
suffering, and desolation. It is not that Jesus's death has justified suffering, and that such suffering therefore is to be sought after. Rather,
those who suffer find in Jesus new self-respect, and humanity. God
counts them worthy to be in solidarity with his Son (Moltmann, 1974,
p. 50). Suffering and pain are redefined. God is revealed somewhat
paradoxically in the feeling of abandonment by God. Depressed individuals who already *feel* abandoned by God need to hear that they
share in the abandonment that Jesus experienced in his ignoble death
on the cross.

Karl Barth (1960) masterfully discusses this idea in his dialogue
with Nietzsche. Nietzsche, who later became deranged, put forth the
idea of the superman, the perfect man, the man with no problems,
the man who rose above all difficulties and struggles. This was real
man, according to Nietzsche.

The figure of the suffering man, the crucified Jesus, was a threat to Nietzsche's "superman." According to Barth, Nietzsche saw in the suffering Christ the direct opposite of his own ideal. First Corinthians 1:1 raised the great danger for Nietzsche, according to Barth, because pain was elevated. Pain did not imply that one had failed:

> But God chose the foolish things of the world to shame the wise. God chose the weak things in the world to shame the strong. He chose the lowly things of this world and the despised things—and the things that are not—to nullify the things that are, so that no one may boast before him. (1 Cor. 1:27–29)

With the discovery of the Crucified, Christian patients can begin to restructure how they see their life. The incest victim no longer needs to bear the guilt. The battered wife no longer needs to fear she has displeased God. The depressed man no longer needs to worry that his faith is weak. Individuals' thoughts about such pain need to be changed. Social psychologists tell us that society believes in the "just world" theory. If we are hurting, we have received what we deserve. The victim, whether it is the rape victim or the anxious person, is usually blamed. The crucified One changes all of that.

One can control one's life.   Generally depressed and anxious individuals feel out of control. Their feelings seem to overwhelm them. They underestimate their ability to control not only their feelings, but their entire life (Seligman, 1975). Not only do they have a low tolerance for pain, but they can see no way out. Cognitive therapy strives to teach individuals that they do have control of their life. Not only do they learn more appropriate skills to help them regain that control, but they also learn to control their feelings. The suicidal individual must be helped to see that there is some way out other than suicide.

The best therapists will communicate to their patients that they, not the therapist, are in charge of their fate. The therapist is a teacher or coach. The patient is in control. It is up to them. Often I like to demonstrate to patients early in counseling that they do indeed have control over their feelings with a brief exercise in the office.

Susan was a twenty-five-year-old woman who had been diagnosed as having a panic reaction. At times she would become so anxious that she would start screaming. She had to move back home because of the problem. Prior to consulting me, she usually spent most nights in her mother's room because of her fears. She felt that there was nothing she could do for herself, and asked for a referral for some medication.

I was hesitant to do this, as the research suggests that antianxiety medications only lessen the individual's motivation to deal with anxiety. Pain is a good motivator. In order to demonstrate her control, I asked her during our first session to describe her fears and anxious thoughts. As she related them to me, she became visibly more anxious. I asked her to estimate her anxiety for me, using a scale of 1 to 100. She said 90. I then asked her to look out the window, and describe to me what she saw. As she described the clouds, sky, and birds, I asked for a more complete description of the colors. She responded. After about 5 minutes, I asked her to tell me how anxious she was on the same scale. She reported a 40.

"What happened?" I asked. "Did I do anything for you? Did I give you a pill, or some type of medicine to make you feel better?"

"No," she confessed.

"What happened, did something change magically in your body?"

"No."

"What was different? What did you do differently?"

"I looked out the window and described what I saw rather than focusing on my problems."

"Was this something you did, or did I do it for you?"

"I did it."

"Are you *sure* you didn't receive a shot or something to calm you down?" I asked in a light-hearted manner.

"No, I did it myself."

"Notice how *you* can have some impact on your feelings. You *alone.*"

"I never realized that," she said, with a smile.

Cognitive therapy is not just thought. Emotions play an important role. Marvin Goldfried (1982) maintains that the therapist cannot merely give the individual intellectual labels to recite to himself when he is down. That is, the patient cannot be taught merely to say, "I am a good person," or "The situation is getting better and better," and expect to feel better. These labels must be attached to actual experiences the individual is having, at that very time. The labels then become associated with certain events. If one has experienced something, that is the difference between emotional and intellectual insight. It is useless to tell a woman she can control her emotions. The therapist must skillfully arrange for the individual to have an experience of controlling those emotions. In this way, the labels become something that we actually understand in our own life.

Linking experiences of change to cognitive labels is important because it generates hope. When we actually experience what the therapist tells us, we begin to hope that the positive changes the healer predicts will also occur. A crucial element in all psychotherapies is this hope, these positive expectations that healing will occur. Without hope we cease to try. Without hope we become mired in our problems. Without hope we despair. We always look to evidence for our hope. The prime evidence in counseling is a change in our behavior, or a change in our feelings. Hope is not in a vacuum. ". . . . We rejoice in our sufferings, knowing that suffering produces endurance, and endurance produces character, and character produces hope" (Rom. 5:3–4).

Basic Components of Cognitive Therapy

Rationale for procedures.   The first important component of cognitive therapy is the communication of the rationale for the procedure to the patient. In order for change to occur it is imperative that the patient and therapist share the same intellectual framework about what is happening. The patient should understand that thoughts largely determine feelings and that she can influence those feelings by changing her thoughts and attitudes. A demonstration from the patient's own experience is most effective for illustrating the model. Patients always need a clear perception of just exactly what their problem is, and how therapy may help. The figure presented earlier in Chapter 2 can be very helpful.

The second component of cognitive therapy is self-awareness. Before one's thoughts can be modified, they must be brought into awareness. Such self-examination has always been a part of both psychological and spiritual healing.

The final component of cognitive therapy is the restructuring or changing of one's thoughts. Changing our actual thoughts, our underlying assumptions, or even the images that continually go through our mind are all part of this process. Learning new behaviors and new ways of dealing with the world are also other ways of changing our view of the world. Often some individuals need evidence that they are not helpless. Such evidence will come only with new risks or new behaviors.

Healthy individuals learn to allow themselves to trust that their own internal and external perceptions are accurate and worthy. They learn to see themselves as one who is in the image of God. They learn to listen less to internal voices from their external world both past and present, such voices which cause them to doubt themselves, or to despair.

The stages of cognitive therapy actually parallel the stages of healing that have existed through the ages. Evelyn Underhill (1930), in her study of mysticism, lays out three stages of mystical experience. In the first stage, there is an awakening of the self. One begins to think of oneself and look beyond oneself. The present existence no longer satisfies. All of the great saints have talked of being conscious of something they have missed until their conversion. Consciousness of need is always a necessary precursor to any type of counseling or therapy.

The next stage of growth allows the individual to gain a detachment from her surroundings. This detachment allows one to look at those same surroundings in a more objective manner. No longer is one to be dictated to by them. Likewise, taking the cognitive therapy position that one's own thoughts and beliefs, rather than the environment, largely determine one's emotional state allows an individual to look at the environment more objectively. This process proceeds as one becomes more aware of one's thoughts.

Underhill terms the next stage on the mystical journey as the purification of the self. Part of this purification is the mortification of one's self. One begins to turn one's heart away from the old loves, the old ways of doing and being, towards new ways. True mortification proceeds from an awareness and an acknowledgment of how one has become mired in the old way. The self-examination of one's thoughts is also a type of mortification. Most patients report a fear of examining those thoughts. They are afraid of what they will discover. Indeed, some individuals become initially more depressed as they begin to face some of their long-held assumptions about the world.

Pain and struggle, however, lead ultimately to light. For Underhill, and indeed, for the mystical tradition in general, this light leads to a greater illumination of self and the presence of God. One gains a new sense of freedom. Indeed, rather than losing ourselves, we find ourselves. All life is lived for God. In cognitive psychotherapy there is light at the end. Realizing that we can change our feelings by simply thinking about them, leads to a greater sense of personal control, of freedom from the environment. Patients begin to have a greater sense of self. As they realize that *they* can have control, that they can make some of the choices, they sit up straighter in their chairs. They are no longer helpless. They have gained themselves. They have regained the image of God within themselves.

Chapter 4

SELF-KNOWLEDGE

> Our wisdom, in so far as it ought to be deemed true and solid
> wisdom, consists almost entirely of two parts; the knowledge of
> God and of ourselves. But as these are connected by many ties,
> it is not easy to determine which of the two precedes and gives
> birth to the other.—Calvin, 1559/1972, pp. 37

Contemporary people hunger for self-knowledge. We long to have
some secret insight into ourselves. We eagerly devour self-help books,
and other volumes that promise to show us what our dream was *really*
about, or why we behave the way we do in certain circumstances. Little
tests that purport to show us whether we are the ideal wife or husband,
or whether we are an introvert or an extrovert, appear regularly in
Sunday news magazines. Many of us eagerly complete them, hoping
that somehow we will understand more fully who we are.

Most of us do not know why we crave self-knowledge. Perhaps
for some of us it is a pastime to fill in our Sunday afternoons. Some
of us may believe that understanding ourselves will lead to greater
personal happiness. We may be trying to overcome a gap in our development, or a personal tragedy that still haunts us. Self-insight, we
hope, will increase our personal sense of contentment or well-being.
Finally, a few of us seek self-knowledge because we somehow feel such
knowledge will give us greater personal power. Perhaps we hope to

learn why we are *really* intimidated by our boss. We hope that this knowledge will lead ultimately to less timidity.

Paradoxically, even though we all crave self-knowledge, we also fear it. We back off from knowing about ourselves because we fear that we may learn something unpleasant. Some of us may fear that new knowledge may lead us in a direction we would rather not go. We fear not only knowing ourselves, but we fear having others know us. We back off from others, fearing either rejection or vulnerability. We thus become marooned on an island of secrecy. We want to jump into the deep waters of our self, exploring ourselves, and allowing others to know us. We would like that link with others. We avoid those deep waters, however, and we often prefer that others do the same, thus maintaining our island.

Self-knowledge (and the self-examination that accompanies it) plays a central and important role in all forms of psychotherapy. Similarly, Christian spirituality has given self-knowledge an important place in the process of spiritual maturity.

Psychological Models of Self-knowledge

This section will review ideas of self-knowledge and self-examination that have been proposed by Sigmund Freud, Carl Jung, Carl Rogers, Rollo May, and those who have considered self-knowledge a learned phenomenon. The definition of mental illness, or psychopathology, for most models of psychotherapy includes the idea of fragmentation. The individual is cut off from aspects of himself, and does not really experience those aspects of self.

The *dynamic* schools of thought have defined self-awareness as the patient's understanding of how his present thoughts and motivations are actually a manifestation of unconscious past experiences or childhood perceptions. Freud and Jung are the major representatives of this line of thought. Both were European thinkers who made most of their contributions in the first half of the twentieth century. Sigmund Freud and his followers are the most well-known advocates of this school of thought. They have contended that the whole purpose of therapy is to make the unconscious conscious—to make the individual aware of his motivations (Freud, 1923/1961). In health, the individual again becomes aware of all motivations and impulses that he has previously forgotten or suppressed. For Freud, awareness of these motivations and ideas means that they are under the rational control of the individual. This process is expressed in Freud's famous statement, "Where id was, let ego be." This means that the logical, coherent, adaptive thought of the ego should control the biological forces of the id.

Carl Jung, a Swiss psychologist, also focused his attention on helping the individual become aware of ideas from the unconscious (often called the shadow). Unlike Freud, however, Jung believes that all unconscious materials are not necessarily biological impulses (cf. Jocabi, 1973). These materials could also be certain universal themes of meaningfulness or ultimate needs important in the history of the human race.[1]

In all dynamic therapies, disturbed individuals are helped to see how their present suffering is a result of something from their *past,* continuously pushing for recognition (Wachtel, 1977). According to the psychoanalytic point of view, certain ideas from the past are repressed because of their unacceptability to the patient. These ideas (such as an irrational fear, for example) remain sources of distortion and conflict. They do so precisely because the individual does not reexamine them in light of present more mature and realistic ideas. The individual continues to be influenced by these ideas from the past, though he is usually unaware of such influences (Wachtel, 1977).

The importance of the role of the environment as the cause of one's problems is the theme of the behavior therapists. While individuals like B. F. Skinner are often associated with this school, a much larger group of social learning theorists such as Albert Bandura (Bandura & Walters, 1963) and Miller and Dollard (1941) are included in this category.

These three thinkers are American psychologists, residing in universities, and thinking and writing in this same general area. During the 1980s, Miller, for example, has been interested in work on the conditioning and learned modification of responses, such as heartbeat rate and blood pressure.

For these individuals, self-awareness consists of understanding just what it is in one's environment that causes one to respond in certain ways. These individuals are known for their emphasis on *faulty learning* as the root of all problems.

A third group of psychotherapy theorists, called the third force in psychology (to distinguish it from either the behavioral or the dynamic schools), has emerged since the mid-twentieth century. This group has historically focused on the present conscious experiences (thoughts and feelings) of the individuals. One example of therapists in this category is the phenomenologist Carl Rogers. Carl Rogers (1961) defines the healthy individual as one who is open to all of his feelings and thoughts. Usually this is possible because such an individual has a concept of himself that defines all feelings, thoughts, and motivations, regardless of their nature, as acceptable. The unaware individual, on the other hand, will not always admit to feelings or thoughts that he may be experiencing. In addition, these individuals have a mind-set (called the "ideal self-concept" by Rogers) that results in the belief that many experiences are unacceptable and should not be present. If such unacceptable experiences are detected, they are denied or ignored.

Recently, the behavioral and the psychoanalytic schools of thought, like the third-force schools, have displayed increasing interest in the individual's present conscious feelings and thoughts as vital determinants of behaviors and motivations.

The behaviorists, for example, (Bowers, 1973) have argued that it is one's present thoughts and perceptions about the environment that influence one as much as the environment itself. The continued development of this theme has resulted in cognitive-behavioral therapy. According to some cognitive therapists (Beck, Rush, Shaw, & Emery, 1979), it is important for the counselor or therapist to recognize and make the patient aware of the patient's idiosyncratic way of organizing the world, and also the patient's faulty perceptions and meanings of the world.

Wachtel (1977) has also brought the importance of present conscious thoughts and assumptions into the psychoanalytic model. He suggests that conflict may actually be something that individuals continue to evoke from their environment. (This view contrasts with the classic psychoanalytic assumption that conflict arises from the unconscious.) According to Wachtel, individuals evoke conflict from their environment because of their distorted idiosyncratic way of perceiving or thinking about that environment. Wachtel suggests that continued contact with that conflictual environment, and a more rational evaluation of one's present perceptions and assumptions about the environment are both necessary. The therapist aids in this reevaluation process. Thus, for Wachtel, therapy would take into account both the dynamic and the cognitive models. This therapy would consist of a direct confrontation with the troubled thoughts arising from the environment, and a rational evaluation of those thoughts. Therapy would also consist of a more realistic evaluation of that environment.

Even this brief survey of these psychological models suggests that common themes have arisen as these theories have continued to develop. The most central theme that has developed, however, has been an increased emphasis on the individual's conscious thoughts and assumptions.

Theological Aspects of Self-awareness

Self-examination is an important theme in both the Old and New Testaments. Psalm 139 appeals:

> Search me, O God, and know my heart!
> Try me and know my thoughts!
> and see if there be an wicked way in me,
> and lead me in the way everlasting!

The psalmist is asking for an understanding of himself, a renewed self-awareness. This request comes on the heels of the psalmist's admission that he is known by God, and that he finds such a realization frightening, or unfathomable.

> O Lord, thou hast
> searched me and known me!
> Thou knowest when I sit down and when I rise up;
> thou discernest my thoughts from afar. . . . .
> Such knowledge is too wonderful for me;
> it is high, I cannot attain it.

In the Christian tradition, self-awareness is linked to God's awareness of us. This means that a greater knowledge of ourselves is derived from a period of retreat into the presence of God. Some individuals may protest that such emphasis on self-knowledge gained in retreat may smack of the "me-ism" that has become rampant in the past decade. However, the spiritual journey is a circle. We must retreat for a time from the voices, opinions, and demands of those around us in order to hear the voice of God speaking within us. It is only through this voice that we gain a renewed sense of ourselves and who we are, and the final phase of this healing always involves the journey back towards others.

This section will discuss the importance of self-knowledge, the role Christ plays in that process, the difficulties and obstacles on the way, and the anticipated results from such a renewal process.

Self-knowledge is the first step in self-definition. Self-knowledge is also an integral ingredient in our learning to respond to God, and take our cues from God. Most of us spend most of our life allowing ourselves to be defined by the community around us. We are a product of our parents, our friends, our education, and indeed, all of the voices of the culture in which we are immersed. We respond to those voices around us, and eventually form our definition of ourselves from those voices.

Certainly being human implies that our self is derived from other human interactions, for it is the human interactions that are the most distinctly human part of our lives. However, if our definition remains only a product of those interactions, eventually we find ourself imprisoned. Eventually, we find that we are diminished because we reflect only that which is around us. We have no unique self. Ultimately, however, we want to become completely who we are. We want to become what God's voice is calling us to be. Ultimately, the Christian hopes to discover who Christ is calling her to be through his example.

This process of reaching authenticity cannot happen unless we first know what it is that keeps us from this authenticity. We must know what voices and what forces currently control our lives. We must know those voices that speak the loudest, those voices that have been calling the shots. This is the role of self-knowledge. Awareness of these voices and the role they play in our lives means that we can begin to speak to some of those voices. Awareness of these voices means that we do not have to be quite as imprisoned by them. Finally, awareness of these voices means that we can even choose not to respond to them. We can begin to have some of those delicate moments when we can take our cues from Christ.

Numerous writers and theologians have stressed the theme that we know God better when we know ourselves. This theme is present across the spectrum of Christian belief from Calvinism to Roman Catholicism. Christian theology, regardless of its flavor, does not allow us to escape this truth. Thus, for example, the beginning of this chapter reminds us of Calvin's observations on this subject. Likewise, St. Teresa of Avila, a Carmelite nun, at the other end of the theological spectrum, has said that if we know our souls better, we will know God better (1577/1961).

Karl Barth provides us with a clear statement of the nature of the relationship between self-knowledge and knowledge of God. He says that it is from God that we ultimately learn that we can indeed know ourselves. Jesus is the source of knowledge about what humanity actually is. All human nature in all its fullness was revealed in Jesus (Barth, 1948/1960, pp. 38–53). Barth later says that to know oneself is to know oneself confronted by God, in Jesus Christ. Jesus shows us who we actually are and who we can be. Knowledge of Jesus stirs something very deep within and arouses us to new heights and unimagined possibilities.

Violet was a very timid little woman in her late fifties. She was being taken advantage of. She was quite upset, but did not see what possibly could be done. I sensed that much could be accomplished if she would go to those concerned and demand that certain actions be taken. Violet was quite religious, and her experiences and the authoritative voices around her had told her it was not a woman's place to speak up. I despaired that anything could be done. However, I suddenly remembered the story of the Syrophoenician woman in Mark 7:25–30. This was a woman who only obtained what she wanted when she persisted in her demands. Jesus rewarded her persistence. Violet was encouraged by Jesus's reaction to this woman's persistence, and was able successfully to demand that the wrongs against her be righted. Violet was able through this encounter with the Christ figure in Scripture to see new possibilities for herself. Indeed, she was able to recognize what she had already become in Christ.

Christ plants the kernel of who we are within us, and working with him, we begin to realize the true self that has been put within us by grace. We find our true selves as we acknowledge our identity with Christ, in his suffering and ultimate exaltation. However, too often we feel that the experiences around us define us. The seed planted by the grace of God does not grow and expand and fill our inner selves. Instead we focus on the outer hull, and thus, we have put bandages around an empty hollow self.

Van Kaam (1976) contends that we become alienated from our own self-direction when we begin to pay too much attention to others' expectations or affirmations, rather than to our inner self. If we examine our inner self and the impact of environmental pressures or others' expectations on our behaviors and feelings, we begin to know our true self. This means listening to our thoughts and ideas and discerning their source. We can begin to sort out the inner voice of God and our own desires from the desires and pressures of those around us. Jesus, rather than external demands, can become the model for our feelings, ideas, and behaviors.

The most important role that Jesus plays in our self-knowledge is as a mirror. As we remain in the presence of Christ, this Christ becomes one criterion by which to evaluate and restructure our self-image. Karl Barth has said that we see ourselves and our sins most fully in the mirror of the grace of God (Barth, 1948/1960, pp. 36–41). Christ is the mirror of who we really are, and what we can become.

As we reflect upon Jesus, we can learn who we were meant to be. Because Jesus is the model of fulfilled humanity, we know more fully who we actually are, though God's grace, as we view Jesus. He is not merely a model out *there*, whom we seek to duplicate or imitate. Rather, as we see God's exaltation and favor bestowed on him, we see ourselves and God's view of us. This is grace. We are accepted. Wholeness is coming to this realization. He is the firstfruits of what we can and will become (1 Cor. 15:21–23,45–49).

Reinhold Niebuhr (1955) borrowed from Augustine the concept that the image of God in the individual is that aspect of the individual which is able to dialogue with itself and is thus self-conscious. At least one meaning of Niebuhr's self-consciousness implies an awareness of one's perspectives and thoughts and an ability to dialogue or argue with those thoughts. In fact, Niebuhr asserts that the essence of humanness is the ability to step back and evaluate oneself, as God sees one. He calls this self-transcendence. True self-knowledge results from this dialogue when God, in the form of Jesus Christ, is used as the mirror. Self-transcendence, in the Christian sense, is thus standing outside of ourselves and seeing ourselves as God sees us.

The dialogue process might involve the following questions. "How does God see me now? What is God's perspective on my thoughts?" Because Niebuhr sees Jesus as God incarnate and perfect humanness, Jesus becomes a perfect mirror for self-knowledge and understanding. A mirror is always more personal than a model. A model merely gives us a picture of another. A mirror gives us a true picture of ourselves. Such a picture is never abstract or theoretical, it is always intensely personal.

Emil Brunner (1947/1964) also has emphasized the role of Christ as a mirror in our self-knowledge process. He states that the actual *imago Dei* is to be found in relationship with God. This relationship includes dialogue both with self and God. By looking at God, we gain the advantage of a mirror, so that we can see ourselves as we are. Thus, as we are in dialogue with God and ourselves (as we examine our thoughts and perspectives and compare them with God's), we see ourselves as we truly are as we are reflected in the mirror of Jesus Christ. Real humanness is the process of examining oneself in the mirror. Although the mirror remains a mirror, it ceases to reflect our image if we do not stand in front of it. That is, if we are not continuously in open dialogue with ourself and God about who we are, we can lose ourselves to the voices around us. Thus, to maintain the *imago*

Dei, we must expose ourselves to God by dialoguing with ourselves in the presence of God. In this way, we receive the image of ourselves back from God. If we abandon God, our self-examination is always less than complete. Consequently, we lose something of the *imago Dei.*

Self-examination is not without its difficulties. First, we fear the pain of a realistic confrontation with ourselves. Health and God, however, are not found by escaping our thoughts or our pains, but in facing them. The realistic confrontation with pain is the uniqueness of the Christian perspective. In Buddhism, we have the Buddha as one who conquers suffering and sin by standing aloof above them, by ceasing to experience them. Christ, however, is one who accepts the ultimate disgrace of suffering and faces all manner of pain. Indeed, Jesus foreshadows the coming kingdom of God by showing that the outcasts, the suffering, and the abandoned are raised. Jesus's death was not peaceful, not noble. He died forsaken. It was only after this confrontation with death and pain that Jesus was raised. His crucifixion gives new meaning to our pains (cf. Moltmann, 1973/1974).

Initially, the idea of self-examination is not seen as a positive experience by either those who enter psychotherapy or those who undertake such an examination for religious reasons. Often individuals will resist this action. Usually, this resistance is on an unconscious level, for they may assert that there is no pain to confront, even as we see the pain in their eyes. If the person is aware of the pain, he or she may strongly protest that nothing is to be gained by talking about it. Analogies may useful to us at this point. For example, one might prefer to put a Band-Aid on an infected wound. However, it is generally better, though more painful, to clean out the wound first before applying a dressing. The same idea is to be applied to our internal thoughts and images. In cognitive therapy, before negative thoughts or images can be dealt with and modified, the individual must be made aware of them and have a grasp of their central content. Pushing unpleasant thoughts from one's mind and "thinking positively" with Norman Vincent Peale, is neither cognitive therapy, nor effective (cf. Mahoney & Arnkoff, 1978).

Often, individuals fear to examine and confront their thoughts. Ideas from our spiritual tradition may be reassuring at this juncture. One such helpful theme for this difficult time comes from St. John of the Cross. In his *Dark Night of the Soul* (1577/1959) he describes that emotional darkness as part of the contemplative path. In traveling that path, we must be willing to give up all understanding of our feelings. There must be an openness to what is experienced. The darkest experiences are accomplishing a purpose.

If we are not to ignore our thoughts, neither need we become overwhelmed by them. It is important to communicate to those confronting their thoughts that self-awareness is a necessary first step in the process of gaining health and that we will not stop there. Individuals should be prepared to expect negative thoughts or feelings that may arise. Self-awareness for the Christian is actually a spiritual exercise. St. Teresa of Avila suggests in *The Interior Castle* (1577/1961) that self-examination should always be undertaken in the presence of Christ. We must remember that God cares for us, regardless of how negative our thoughts and images may be. It is important to create an atmosphere of benign, hopeful anticipation regarding the self-awareness process. Self-awareness can be seen as a process of opening one's self to the light of the Holy Spirit within one's self.

A second obstacle in self-examination is a refusal to admit our finiteness. When we begin to understand that we can stand back and examine our thoughts from an objective perspective, we are tempted to see ourselves as totally outside the process. Because we can transcend a situation or stand above it, we falsely think that we know everything about it. We mistakenly come to believe that we can be completely free of a situation. We mistakenly put ourself in the place of God. Reinhold Niebuhr (1953) feels that our refusal to recognize our finiteness is the source of our problems. Because we stubbornly hold on to the illusion that we are infinite, that we are not limited, we never bother to learn more about the forces that are actually limiting us. Ironically, by refusing to admit that we are not free, we limit our freedom.

One final obstacle that prevents a free self-examination is our fear that God cannot reach us. We fear that we are alone; therefore we fear going into our abyss alone. We fear having no same perspective by which to evaluate ourselves. We fear losing our bearings. As noted in Chapter 3, a good relationship with a healing other, and a good relationship with God will provide a reference point and a healthy perspective in the darkness of our own pain. We are not alone. Christianity strongly asserts that the human spirit in its depth and height reaches into eternity and God (Niebuhr, 1953, p. 157). As Psalm 139 declares, we cannot retreat into ourselves. We are always utterly reached by God (Barth, 1948/1960, pp. 141–142).

Self-awareness is a difficult process, but the end product is valuable, and indeed indispensable to our mental health. As we become aware of our thoughts and assumptions, we can learn to dialogue with them and influence them. We become the influencer as well as the influenced. Thus, awareness grants us more freedom over those external voices that would control us. Additionally, as we move towards God, we are in a better position to see ourselves more clearly, because we have more detachment from what we might see. We are less invested in a certain picture.

Methods of Self-Knowledge

Cognitive psychotherapy focuses on helping the individual become aware of his underlying assumptions about life. We must understand how we really view life. We must have some insight into what color the glasses are through which we look at things. The first step in this larger process is to make the individual aware of his individual thoughts and images. The methods proposed below are geared to this purpose. Some of the methods have been adapted from those advocated by other cognitive therapists, while others are procedures that have been found particularly useful for religious patients. All of the methods emphasize that we must *face* our pains.

The important factor in all of these methods is a shift in the individual's mind-set. Gradually we must become aware of what we are saying to ourselves. As long as we are approaching this goal, flexibility of method is always best. For example, some individuals may have difficulty recording thoughts on paper; but these same individuals may quickly shift to checking their own thoughts when they occur. Other individuals may be quite good at recording their thoughts. Some of these individuals, however, may find it more difficult mentally to observe their thoughts without the benefit of a pencil and paper to record them. Each procedure must be adapted to the style of the individual.

"Catching" thoughts as they occur, and modified journaling, the first two procedures, may be useful for anyone, whether or not they are seeing a counselor. The imagery procedure is probably most effective with a guide.

Here-and-now interactions in the therapy session. As the name implies, this method attempts to make the patient aware of the thoughts or images he may have at one specific moment in the therapy session. Using the patient's actual thoughts in a session, either to convince him of the validity of thought-monitoring, or to make him aware of some of his thoughts, has been used by many cognitive therapists. Generally, the therapist stops the ongoing conversation and asks the individual about his thoughts.

Examining one's thoughts *as* they occur fits Van Kaam's (1976) directive that we be open to messages from each situation. Openness to our thoughts as they occur is analogous to being open to God in the present moment.

The following is a sample transcript of how the therapist may sample the patient's moods and thoughts right in the present moment.

> As we are sitting here right now discussing _____, I wonder what your mood is right at this moment? Could you give me some estimation of that mood by using a number where zero would be the worst you have ever felt and 10 would be the best?
> [The therapist should write on some sort of monitoring log the present topic of conversation, and an indication of the patient's mood. This models monitoring, which the patient can later do on his own.]
> Would you now tell me some of the things that have been going through your mind? What are some of your thoughts?
> [The therapist should write down everything the patient tells him. The self-monitoring form discussed in the next section is useful for this purpose.]

Asking individuals for thoughts right at the moment is especially effective on two specific occasions:

1. *When the therapist is introducing the self-monitoring of thoughts, and wants to give the patient a sample of what the process involves right at that moment.* Most individuals are unclear as to what the self-monitoring of thoughts involves, and require such an example so that their mis-understandings are cleared up.

2. *When it appears that some event in the previous few minutes has resulted in mood changes.* It is, at this point, a good idea to document for the patient the change in mood, and also the underlying thoughts that may have contributed to that change. This is especially important when, for example, a counselor is working with someone who has been extremely discouraged and has become, as a result of the previous few moments, somewhat encouraged. This is also very useful for an individual to do on his own, when he suddenly feels a shift in mood. It is important to know the source of those mood changes.

Looking at present thoughts is particularly useful in monitoring a dramatic change in mood. Joe, for example, was a salesman who felt that it was important that he always be perfect and perform at a high level on the job. As a result of these unreasonable expectations for himself, he became depressed because he was not always able to perform perfectly. He came to one session extremely despondent about a failed interaction at a recent sales meeting. In the process of discussing the unreasonableness of any individual being perfect, his expression became more cheerful. Noticing this, I decided to check out his feelings and thoughts. He indicated that indeed he suddenly felt better. When queried about his thoughts, he replied, "I guess it is absurd to think that I can be perfect. I guess no one can be perfect. Perhaps only God, and I am certainly not God." Linking his shift in mood to his shift in thinking, reinforced for this individual the idea that thoughts do indeed affect moods.

Individuals on their own may find a modification of this procedure very helpful. Often when I am down, and I become aware of my mood, I stop myself and say, "Now, Propst, what are you saying to yourself that is making you upset?" I am usually able to come up with several negative thoughts. I then argue with those thoughts, using some of the procedures in the following chapters.

Modified Journaling.   A second useful procedure for becoming aware of one's thoughts is to keep a monitoring log over a period of time. This is a very specific type of structured journaling. The goal is to write down periodically any thoughts that may occur between counseling sessions, right at the moment of the thought. Surrounding circumstances and mood is also recorded. This exercise provides information on experiences when they are occurring, which can then be used later in the counseling session. This exercise can be useful for anyone, whether or not they are currently seeing a counselor. Figure 4-1 is one type of monitoring form that may be useful for monitoring one's thoughts. Note especially items 1–5.

The goal of cognitive therapy is to examine one's view of the world and one's core assumptions about reality. According to cognitive therapy, our core assumptions are most clearly seen in our individual thoughts and fantasies about a situation. Cognitive therapists, unlike earlier behavioral or psychodynamic therapists, accept a person's conscious thoughts about an event as rock-bottom data about their core assumptions and motivations (Bedrosian & Beck, 1980). The more individual thoughts collected, the more clues we have about an individual's life themes or basic belief systems. Indeed, in the very act of self-observation, "patients begin to adopt a position of greater distance and objectivity vis-à-vis their thoughts" (Bedrosian & Beck, p. 131).

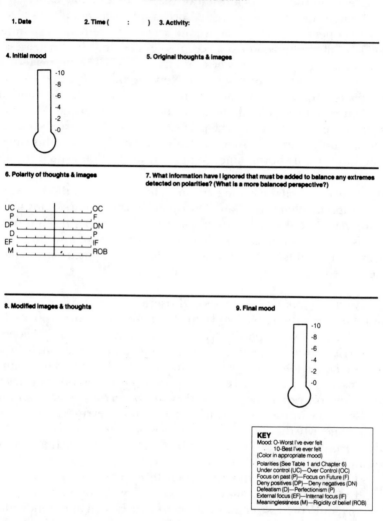

Figure 4-1

An example of a thought monitoring form that may be used to record activities, mood, thoughts, and images, and to evaluate and modify those thoughts and images.

The confrontation and acknowledgment of the darker thoughts is important. "Confess your sins to one another . . . that you may be healed . . ." (James 5:16). The Greek word for confession, *exomologeo*, stresses the idea of acknowledging what is there, and revealing what is hidden. An acknowledgment of the evil, the dark, the unpleasant, and of the failures leads to healing. To the extent that a failure is known and examined, to that extent it may be changed or healed.

As noted above, the self-monitoring process should begin with some type of self-monitoring log. Figure 4-2 below is an example of a self-monitoring log which has been completed. The reader need only make note of items 1–5 at this point. The remainder of the items are discussed at the end of chapter 6. Note that not only are activities and thoughts recorded, but so is the individual's initial mood.

Using a specified form like Figure 4-1 is important in the beginning of the thought-monitoring process. Such a log structures the type of material that is recorded. This same log can then be used for restructuring thoughts later.

The process is very simple. The counselor asks the patient to record thoughts between sessions. Thoughts can be monitored either at specified times of the day, or merely when an individual is feeling upset or is in a potentially upsetting situation. Assigning specified times is usually best at the beginning of the process. The use of such times insures that a given number of thoughts will be recorded. This process also structures the situation for the depressed individual who may need such a structure to prod him into acting. The disadvantages of prespecified times is that those may not always be the ones that are the most difficult or the most upsetting for the individual. Assigning self-monitoring during difficult periods, on the other hand, allows an inspection of thoughts at those times. This procedure has the disadvantage, however, of not providing as much structure for those who need it.

It is usually better to start self-monitoring with a precise and definite schedule and then switch to monitoring during difficult times after improvement has started. Those individuals who are having difficulties with depression or anxiety will generally have negative thoughts or images at any time during the day.

In assigning self-monitoring as homework, the counselor may say the following:

This week (or until I see you next time), in order to help you become aware of what you are saying to yourself, I would like

SELF-MONITORING CHART (example completed)

1. Date: Tuesday, 3/28   **2. Time (** 6 :15 **)**   **3. Activity:** Sitting in the living room looking through the want ads.

---

4. Initial mood

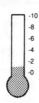

-10
-8
-6
-4
-2
-0

5. Original thoughts & images

I will ultimately never be able to succeed in my chosen profession because I have not been able to find a job I want, therefore I am a failure.

---

6. Polarity of thoughts & images

UC ____✓____|_____ OC
P _____|____✓___ F
DP ____✓____|_____ DN
D _____|___✓____ P
EF _____✓__|_____ IF
M _____|_____ ROB

7. What information have I ignored that must be added to balance any extremes detected on polarities? (What is a more balanced perspective?)

I really have the choice to modify what I will accept as an acceptable job. I also have the opportunity to go back to school and learn a slightly different trade that seems to be more enjoyable. I can make that choice. I can also continue to look in more places and not leave any stone unturned. If I continue to do that, it is only a matter of probabilities until I find a job. I am good at some of the things I do, and I am willing to learn, so I could easily develop these skills in a slightly different direction. Are there any positive things I have ignored? Yes, I have had some positive feedback about my work from several sources including Mr. Smith and Mrs. Jones. Finally, it is important that I look at my priorities. If it is more important that I do this work than have full-time employment, then I should be willing to accept part-time employment. If a full-time job is necessary, then I need to be more flexible about the type of work I am willing to do. The choice is mine. I am free to make it. Not succeeding in one thing doesn't mean I am a failure at everything.

---

8. Modified images & thoughts

I will check out possibilities in this area for six months and during that time resolve not to leave any stone unturned. If there is nothing by then, I will choose to go into one of the two other types of jobs that I have been interested in. Rarely do we ever find a perfect solution and this solution is as good as any.

9. Final mood

-10
-8
-6
-4
-2
-0

KEY
Mood: 0-Worst I've ever felt
10-Best I've ever felt
(Color in appropriate mood)
Polarities (See Table 1 and Chapter 6)
Under control (UC)—Over Control (OC)
Focus on past (P)—Focus on Future (F)
Deny positives (DP)—Deny negatives (DN)
Defeatism (D)—Perfectionism (P)
External focus (EF)—Internal focus (IF)
Meaninglessness (M)—Rigidity of belief (ROB)

Figure 4-2

An example of a thought monitoring form that has been completed to indicate the individual's activities, moods, thoughts, and his or her evaluation of those thoughts according to the procedures discussed in Chapters 4-8. (See relevant chapters).

you to write down your thoughts following the model which we have just completed here. [Show him the example of the recorded thoughts.] Remember that it is important to write down the troublesome thoughts immediately as they occur, rather than waiting until sometime later, and then, for example, trying to remember what you were thinking an hour ago. This immediate recording insures that there will be less distortion. In addition, be sure to be very specific. Write down your negative as well as your positive thoughts.

Figure 4-1 also contains space for the recording of the initial mood via a thermometerlike figure. It is always important to record initial mood, so that one has an experience of seeing one's mood change when it is recorded again at the end of the cognitive restructuring process.

Some examples of specific and nonspecific thoughts are listed below as a model. It is important to discuss these differences with the patient. More specific thoughts are more useful, because they can be more effectively argued with. For example, to say that one is a lousy housewife is not specific enough. Usually one is saying that because of some specific experience or piece of information. It is important to refer to that specific information when recording the thoughts. For example, it would be better to say, "I am a lousy housewife, because my mother-in-law remarked that I had dust on my bookcases." This thought can be more effectively argued with and evaluated using the procedures in the next few chapters. In addition to being very vague with one's thoughts, individuals also commonly record feelings or activities rather than *thoughts*. Sometimes they also avoid writing down the negative aspects of their thoughts. This is especially the case with individuals who are reluctant to admit their difficulties.

Nancy had been in counseling because of a poor self-concept, and a sense that she was basically unlovable and had failed as a housewife. At the beginning of the counseling process she offered some of the following examples of thoughts.

Of an interaction with her children, she recorded, "I blew it, I am making it hard on my kids. I am ruining their lives." We examined her thoughts and recorded a more specific version: "I lost my temper at Johnny on Tuesday when he spilled the paint, therefore I blew it." This second thought is really the source of her recorded thought. This more specific thought is also more effectively checked for cognitive distortions.

In response to an argument with her husband, Nancy had recorded, "Leave me alone." Later we clarified that thought to "I don't
know how to argue with you. I don't know what to say. There must
be something wrong with me. I don't want to argue. Leave me alone."

Early in the counseling, when Nancy was filling out an application
for work with a religious organization, she had recorded, "I have failed
you, Lord," on her thought-monitoring sheet. Later, during our therapy session, she was able to elaborate on the specific reason for her
perception of self-failure in the religious sphere. She noted in the
therapy session, "Because I am depressed now, and need to be in
therapy, I am a bad Christian. A good Christian would not have these
problems."

In all cases above, the more specific thought outlined a specific
event or reason which prompted the negative statement about the self
or the situation. Both the negative statement about the self or situation,
and the specific event or reason which prompted the statement, should
be written on the monitoring log. Such a specific thought can be more
clearly evaluated for distortion. That is, the irrational negative conclusions drawn from one event will be more evident.

After a number of sessions, Nancy became more specific and more
aware of her actual thoughts. For example, when reflecting on the
fact that she had signed up for a CPR Course, she recorded the following thoughts: "I don't believe I got myself into this. I'll never be
able to learn this material. I'll make a fool of myself." Earlier she might
have merely recorded something like, "I should not be taking this
course." She would not have recorded the reasons for her hesitancy.

Another example of her thoughts occurred when she was baking,
and reflecting on her· work. She recorded, "I really got a lot done
today. I am doing better, but really it is not much compared to what
others get done." Another example occurred when she was sitting in
her living room reflecting on her faith and her feelings about God.
"I feel so far from God, so there must be something really wrong with
my relationship with God, and my Christian life." Earlier, she would
probably have just written, "I am a bad Christian," and would not
have recorded the specific reasons or events that led to that conclusion.
More specific thoughts reflect more accurately the heart of the problem, and are also more amenable to change.

Monitoring of images.   Mental images and fantasies play an important therapeutic role in the psychodynamic, behavioral, and cognitive models of psychotherapy. Images and fantasies are also im-

portant in the ascetic and mystical theological literature. An individual's report that she could visualize in her mind a nice red apple that was wet on the outside and smelled fresh would meet the criteria of the definition of an image.

According to both cognitive (Lang, 1979) and psychodynamic theorists (Horowitz, 1978), images are not unlike thoughts, except that they have sensory components. If this is so, then images can be monitored and examined like thoughts. According to Lang (1979) images usually include both a stimulus component, which is an actual description of a situation, and a response component, which is the individual's emotional, behavioral, and physiological reaction to the mental image. Images usually evoke stronger physiological responses than do nonimage thoughts. This may make images more powerful.

There is an extensive use of images in the ascetic and mystical theological tradition of Roman Catholicism. Studies of meditation, for example, in the Carmelite tradition, have found that such meditation includes images not only of Christ, but images of the individual in various situations, as well as associations with each of these images (Mallory, 1977). Images are also used extensively in the spiritual allegory tradition in Protestant Pietism. *Pilgrim's Progress* by John Bunyan (1678/1911) and *Hind's Feet on High Places* by Hannah Hurnard (1977) represent two classical examples of this tradition.

One well-known example of imagery use in the Christian tradition is recorded in *The Spiritual Exercises of St. Ignatius* (1548/1951). St. Ignatius reports a series of imagery exercises which individuals can use for both self-examination and to aid themselves in making decisions or understanding God. St. Ignatius increases the focus and intensity of an individual's image by focusing on the five senses. For example, for the meditation on hell, he suggests that participants "see" the fires, "hear" the wailing, "smell" the smoke, "taste" the bitterness of tears, and finally, "touch the flames."

The focus on the five senses is precisely the technique that Milton Erickson, the father of modern clinical hypnosis, has advocated to increase the individual's involvement in images. The procedure is simply to help the individual focus on enough cues in the situation so that the situation becomes vivid for him (Zeig, 1982). Cues are obtained by having the individual turn on the various senses, such as sight, sound, and smell. The cues of the image can also be used to help the individual get in touch with his thoughts and feelings about the situation at the time of its occurrence.

Below is a transcript for helping the individual become aware of various troubling memories or images. Note that the entire procedure is set within a religious context.

> I would like to help you remember in a little more detail the situation that is bothering you by helping you focus your attention on it. Could you please tell me where the situation occurred? . . . .I would also like for you to try to become as comfortable as possible in the chair and close your eyes whenever you would like.

The location information obtained is used to help the other person focus more clearly on the situation. The amount of emphasis which the counselor can choose to put on physical relaxation may vary. If one wishes to put more emphasis on relaxation, parts of some of the sequences in Chapter 9 could be used before continuing with the image. It is also very important at this juncture to introduce an attitude of permissiveness. By your attitude you emphasize that the individual has your permission to explore as little or as much as he or she wants to. Such an attitude sets up a framework of mutual cooperation, in which the other person makes the decisions, and you are the guide. Individuals exploring thoughts and images, some of which may be frightening, need permission to go at their own rate.

> After you have made yourself comfortable in the chair, try to picture yourself right now in the presence of God. Realize that you are not alone in this process. Now I would like for you to try to visualize yourself in _____ [location previously identified by patient.] Can you see yourself in that situation?

When the patient responds, "Yes," it is important to reassure them with "Good," and then proceed to ask them the next question.

> As you see yourself in _____, what do you see around you?
> [This procedure is very different from a standard hypnosis procedure, in that questions are repeatedly asked the individual which he can verbally answer. A hypnotic state is neither required nor desired. We are merely using some procedures borrowed from hypnosis that are an aid for the focusing of attention. At this point the counselor could continue by linking each of the patient's responses to another object, in Ericksonian fashion.]
> As you see _____, what else do you see? [patient's response]
> Good, now as you see _____, what else do you see?

[The process should continue until the patient cannot report anything else and/or the counselor perceives that the counselee is more absorbed in the image. At that point, the counselor should shift to another sensory modality.]

Good, now as you see _____, can you hear anything?

As you hear _____, can you smell anything?

As you smell _____ can you feel anything?

The counselor should allow for a few responses in each of the sensory modalities. If the patient does not report anything, it is important to communicate the idea that that is also okay. Whatever the individual perceives, or fails to perceive, is okay. Such a process encourages exploration of the image, and relieves any fears that the individual may have of failing. Most individuals view this as a very vulnerable activity. Such vulnerability requires great acceptance on the part of the counselor. The acceptance we have obtained from God must flow from us to the other person.

After the counselor has inquired about responses in each sensory modality, he or she should then switch to feelings and thoughts.

As you are aware of feeling [repeat bodily sensations described previously] ____ what kinds of emotions are going on inside? As you are feeling ____, what thoughts are going through your mind? What other thoughts do you have?

The counselor should ask for a number of different thoughts and record them on a monitoring chart. When the process is complete, the counselor should ask the patient to open his eyes. A very brief discussion of the individual's feelings about imagery should ensue, and then attention should be directed to the recorded thoughts.

Chapter 7 discusses further imagery-monitoring and the accompanying modification.

Awareness of bodily sensations.   Sometimes it is useful to become aware of bodily sensations. Such an awareness may provide a clue as to our actual feelings and thoughts. Additionally, however, this awareness in and of itself may help relieve nervous tension. Part of this procedure described below was derived from *Autoanalysis* (Jencks, 1974). It has been modified, however, to include an emphasis on the presence of God. The following is one possible transcript of how this might be done.

Sit or lie down as comfortably as possible. Then slowly become aware of God's presence in the room with you. The whole process can be seen as a self-abandonment of your body to Divine Providence. . . . [The counselor may pause after each of the following phrases.]. . . . As you become aware of the Divine presence, close your eyes, and pay attention passively to anything that occurs in the body. The attention must not be active, but rather a passive observation of these experiences. You may, if you wish, give up the need to be concerned about what your sensations are. Merely ask God to show you what they are. Adopt an attitude of waiting. Put into audible words whatever happens. Do not analyze, or intellectualize, but just pay attention, and verbalize the sensations. As you verbalize each sensation, gently let go of the sensation into the control of God. This should not be an active letting-go, but a passive surrender.

Scan the body and feel more clearly what is happening in different places. Some examples of what you might feel include, "eyes tight; pressure in the chest or stomach; throat tight; left arm itches; neck hurts." Omit all unnecessary words and merely whisper the sensation, omitting all reference to yourself. This attending should lead to relaxation.

After a few minutes, the sensations will become fewer and a calm state will follow. Allow yourself to enjoy the calmness and relax in the warm divine presence. Facility in this' exercise will increase with repeated practice.

Concluding comments.   A number of general issues should be kept in mind while considering the thought-monitoring process. First, the goal of self-monitoring is ultimately to become aware not only of our most specific thoughts, but also the basic underlying assumptions that influence our entire lives. More in-depth thoughts will only come with time, however. This does not mean that an individual should avoid any cognitive restructuring until he or she is aware of these deeper assumptions. On the contrary, sometimes some of the more deeply held assumptions we hold will only come to light when some of our more superficial assumptions and specific negative thoughts have been successfully challenged. Gradually, as individual assumptions are challenged, the underlying major ideas held by the individual are brought up for consideration and eventually changed. This change process is not unlike the creativity or the religious conversion process as suggested by Batson and Ventis (1982). Our normal way of thinking is subtly challenged by bits of data or alternative thoughts which gradually build up. Over time, the discrepancy builds, and at some point the entire old underlying structure is brought up for reconsideration.

Secondly, we sometimes hesitate to examine our thoughts because of a fear of what we might discover. Such fears should be discussed at the beginning of counseling, and defused. Several factors should be considered. It is important to realize that the thoughts we discover have already been exerting a great influence on us. Our discovery of them actually relieves them of some of their potency, and lessens their negative control over us. Additionally, any self-examination process can be seen as a spiritual exercise and should be done within the context of the divine presence. This theme of protection often provides the extra needed emotional buffer that many individuals need to continue the process.

Third, it is important to realize that there is no magic amount of thought-monitoring. It is more important to monitor correctly a few times than many times incorrectly. Homework assignments should never be overwhelming.

Fourth, since showing one's thoughts to another is a very vulnerable exercise, all recorded thoughts should be treated gently and with respect. It is always important to affirm an individual's attempts.

Finally, thought-monitoring is probably the most important part of cognitive-behavioral therapy. It is a building block for changing both thoughts and behavior. It is therefore very important to feel comfortable with thought-monitoring before moving on to additional procedures.

Self-examination is not the goal of cognitive therapy, however. Neither is it the ultimate goal of spirituality. After one gains more self-knowledge, that knowledge must then be evaluated. The hope is that the outcome of this evaluation will be personal change and growth. Processes for that change and growth will be the focus of the next several chapters.

Chapter 5

TRANSFORMATION OF OUR POINT OF VIEW

Deep within us all there is an amazing inner sanctuary of the soul, a holy place, a Divine Center, a speaking Voice, to which we may continuously return. . . . It is a Light Within which illumines the face of God. . . . For the religious man is forever bringing all affairs down into the Light, holding them there in the Presence, reseeing them and the whole of the world . . . in a new and over-turning way.—Thomas Kelley, 1941, pp. 29,36

Change and Transformation

Thomas Kelley suggests that we become responsive to God by "centering down." This traditional Quaker term means that we let go of all competing distractions until we are truly centered, until we are truly aware of ourselves and the voice of God speaking to us in the present. As we begin to focus, we begin to listen. We begin to listen to our thoughts, and to God's thoughts.

It is only after we have listened that we can begin to respond. It is only after we have begun to understand ourselves, and God, that we can begin to change. It is only when we have actually brought our thoughts and concerns into the divine presence that we see them differently. Kelley asserts that living in the divine presence is awkward and painful at first. It is awkward, because it takes constant vigilance, effort, and practice. It is painful, because we so easily forget that presence.

Changing or transforming our ways of seeing and thinking are never easy, but it is this renewed way of seeing that forms the basis for a renewal of the spirit of God in one's life. "Repentance," the necessary precursor of our redemption, is actually *metanoia* (literally, to change one's mind). This is not merely the experience of remorse, or an uncomfortable feeling. Rather, repentance implies that one has arrived at a different view of something, an entirely different perspective on the matter (cf. Michel, 1942/1967, pp. 626–629). Human repentance results merely in remorse and regret. Divinely inspired repentance is a true change of perspective. A new life does not come from mere remorse, but from a change of perspective.

Psychological Theories of Change

Changes in perspective are at the heart of most theories of counseling and psychotherapy. All are agreed that the suffering individual has a faulty understanding and incorrect ideas about himself and his world. All agree that such an individual is stuck in less than adequate ways of thinking about himself and others. Furthermore, most major theories see as their goal the changing of this faulty mind-set. Theories differ, however, in how this change of mind may be encouraged in the counseling session.

Dynamic theories.   As noted in the previous chapter, Freud desired to bring unconscious impulses under the control of the powers of reason. In Freudian analysis, the process of transformation is actually a by-product of the self-awareness process. As individuals gains insight into their real motivations, the motivations themselves are transformed. They lose their power to create chaos in persons' lives, because they are now under rational control.

The actual change process occurs as all of the patient's thoughts about the therapist and other persons and situations in the present are interpreted by the therapist as representing concerns from the past. For example, the therapist may state that the patient's reactions to her represent the patient's felt expectations from a parent. There is usually resistance to such new perspectives. Troubled individuals prefer to continue to see things from their point of view, even though this viewpoint causes them pain. Eventually, however, the patient has to give up control, give up seeing things from his perspective. He adopts the therapist's perspective (cf. Barton, 1974).

In psychoanalysis, there is nothing overt about this change process. The therapist does not typically tell the patient that he will come to see things from the therapist's perspective. Neither does the therapist actively challenge the patient's perspective in most cases. Instead, the psychoanalyst maintains a very distant stance, a kind of evenly hovering attention, regardless of what the patient shares. Ideally, the therapist maintains enough distance so that any response on the part of the patient is ostensively not to the therapist, but rather to the patient's internal ideas projected onto the therapist from the past. Gradually, because of this lack of external input, the patient comes to realize that his perceptions and ideas are just that, *his*. He is the one doing the interpreting. The patient's mind has been changed. His perception that his present difficulties are due to present circumstances, and not his own distortions borrowed from the past, is challenged.

Jung is another important dynamic therapist. In Chapter 4 we noted that self-awareness for Jung implied more than simple awareness of biological impulses and the influence of our personal past. According to Jung, the psyche of each individual is striving for wholeness (Jocabi, 1973). This wholeness comes about through the freer expression and awareness of psychic energy. This energy is not merely biological or sexual, as was the case with Freud. It is composed of the intentionality of all living things, a creative life force, the same force that underlies myths, religions, and neurosis.

Any blocking of this creative life force results in neurosis. This may occur when any individual has overemphasized one side of his life, and denied another side. This denied side of life haunts the individual through neurosis, bad dreams, or complexes. Therapy aims to put the individual back in touch with the creative forces in this denied side of his existence. In opposition to Freud, Jung did not believe that the goal of therapy was to bring all of one's existence under the control of rational thought. Rather, the patient in Jungian analysis was helped to develop a more comprehensive self that would encompass those parts of himself that he had previously denied.

Jung does not specifically talk about the actual process of psychotherapy. He prefers to describe inward events. He merely states that individuals need to share their dark side with someone, or relive part of themselves. But Jung believes that it is not just reliving part of oneself in therapy that is valuable. One must also have the strengthening support of the other when this process is happening.

The other individual leads the patient into courage and helps him to accept what he discovers (cf. Jung, 1928/1972).

In contrast to Freudian analysis, the Jungian therapist is not invisible to the patient. Also, the therapist does not claim or assume that she has priority with respect to the interpretation of reality (cf. Barton, 1974). Both the therapist and the patient collaborate in interpreting the patient's experiences, thoughts, or dreams. Transformation happens as the hurting individual is able to reconcile the often conflicting sides of him into a larger whole. The therapist may hint at possible meanings of the patient's experiences. However, the patient decides finally what the meanings are.

Jung very strongly states that the process is one in which both the patient and the therapist sit back and watch the unconscious work. There is a process within the individual that is pushing him towards wholeness, and the patient is encouraged to become open to that force. One's behavior is thus often a product of some of these internal creative urges towards wholeness. Some Christian Jungians see the source of this creative urge as God. One of the goals of Jungian therapy is for the patient to discover the direction in which his life is going. Dreams and associations give hints of this direction.

For Jung, the call of God is really the internal psyche of the personality striving towards wholeness. This striving for meaning and wholeness becomes stronger as the individual becomes more aware of himself. The goal is for the patient to recognize the irrational, to recognize that solutions are often bigger than his conception of them. The patient must realize that not all problems have rational answers. Ultimately, this process also involves changing our minds about what is acceptable to us. I contend that this changing of the mind, resulting in the acceptance of a different way of seeing reality, is the goal of Jungian analysis. I am unsure, however, whether Jung himself would admit to such a strong role for rationality and thinking in his therapy.

Even though Jung asserts that rational processes are not the goal of therapy, it seems that they actually play an important role in his therapy. Jung's genius is that he very permissively allows the patient to arrive at his own new views of himself and his life, rather than directing the therapist to impose a new view in an authoritarian manner. This nondirectiveness may obscure the fact that the therapist is encouraging the patient to change his mind. Actually, the process of unifying the opposites and the contradictions in our life is a cognitive process. One develops a larger framework or perspective in which the various opposite ideas, experiences, and processes are admissible.

This process is not unlike the acceptance of imperfections in ourselves. By the therapist's refusal to be dogmatic about the needed interpretation, the patient feels less pushed and is actually more willing to accept the therapist's interpretations. I thus disagree with Jungians who assert that *rational* processes are not ultimately the source of psychological change. However, I do concur that *rationalistic* solutions or solutions from rationalism are not always necessary for our problems.[1] Certainly to assert that God accepts us and continues to love us only when we experience a "dark night of the soul" is not a rationalist solution to a feeling of desolation; but it may be a rational solution, depending upon our underlying assumptions.

Social learning theory.   The second major school of therapeutic change is social learning theory. One prime exponent, B. F. Skinner, is not concerned with any internal mechanisms or thoughts. He is concerned only with contingencies of reinforcement, that is, how positive or negative changes in the environment change the individual's behavior. Transformation is changing the environment, so that the individual's behavior is changed. Therapy, for social learning theorists, consists of teaching the individual new skills so that he may obtain the needed rewards from the environment. In some cases, the patient may learn to change his environment.

Some social learning theorists such as Miller and Dollard (1941) combined the notion of biological impulses, posited in earlier dynamic theory, with learning theory. Individuals learn responses so as to reduce certain internal urges or drives. For example, an individual may learn skills to obtain food, to satisfy the hunger drive. If the drive is thwarted in any way, frustration and aggression will result. Each time a drive is reduced, any behavior that reduced that drive is reinforced. For example, an infant soon learns that placing a bottle in his mouth and initiating a sucking behavior results in a pleasant taste and lessened hunger pangs. That behavior has been rewarded and it is likely to be repeated.

Bandura and Walters (1963), two other American contemporary social learning theorists, later suggested that the actual behavior did not have to be performed. If one observed behaviors of another person being rewarded, one was more likely to pick up those behaviors. According to Bandura, the individual forms internal ideas, or symbolic representations of observed behavior. These internal ideas are then the source of later behavior which imitates the observed.

This was the beginning of the cognitive revolution in social learning theory. According to Bandura, an individual changes his mind about which behaviors to perform, in order to obtain certain expected rewards. These expectations are changed when others' behaviors are observed being rewarded. Changed expectations, or a changed mind, results in changed behavior. For example, children usually do not expect certain aggressive behaviors to be rewarded. However, when they observe that another child's aggressive behavior results in his being given more attention and greater rewards, they change their expectations as to what results from aggressive behavior. They have changed their minds.

Phenomenological and Existential therapists.   As emphasized in Chapter 5, a third group of psychologists, including both the phenomenologists and the existentialists, have defined self-awareness as being open to all of one's experiences as they occur. In contrast to dynamic theories such as Jung's, however, nothing is said in these theories about the existence of archtypes or unconscious psychic energy. Explanations are limited to what can be actually observed occurring in the individual.

For Carl Rogers, transformation occurs as the therapist helps the patient to experience his natural processes and experiences. A neurotic individual has denied many of his experiences because they are not acceptable to others. Acceptance of those experiences occurs, however, within the context of a therapeutic relationship in which the therapist communicates to the patient that his previously denied experiences *are* acceptable. This acceptance actually redefines the patient's experiences of himself, by communicating to him that his experiences are acceptable. This is Rogers's *unconditional positive regard.*

Typically, the Rogerian is a good listener. Like the Freudian analysts, she maintains a somewhat distant, even attitude toward whatever the patient shares. Unlike the analyst, however, the therapist always shows positive acceptance. The Rogerian emphasizes that it is the patient's feelings, not his thoughts, that are the important ingredient of therapy. The therapist merely expresses acceptance of those feelings (Rogers, 1961), but through this acceptance, the therapist is able to give the patient a different *label* for his feelings.

As George Mead has said in *Mind, Self and Society* (1934), we see ourselves as we see other people seeing us. The patient is given a different label for him or herself from the therapist. For example, rather than seeing her anger as an example of her "badness" or "immaturity," as such emotions may have labled by her parents, a young woman may begin to label her anger as part of her need for self-respect and the need to be taken seriously.

The existential and phenomenological psychologists focus on the individual's own experience of himself, rather than attempting to explain those experiences from their own perspective.

Existential therapists do not emphasize techniques (May, 1958). Instead, they "seek to understand the patient as a being and as being-in-his world" (p.77). The therapist attempts to help the patient become more fully aware of herself and who she is. She is helped to see that she can make the choices about her life. The patient, like Judy in the preceding chapter who was continually asked, "What do *you* want?" is confronted. Transformation is making the patient aware of her own self, and her freedom to make her choices. Experiences in therapy are used to change the individual's mind about who makes the decisions in her existence.

Victor Frankl (1959), a Jewish Existentialist, has also emphasized the role of choice. According to Frankl, becoming conscious of oneself and one's ability to take a stance results in emotional health. He believes the human personality has within it the ability to stand outside of itself, to transcend itself, and take a stand or attitude towards its situation. It is these attitudes that we take towards our life that will ultimately determine whether we see our life situations as meaningful. It is these changes of mind that ultimately make us content or miserable.

This brief review of the three major schools of psychotherapy has emphasized that all of them are concerned with helping individuals change their mind about themselves or their life situations. Psychoanalytic theorists want to modify the individual's distorted internal mental constructions derived from the past, so that these thoughts more closely match present reality. Behaviorists focus on the individual's expectations about whether his environment will reward him. Finally, existentialists believe that health comes when a person adopts the perspective that he is no longer helpless, that he can choose a meaningful perspective on his existence.

Cognitive therapy.   Changes in assumptions and perspective are an important ingredient in cognitive therapy. Michael Mahoney's 1980 volume *Psychotherapy Processes* construed change within the cognitive therapy paradigm as starting with single cognitions. Ultimately, however, cognitive therapists talk about a shift in the individual's overall mental structures, a shift in the way one construes reality. Cognitive therapy is not simply a superficial technique that teaches the individual to say certain thoughts to himself. Cognitive therapy aims to shift the person's core assumptions.

Aaron Beck (Beck, Rush, Shaw, & Emery, 1979) talks about this deeper process as changing the individual's depressogenic (depression-causing) assumptions. These assumptions are the basic beliefs that predispose the person to depression or anxiety. Each individual has a unique set of personal rules about how he and his world should be viewed. If these rules or assumptions are not changed, even after the depression has abated, the individual will remain vulnerable to future problems. These underlying beliefs must be identified and changed. Usually these assumptions are inferred from a sampling of the individual's cognitions. Often, once these assumptions are identified, many individuals see their absurdity. However, arguments must often be continually presented against these assumptions whenever they occur until the old assumptions are gradually replaced with more adaptive ones (pp. 252ff.).

Regardless of orientation and specific techniques, the common road to health across these differing approaches to psychotherapy is "repentance." Repentance means the changing of one's mind about how one's self and the world is to be viewed.

Theological Models of Transformation

> . . . Do not be conformed to this world but be transformed by the renewal of your mind, that you may prove what is the will of God, what is good and acceptable and perfect (Rom. 12.2).

Theological models of transformation actually contain many of the same themes of change as appear in psychological models. We are admonished to find ourselves, not to allow the world to squeeze us into its mold, to examine that world and become aware of its actual influence upon us. We are counseled to cease living a constricted existence, to cease allowing old ways of seeing things, or doing things, to dominate our existence. Finally, we are asked to step outside of ourselves, to transcend ourselves. We are challenged to risk, to make a commitment, to change our minds, to choose, to choose life.

Theological models of transformation emphasize change in two areas. First we learn to look at ourselves differently. We gain a renewed perspective on what we can be. We cease to define ourselves merely in terms of who we are. We cease to define ourselves merely in terms of our own limited goals. Ultimately, we struggle to define ourselves according to the will of God.

Initially, this struggle for self-definition involves a move away from people. We must learn not to respond or conform to others' expectations of us. We must seek a desert of solitude where we can reflect on who we are, what we *really* want, what God expects of us. We must learn what our inner voices are. We must learn what we *really* say to ourselves when we are tired, or confused, or simply caught up in the business of the day.

Transformation of self.   Self-dialogue and the gaining of a transcendent divine perspective whereby that dialogue may be influenced are two important ingredients of self-transformation. I wish to focus on two thinkers who have emphasized both of these themes.

Reinhold Niebuhr.   Niebuhr borrowed from Augustine the idea that self-dialogue represents the *imago Dei* in the individual. Niebuhr (1955) further contends that self-knowledge and transformation occur for the individual when he knows himself confronted by God. How is it that a self-transcendent belief system results in a greater sense of self? "Only in that confrontation does he become aware of his full stature and freedom and of the evil in him. It is for this reason that biblical faith is of such importance for the proper understanding of man" (p.131).

It is only in confrontation with a greater transcendent being, that our own feelings of self-transcendence and freedom are verified. We really do stand outside of it all. We really can make some choices. We are responsible—and we can make some wrong choices—we can choose evil. In this confrontation with God we are empowered. We are transformed. We begin to change our minds about ourselves.

This confrontation can't be in theory only. It must be experienced. The good psychotherapist will enable the patient to experience the empowerment that comes with the realization of the *imago Dei* in her life. Self-transcendence, for Niebuhr, thus means to stand outside of oneself and to see oneself as God sees one. An individual will stand straighter as she realizes that she is important, that she can make her own decisions for her life.

Because we are able to stand outside and beyond the world, we are tempted to regard ourselves as gods. Yet we also see ourselves as involved in the flux of the world. We have "a sense of being seen, commanded, judged and known from beyond ourselves" (p.128). This was the experience of the psalmist. "O Lord, thou has searched me, and known me. Thou knowest when I sit down and when I rise up. . . . and art acquainted with all my ways" (Psalm 139). This sense of being spoken to is interpreted by biblical faith as a relation between God and the person.

The view that there is something beyond us derives from our

experiences. We often sense that there is more. "It is a fact that man is judged and yet there is no vantage point in his own life, sufficiently transcendent, from which the judgment can take place . . ." (Niebuhr, 1953, p.129). All common human experience requires *more* than the immediate experience to help us *understand* our immediate experience. We must make *sense* of our experiences. We must evaluate them. Only something bigger than our experiences will be accepted as a legitimate judgment of them.

The patient who experiences intense darkness and struggle in his life needs a word much bigger than those experiences to help him change his mind about them. We need a word outside of ourselves. We need to see our experiences in a new light. Without these transcendent interpretations, we would not acknowledge another perspective that would challenge our own. We would then excuse ourself, accept ourselves as we are. We would feel justified, comfortable in our present existence. But, we do not feel comfortable. We often feel judged, challenged, condemned. We need a word to challenge those judging voices.

This need for a transcendent perspective is true of the depressed perfectionistic individual. *With only self to confront self, there is no believable word that will allow one to step outside of the self-condemning darkness.* There is no word to contradict our words of despair to ourselves. We never have a broad enough perspective with which to stand back and get a clear picture of ourselves. We only know ourselves truly, and begin to grasp our potential, as we know ourselves confronted by God—as we see ourselves as God sees us.

When we actually discover ourselves, we realize that we do not know all of ourself. Our limits lie outside of ourselves. "Man's powers of transcendence place man so outside of everything else that he can find a home only in God . . ." (p. 154), Niebuhr echoes Augustine.

Augustine (c.401/1963) finally had to realize that the limits of the self lie outside of the self.

> Through all this I range; I fly here and I fly there; I dive down deep as I can, and I can find no end. So great is the force of memory, so great is the force of life in man who lives to die. What shall I do, you true life of mine, my God? I will go past this force of mine called memory; I will go beyond it so that I may draw nearer to you, sweet light. . . . I will pass beyond memory to find you." (pp. 227–228)

According to Niebuhr, Augustine understood that "the human spirit in its depth and height reaches into eternity" (p.157). Niebuhr warned, however, that "Human life points beyond itself. But it must not make itself into that beyond" (p. 158).

Niebuhr noted that because our experiences point to something outside of the natural, and because we can transcend our world, we want an ultimate key to understanding that world that comes from beyond even our own limited capacity to understand or transcend. He adds that Jesus provides this key only if he is not merely a human Jesus. The source of meaning and confrontation must always lie outside of things, because something inside the flux is not adequate to explain everything. Ultimately, our perspective on ourselves is changed only as it is challenged by another perspective.

Jesus both elevated humanness and also pointed beyond humanness. Without Jesus, there is a tendency either to deny nature and our physical humanness, or to make it God. Biblical faith alone sees a discontinuity between God and man. Jesus is different from us. He gives us complete knowledge of what we can be. Otherwise, our own knowledge is partial. Jesus, who stands outside of us, challenges us, provides us with a new way of acting, thinking, and feeling. Only as Jesus is divine is this alternative seriously considered.

For Niebuhr, our minds are changed about ourselves as we are confronted with another alternative concerning ourselves—Jesus.

Karl Barth.   According to Barth, (1948/1960) humanity is not only a body, but a soul. This soul within the individual is aroused by the spirit of God. Thus humanity also has a spirit. Barth does not say that the person is a spirit, but that the person has a Spirit. This means that the individual can reflect upon herself and understand herself. This individual can also take responsibility for herself, and act.

The soul is given special abilities by the spirit of God. According to Barth, the body desires, but the soul wills. The soul stands at a distance from his desiring. He reviews himself. He becomes an object to himself. This freedom to stand at a distance from oneself, and reflect upon oneself is given by the spirit of God.

For Barth, the divine also opens up the possibility for transformation in a second way. As we are summoned by God, we are awakened, aroused. We are called out of ourselves, beyond ourselves. As we go beyond ourselves, we embark upon a new way of seeing ourselves. We see ourselves in the proper context. As we act responsibly beyond God, we have a greater sense of self. Life tears less at us, because it is no longer our primary orientation. As we go to God, we step out of ourselves. The result is that we have a clearer perspective by which to look at ourselves.

The divine spirit thus leads to transformation because it drives us to confront ourselves. This confrontation and transformation occurs through the call of God that comes from Jesus. Jesus provides a call when he asks us to step out of ourselves and look at ourselves and when he demonstrates the possibilities of transformation.

The spirit of God, indeed, gives us a new self-definition and a new direction. As this newness is experienced, new possibilities come into being. "As a man is freed interiorly, then nothing can imprison him or prevent him from expressing his authentic life" (O'Hara, 1984, p. 19). Even if nothing changes externally, somehow we can free ourselves. We can cease to allow ourselves to be defined by the community around us. Such a promise provides hope for the depressed individual who is beset by the thought that, "I must have the approval of everyone around me. If I am not liked by someone, I have failed. I wonder what so-and-so thinks about me. I am sure they don't like me." God calls us to step outside of the evaluation placed upon us by others. God purifies us from childhood and infantile patterns and dependency and extreme need for approval and security. When spirituality comes to its fullness, we learn to transcend these images of the past (cf. Van Kaam, 1976). We learn that we are someone graced with God's acceptance and God's calling forth. Our disappointments in others need not devastate us. Our happiness no longer depends upon having our desires for affirmations and acceptance from others completely fulfilled. (They never are, anyway.) Only as one moves away from relationships to obtain an objective perspective on oneself from God, can one move back into the community with a message of wholeness.

A true realization that our call is from God does not mean that we then live a perfect life, immune from pains, from disappointments, and the inevitable failures and rejections that form part of human experience. Our call is from Jesus. To receive a call from Jesus means that we expect some pain, disappointment, failure, and rejection. The difference, however, is that pain does not lead to despair, because it only reminds us of Jesus's pains. Failure does not lead to giving up, because ultimately the failure of the cross was a success. Disappointment is not devastating, because our focus is on God. Finally, rejection only serves to increase our identification with Jesus, who also suffered rejection.

Healing our relationships with others.   If the road to transformation appears initially to lead away from others, this is only part of the journey. Ultimately, true spirituality and true mental health form a circle. First, we are called away from the group. We cease to respond to other persons' expectations of us, and begin to respond to the call of God in our lives. Ultimately, however, we come back to society. We must relate as a whole person to the community.

Karl Barth.   Barth's theology focuses as intensely on our relationship with others as it does on the notion of self-dialogue, and confrontation with Jesus. Just as we are a soul who dialogues with God, so we are a body who dialogues with others. It is with our bodies that we know others and are known to the community. The body and soul are not in opposition to each other. The spirit of God in our lives brings them into harmony with each other.

Again, just as Jesus is the model of who we can be with ourselves, so Jesus is the model of who we can be for others. The body and the soul were not in opposition in Jesus. Jesus gave both his soul (Matt. 20.28) and his body (Luke 22:19) for others. Jesus was a loving servant of others, though he was not a slave to them.

Barth includes caring for the other person in mental and spiritual health. Wholeness is honoring and treasuring the other person. However, wholeness is not ultimately oriented towards the other person. Ultimately, we gain our self-definition from God.

Object relations theorists (e.g., Fairbairn, 1952) state that we long to be in a perfect relationship. We long for perfect parents or significant others in our life. We want perfect affirmation. These relationships always disappoint, however. White (1984) says this is because our longing for a perfect relationship is ultimately a longing for a relationship with God. We have a craving and longing for a relationship with the perfect Deity. Often we carry within us an internalized image of a parent who is seen as all bad simply because they were not perfect. When others also fail to fulfill all of our expectations (which they will inevitably), we see them as all bad. We place demands upon relationships that disrupt their harmony. Our thoughts and images about others must be healed. We must change our minds about them.

As we turn our attention to God, some of our longings may be fulfilled. Developing a healthy picture of God results in a picture of a God who delights in us and is pleased to dwell with us. Jesus's redemption of us is seen as evidence of this love. As we gain affirmation from God, it can be less important to us that the relationship with the other person, or indeed the other person himself, be perfect. We are able to relate to them with lessened expectations. Healing results because we can relate freely to others without intense demands that they be as we wish. We can allow other people to be themselves, because our self-definition does not come from them. We relate as an "I and Thou" (cf. Martin Buber's concept of "I and thou," 1937/1958). We have begun to see the other as they really are. Our relationships are transformed.

Techniques of Transformation

Psychological theories of transformation urge us to adopt a less restrictive mind-set. They caution us not to be influenced by the past, to understand how our present world would dictate our behaviors, and to resist that dictation, not to allow ourselves to be defined by our roles.

Theology also states that true transformation occurs when we cease gaining our self-definition from those around us, but begin to take our cues from God. Such a process results in a new freedom. We are less dependent upon others' approval. We have less need for all relationships to be perfect. We can be a servant of others, and not a slave.

The remainder of this chapter and the next two chapters will describe methods whereby individuals can begin to learn alternative ways of viewing themselves.

There are three types of techniques discussed in this chapter: First, meditation techniques are discussed; several techniques that emphasize cultivating a type of attitude ("problem solving" and "facing" the worst) are next; finally, two techniques ("stress inoculation" and "checking out reality") adapted from the cognitive therapy literature are included.

It should be noted that within the context of counseling, these techniques are often taught to the patient during the session. After he has had a chance to practice them in the session, they are then assigned as homework. Such homework is described to the patient as an *experiment.* He can use these procedures to examine some of his thoughts or to test out some of his hypotheses about himself.

Techniques for change or transformation presented in the remaining chapters of the book will be accompanied by the following information:

1. A description of the technique, including a brief discussion of its psychological background;

2. A brief theological discussion of the technique; and finally, in some cases,

3.   A transcript of how the technique can be used, and/
or an example of the use of the technique.

All of the techniques in this chapter are suitable for use by the
individual on his own for self-growth.

Meditation.   Meditation has been defined as focusing one's attention in one direction. In meditation, an individual may either focus
her attention on a single unchanging stimulus (concentrative meditation) or on whatever passes through her awareness (awareness meditation) (Woolfolk & Lehrer, 1984). As we noted in chapter 2, both
methods have been compared to cognitive restructuring. For example,
in awareness meditation, as we stand back and examine our thoughts
in a detached manner, we can more objectively evaluate them. We
need no longer be overwhelmed by the thoughts that come into our
mind. Concentrative meditation accomplishes the same purpose. As
an individual focuses attention on one object, other thoughts that intrude into the mind are merely dismissed as they arise, and the med-
itator is taught to focus his attention back on the object. Such a reaction
to intrusive thoughts gradually leads to a neutralization of those
thoughts or ideas. One merely allows the thoughts to "float by," and
does not become upset by them. In actuality, we have adopted the
attitude that we are not going to worry about them.

Research in the physiology of stress and stress management
has begun to define what appears to be necessary in order to evoke
the "relaxation response" in individuals. One of these researchers,
Benson (1975), suggests that what is needed is a quiet environment,
a comfortable position, a passive attitude, and a mental device to engage one's attention in order to relax. For a mental device, Benson
suggests that one pick a work, or gaze at an object, to occupy one's
attention. If one picks a word—he recommends the word "one"—
Benson suggests saying the word with each exhalation. In this exercise,
one's attention is turned away from all the worrisome concerns of
one's day, and focused comfortably in a direction where anxieties will
not be aroused.

Meditation has been part of the Christian tradition since its in-
ception. Richard Foster (1983) quotes Theophan the Recluse, a nine-
teenth century Russian Orthodox monk, as saying, "To pray is to de-
scend with the mind into the heart, and there to stand before the face
of the Lord, ever-present, all seeing, within you" (p. 7). The object
of attention in Christian meditation is God. As we think about God,

we learn to push out other thoughts. True Christian meditation is not the cessation of thinking, but rather the focusing of our attention on God. Indeed, eventually other things come to be seen in the light of God's grace. If the focus of our attention is on Christ, any other thoughts that intrude upon our consciousness are seen in light of Christ. We resolve simply to keep Christ present in our minds.

A. W. Tozer (1948) has defined faith as the gaze of the soul upon God. Indeed, we are admonished by the writer of Hebrews: "looking to Jesus the pioneer and perfecter of our faith" (Heb. 12:2). Even Jesus's power lay in his continuous looking at God. Gazing at God, however, is not always easy for people. It is something that must be developed. It does not come without struggle and practice. Regardless of what one may be worrying about, one is always to bring one's attention back to focus on God. Beck (Beck, Rush, Shaw, & Emery, 1979) also advocates a central focusing of one's attention. He states that any specific thoughts worrisome to the individual should always be related to some of the individual's larger life questions. All troublesome thoughts can be brought back to God.

The actual process of meditation involves an attitude as much as a specific technique. These attitudes are discussed below. Chapter 9 describes a similar process called recollection, which also includes elements of the present exercise plus an additional focusing on the body.

The attitude needed for meditation consists of the following elements:

1. *It is all right to allow ourselves to surrender to God.* Some individuals fear any type of letting go. They fear letting go because they either fear external negative influences or they fear facing some feelings within themselves. They fear either that others will reject them if they become vulnerable or that they will reject themselves. That is, they fear they will stir up all kinds of negative label feelings about themselves (which are really negative thoughts and ideas). In either case, it must be remembered that in Christian meditation one is surrendering to one who loves us and delights to be with us.

2. It may be helpful for some individuals to *begin the practice of meditation in the presence of a caring other.* Often we cannot experience acceptance from God until we can experience acceptance from some other person.

3. Beginners need to be *accepting enough of themselves to be prepared to struggle,* to realize that the focusing of attention does not come without practice, as is the case with any skill. They must be able to say to

themselves, "It is not necessary that I be perfect at this as soon as I start."

4. *It may help some individuals to relax themselves first.* One may include the recollection procedures of Chapter 9, if desired. It is always important to begin any type of meditation by telling yourself to slowly and deliberately allow all tension and anxiety to drop away.

5. *Become aware of God's presence.* Perhaps one way to do this may be to imagine or visualize Christ in the room with you. Allow yourself freedom to develop this image. Another way to become aware of God's presence may be to say a brief prayer and focus on the meaning of the words. It is important to stay with the same words, so that one can focus one's attention intimately on the meaning of the words rather than on new words. An example might be, "Lord Jesus Christ, have mercy upon me." This prayer is from the Eastern Christian traditions, and has been called the "Jesus Prayer" (Brianchaninov, 1860/1952). You could also choose any other brief prayer that is special to you.

6. *Be prepared for the frustrations and distractions that will arise.* As each thought or problem comes to mind, you may try several things. First, you may simply give them to God, and return to your prayer or image. ("Cast all your anxieties on him, for he cares about you." 1 Peter 5:7.) You may imagine God taking them and return to your image or prayer. You may also just let go of the thoughts and return to your prayer or image. If any guilt arises, give that to Jesus, being mindful of his redemption, and return to your thoughts of Jesus. It is important to cultivate the attitude that nothing matters except attending to the Lord.

Meditation can be most useful for anxiety states. It can be particularly useful for some Christians who may feel uncomfortable focusing primarily on the parts of their body, or engaging in any type of hypnosis. Finally, meditation is also useful for those achievement-oriented individuals who find ordinary muscle relaxation exercises difficult, because they take everything as a challenge. They may work so hard at relaxing their muscles that they actually tighten them.

When I find myself becoming preoccupied with too many different thoughts or concerns, I have found a little meditation exercise helpful. First, I allow myself to relax, and try to let go of any tension. I am always amazed at how much tension has accumulated. As I exhale deeply a few times, I imagine surrendering myself to God with each exhalation. This little exercise is merely one of the numerous ways meditation can be used by an individual.

Looking at the present moment.   This second type of meditation is actually an abbreviated version of the first.

Most of the time, our thoughts are directed either toward anxious concerns in the future, or at sad regrets over the past. We constantly set expectations on how a situation will work out. If we tend to be anxious or depressed, these expectations tend to be negative. We constantly review our past actions, rehearsing what happened and what might have happened. If we are the depressed type, we often say, "If I only would have. . . .". Looking at the present moment however, means directing our thoughts at what is happening right now.

Margaret Dorgan (1984) calls this present centeredness the sacrament of the present moment. She quotes an earlier spiritual director as saying, "This is God's moment, he made it, he sent it, he watches its effect." We must say God is in this present moment.

The easiest way to teach someone about the value of the present moment is to demonstrate it. It is important first to remind yourself that this present moment is God's moment. Then one has merely to ask, "What are my thoughts and feelings right now? What is going on around me right now? What are my bodily sensations right now? What are my desires right now as we sit here?"

For you, the reader, as you read these lines, remember that even this moment, as you read, is God's moment. God is watching its effect. What are your feelings right now? What are your concerns right now? What do you desire right now? What is going on around you right now? What do you feel right now about what is going on around you right now? This is not too different from the here-and-now thought-monitoring discussed in Chapter 4. Here, however, the emphasis is on relaxation, as well as awareness.

Looking at the present moment is best for anxiety or restlessness. As I am writing these lines this afternoon, I am aware of restlessness. I am aware of part of me wanting to sit outside because it is a warm pleasant day. However, I am also aware of an inner desire to communicate more about mental health and its relationship to spirituality. I am aware of incidents in which the intensity of Jesus's love has touched the mental anguish of my patients. I want to communicate that.

Even as I reflect on this, my restless desire to be sitting outside has lessened. If I were sitting out there, I would probably only get frustrated, because I would want to be back in here writing. Often, merely describing our present feelings and desires, or describing something around us, can be a healing response. In doing this, we are ceasing the constant cognitive ruminations that are always part of anxiety.

Adopting a problem-solving attitude.   The technique of problem solving is both an attitude and a behavior. Correct attitudes and correct behaviors are both necessary for the success of this skill.

Problem solving means adopting the general orientation towards life that problems are a natural part of life, and that coping with those problems is only a natural part of living. This attitude means that one will take an active stance towards life. Any problem will signal a mental response of attempting to list the steps needed for problem solving.

Theologically, we must realize that life is not perfect (cf. Chapter 2). Life has a tragic element, and rarely will we be problem-free, or even find a perfect solution to our problems. Faith itself is only a product of difficult situations (cf. Heb. 11). Even Jesus, the one declared good by God, had many problems. Problems can be actively solved, however. Karl Barth has said that we are not merely thought and desire, but also choosing and willing (Barth, 1948/1960, pp. 406ff.). This means that we ultimately make some choices in terms of solutions to problems.

A problem-solving attitude consists of five phases. First, we must adopt the habit of stopping and thinking about a problem, rather than rushing headlong into solving it. Secondly, we must concretely define the problem. We often worry needlessly about tangential issues. The problem should be defined in terms of obstacles to be overcome and goals to be achieved. Third, it is important to think through a number of alternative ways of solving the problem. An individual should never decide on one solution until a number of possible solutions have been examined. Such an action reminds us that there are many ways to solve a problem, it breaks up our mental set of helplessness, and it allows us a bit of emotional distance from the problem itself. Fourth, we should predict the possible consequences associated with each act or alternative solution. Only after the above thinking has been done, should action be taken. The goal-setting section of Chapter 9 focuses on actually choosing an alternative, acting on it, and evaluating its effectiveness.

Problem solving is most effective for those individuals who might tend to overreact emotionally to a crisis, or for those who feel helpless.

Jim sought counseling because of his uncertainty about himself, and a mild depression. During the counseling, a problem came up in his work that allowed an opportunity for Jim to begin to develop a problem-solving attitude.

Jim was chosen to be part of an engineering team to design a large industrial complex. He was quite pleased to be participating in the project because of its importance. He was impressed with the manager of the project, who was well-known for his skills. Jim felt he would learn much in working with this manager.

He came to my office one day upset because he had discovered that the developers of the project had fired the manager. His dilemma was whether or not to continue working on the project in the absence of the manager he much admired. His initial emotional reaction was to tell the developers to find another project engineer. I asked him what his goals in the situation were.

"I would like to have the original manager back on the project."

"Do you have any other goals?"

"Ultimately, I am concerned that the project be completed in a manner consistent with my values, and my concerns for ecology. If the owner wants to change the direction of the design, I am not sure I could participate. I must feel a sense of integrity about what I do."

"What are some alternative ways you could meet those goals?"

"Well, I could confront the developers with my dissatisfaction about the loss of the manager."

"Any other ways?"

"I could talk to the other engineers and technicians in the project and see how they feel. If they feel the same way I do, we could confront the developer together."

"What if this developer does not change his mind about hiring back the manager? Do you have any other goals in this project?"

"I guess I would have to work on my second goal, which is to do the project in a manner consistent with my concerns about the environment and ecology."

We discussed ways in which he could determine whether or not his concerns about ecology were reflected in the developer's plans, and ways in which he could be direct with the developer about those plans. Finally, I reminded him that, regardless of the outcome of this problem, he should realize that by deciding to define the problem and attempt to find a solution, he would feel better about himself in the end, and that was ultimately what he wanted anyway. There will always be problems. What we want is to feel that we have approached them in the best way possible.

Facing the worst.   Another attitude that has proved helpful in overcoming anxiety is the willingness to see that even if the worst thing we could imagine happened, we could still cope.

Often, depressed or anxious individuals continually anticipate the worst. They brood over the imminent possibility of this unlikely event happening. Always, behind any other feared thoughts, is the possibility that the *most* feared event will happen. Often, the only solution for such individuals is gently to direct them to face the worst. They must look at what would happen if their worst fears happened. There is usually resistance, however. They can't imagine surviving in the face of their worst fears. "Learning to face the worst" is actually a cognitive technique. We examine the evidence for the individual's thought: "If such and such happens, I won't be able to stand it," or "I'll go crazy." Usually, they discover the miraculous—that they indeed can cope.

Often, out of a great sorrow, or darkness, a miracle arises. Juliana of Norwich (1392/1977) writes, "Before miracles come sorrow, anguish and tribulation" (p. 139). She adds, "He [God] does not will that we be overly depressed by the sorrows and storms that come our way, because that has always been the condition before miracles come" (p. 139).

Hope for depressed and anxious people is weak, or nonexistent. Their expectations are dreary. Their thoughts about the future lead to a dead end. Hope in the biblical sense, however, does not necessarily mean positive cognitive expectations. Biblical hope means *trusting.* The trust is in God.

Trust in God need not arise as long as there is trust in anything else. Often, when an individual has gone through all the possibilities, and realizes that he can still cope, a trust develops. In order for an individual finally not to be depressed by external situations, he must give up all links to that external situation. That situation must seem less important.

Because this technique may seem insensitive to those who are hurting, it is important that it should never be used until you have spent some time with the individual, and demonstrated your care and understanding of the problem. This is not a technique for the first few sessions.

It is usually best to face our worst fears in the context of a supporting relationship.

The best way to help an individual face the worst is to take him gently through each step of the process. As each step is discussed, or each loss listed, the individual is to write down or discuss with the therapist a number of reasons why each particular step would not be a disaster. It is usually good not to go on to the next step until the individual has been able to give a number of reasons why the previous step was not a disaster.

John was a former psychologist, and a recovered alcoholic. His reason for seeing me was extreme anxiety, which interfered with his sleep and any type of work he attempted. He usually perspired profusely during our sessions together.

After we had worked together for a while, he continually alluded to the fact that he was afraid that his wife would lose her job and they would really be in big trouble. At present he was working at odd jobs even though the primary source of family income was his wife's job. Even though we had discussed how unlikely this event would be (see procedures for reality testing below), he was still quite fearful, and ruminated extensively about the possibility.

"Let's suppose that your wife did lose her job, what would happen?"

"We would not be able to make our car payments and we would lose our car."

"Suppose that happened, how is that not a disaster? What are some ways you could get along without a car?"

"I guess I could take the bus to things we had to do."

"What are some different activities you could take the bus to?"

"The bus line does go to my part-time job, and it does go to the city parks for recreation. Also we could still go to the grocery store."

"What else would happen if your wife lost her job?"

"We would no longer be able to pay rent on our apartment and we would have to move in with my wife's family. The worst thing about that is that they would give me negative vibes about my failure to provide."

"I realize that would be not entirely pleasant, but how is it not a disaster?"

"I think that would be pretty bad. I don't see how I would survive."

"Let's look at it. Let's look at what would happen."

"My father-in-law wouldn't say anything overt, but he would look at me like I was a failure."

"That is happening right now?"

"He continually looks at me right now like I am a failure anyway."

"I am sure that is unpleasant, but you are surviving, aren't you?"

"Yes, I am, but I don't like it."

"I realize you don't like it, but you are surviving?"

"If I lived with them, it would be more intense. I would be around them more."

"What could you do to cope with that?"

"I guess I could arrange to be out of the house more. I could go to the library more. I could also take my walks, which I have been trying to do anyway."

"So you are saying that there might even be one slight advantage in this worst possible situation?"

"Yes, I had not thought of it that way."

"What else would happen if your wife lost her job?"

"It would be hard to buy food and clothing for our kids."

"Are there any other sources of food and clothing?"

"Well, there is always Welfare, and food stamps, but I would hate that."

"I understand it would be unpleasant, but you would survive, and it would not be a complete disaster?"

"I guess not."

The above is a shortened version of our transcript. The actual exchange took over an hour. We went through all of the possible ramifications of the worst possible happening.

At the end of the sequence he was noticeably less anxious. "I guess that there is not as much to fear as I thought there was.".

"You faced the worst, your ultimate darkness you were afraid of, and you survived. That is important for you to remember. Whenever that fearful thought arises again, you now have something to counter it with."

Stress-inoculation training: Statements when handling a stressor.   It is very freeing to realize that we have the ability to talk with ourselves in the midst of a crisis and thereby cope more effectively with that crisis. Meichenbaum and Cameron (1973) called this stress-inoculation training. With our own words, we can actually inoculate ourselves, and thus more effectively deal with our stressors.

The psalmist was certainly familiar with dialoguing with himself. He asks himself, for example, "Why are you cast down, O my soul, and why are you disquieted within me?" (Psalms 42:5). He then goes on to encourage himself, "Hope in God, for I shall again praise him, my help and my God." This is a kind of stress-inoculation training. The psalmist is saying things to himself in order to bolster himself up so that he might cope with distressful feelings.

Stress-inoculation training (cf. Novaco, 1979) actually has four phases:

1. *Preparing for the stressor:* For example, one might say to oneself, "I know this is going to be hard, but I'll be able to handle it simply by focusing my attention on what has to be done next."

2. *Handling a stressor:* One might say to oneself, "I am handling this stressor okay. I need only concentrate on what I have to do next."

3. *Possibly being overwhelmed:* One has to prepare for the eventuality that one may feel overwhelmed. An example of what one might have ready to say might be, "This is really tough, but doing anything challenging seems too much to handle. I'll just continue the best I can, regardless."

4. *Reinforcing oneself for having coped:* "I *did* it! I was able to carry it off. I have really grown a lot in solving this problem."

Stress-inoculation training is particularly useful when we anticipate confronting a demanding situation. It may even be useful to write down some coping sentences ahead of time. In addition to the possible coping sentences listed above, it is also possible to draw from one's spirituality. For example, one might say, "I must realize that God is with me in this situation," or "As I prepare for this situation, I can remember that I need not be overwhelmed, because God's love has taught me that I will never have more than I can bear." (These techniques were used in an earlier study by the author (Propst, 1980) and found to be effective.) An example of how these stress-inoculation procedures may be applied to uncontrollable anger is presented in Chapter 8.

Checking out reality

We always need to question whether our thoughts about a situation actually have any basis in reality. Regardless of what we may tell ourselves, the most healing thing for us to do may be to determine whether or not the world, or people, are actually the way we think they are. There are a number of ways this can be done. One technique is Beck's triple column technique (Beck, Rush, Shaw, & Emery, 1979).

Four steps are involved in Beck's triple column technique: Patients are asked sequentially:

1. To estimate the intensity of their negative emotion (0 to 100).

2. To record their negative thoughts.

3. To estimate how much they actually believe those negative thoughts (from 0 to 100 percent).

4. To think of an argument or evidence that is counter to the original negative thought.

5. To estimate how much they believe this counter-thought (from 0 to 100 percent).

6. Finally, to estimate how much they believe in the original thought and the intensity of the original emotion.

Patty came to see me because of her anxiety level. She was an extremely anxious young woman who feared going to new places. Her fears did not prevent her actually going to the new places, as in a phobia, but she often suffered great anxiety while there. One place that made her particularly anxious was visiting a friend's city apartment which was on the first floor and faced a busy street. At night, each voice she heard from the street led her to believe that the apartment was being broken into.

"As you visualize yourself in your friend's apartment, how anxious are you on a scale from 0 to 100?" (See Chapter 4 for this visualization procedure.)

"About 70! I feel really anxious and am aware of my heart pounding."

"What is the thought that makes you anxious?"

"People are trying to break in here, because I hear their voices from the street."

"How much do you believe that on a scale from 0 to 100?"

"About 60."

"Now open your eyes and let's evaluate your fears. Can you think of an alternative explanation for the voices?"

"Well, yes, people are just walking by on the streets, going wherever they are going, and talking freely."

"How much do you believe that that is the reason for the voices?"

"Oh, about 90 percent. It's really silly. I guess if they were trying to break in, they would be very quiet."

"How much do you now believe your original thought that hearing those voices from the street means someone is trying to break in?"

"Not very much, but still about 20. I'm not quite sure."

"As you think about it this way now, how anxious are you?"

"Only about 15, but I might feel more anxious if I were back in the situation."

"Notice, however, how you and you alone were able to reduce your feeling of anxiety. You did not have a pill or anything, but you actually feel less anxious. How is that possible?"

"I actually thought about the situation differently."

"Good! You can do that when you are actually in the situation. Why don't you try that the next time. Actually keep track of it on this chart." (The therapist may provide a chart for the patient that has a column for each of the steps listed above. See Beck, Rush, Shaw, & Emery, 1979.)

We have examined some ways we may change some of our thoughts, and focus our attention in a different direction. Ultimately, we also need to look at some of our underlying assumptions. That is the subject of the next chapter.

Chapter 6

MAINTAINING THE HEALTHY MIDDLE GROUND

> For the Holy Spirit knows that a thing has only such meaning
> and value for a man as he assigns to it in his thoughts. . . . .
> Therefore He endeavors with all His might to draw us away from
> thinking about things and from being moved by them. . . . Now
> this drawing away is best accomplished by means of the Word,
> whereby our thoughts are turned from the thing that moves us
> at the present moment to that which either is absent or does not
> at the moment move us.—Martin Luther, *Consoling an Anxious Man*
> (1520), quoted in Jaeckle & Clebsch, 1964. p. 213.

Underlying Assumptions

In the last chapter we examined some ways in which we may
transform our point of view. Ultimately, a new attitude is needed.
Ultimately, our worlds must expand so that we can see beyond those
limited thoughts that trap us in despair or hopelessness. We must
catch the vision of a sense of a unique self empowered and emboldened
by the spirit of God, not the self besieged by others' nonacceptance
or our own helplessness.

Despite our best efforts, however, this transformation is often
fleeting. At times we do say new words to ourselves. At times, it may
even be possible to step back from our anxious ruminations and say,

"These are mere thoughts, they do not matter." We are pleased with ourselves. Inevitably, however, a pattern always comes back to haunt us—a pattern that has germinated from a seed planted deep within us long ago.

This inner kernel is unknown to us. All we know is that despite some changes, things never seem quite right. The day's activities have a sour ring to them as we continually push to complete all of them. Often we feel an extra burden that we somehow suspect we do not need to carry. We feel that we have missed something.

Some days are better than others. Finally, we think we have overcome this block, this blind spot, or this "lousy attitude." Usually, however, the attitude comes back. Again we are left with the constant feeling that we have failed, regardless of how much we achieve, or a twinge of guilt because our best friend is always willing to listen to *our* problems. We begin to suspect that we are going from day to day, repeatedly treating a superficial wound, when the deep wound has not been touched. Or we are like the individual who continually rubs his irritated eye. Occasionally the eye will feel better. We eagerly conclude, at that moment, that the problem is remedied. Until the actual hair or dirt caught in the eye is removed, however, this irritation will continue. Until the real wound is cleaned out, the emotional pain will persist. Until we change those deeply imbedded, distorted ways of looking at ourselves, or our underlying assumptions about ourselves, the problem will not be alleviated.

A number of cognitive psychologists have given us extensive maps of the types of underlying assumptions that may subtly influence our thinking and lead to anxiety or depression. Two prominent examples of lists of troublesome assumptions include Albert Ellis's proposed categories of irrational ideas (Ellis & Harper, 1975) and David Burns's (1980) categories of thought distortions. Both contend that difficulties result when an individual irrationally distorts his ideas and view of the world.

Basic Thought Polarities of Mental Health

Emotional pain results from certain underlying patterns of distortion. The present chapter combines Ellis's list of common irrational ideas, Burns's thought-distortion categories, and the work of Bandura (1977) and others into six basic patterns or polarities of thought. The meaning of these polarities and their connection to Christian spirituality will also be presented.

Each type of thinking has its polar opposite in the same category. Dysfunction, distortion, and pain result when our thinking in any of these categories is at one of the polar extremes. In all of the categories, mental health is always the middle ground. Table 6-1 lists these polarities.

These categories are merely intended as an aid to self-examination and should not be viewed as the only possible structure or division of these ideas. There does seem to be support in the research literature, however, for viewing each of the extremes of thought expressed here as a source of pathology.

Undercontrol versus overcontrol. Woolfolk and Richardson (1978) described the active role played by the individual in the creation of stressful experiences. This view of stress does not see the individual as a passive recipient of stress from the environment, but rather as an active generator of his stress through maladaptive beliefs, attitudes, and patterns of action. One set of beliefs that has been found to lead to the most stress has been the perception of helplessness. Seligman (1975) has found in his learned-helplessness research that depression results when the individual has learned to perceive himself as helpless in the face of his environment.

Similarly, Kobasa (Kobasa, Maddi, & Courington, 1981) found that one of the three essential ingredients of emotional "hardiness"

Table 6-1. Basic Polarities of Thought in Mental Health

Perception of undercontrol	Perception of overcontrol
Attention focused on past	Attention focused on future
Avoidance (or denial) of positives	Avoidance (or denial) of negatives
Defeatism	Perfectionism
External focus	Internal focus
Meaninglessness	Rigidity of belief

or "transformational coping" consists of a perception of control as opposed to powerlessness. Hardy persons believe that they can influence the course of events. Likewise, Bandura (1977) states that the probability of persisting in coping behavior is determined largely by the relative degree of self-efficacy. A sense of self-efficacy involves confidence that the individual can produce the required behaviors to influence the desired outcome. In other words, the individual believes that she can have some control over her environment.

Although the perceived ability to be in control of our world does lead to health, there can be too much of a good thing. The extensive literature on the coronary-prone behavior pattern ("Type A") has indicated that Type A individuals are much more vulnerable to heart attacks. (See Matthews, Glass, Rosenman, & Bortner, 1977.) These individuals feel that they must always be in control of their environment. They are also more likely than the average individual to believe that they do have such control. In other words, they accept greater than average responsibility for circumstances in their environment.

Sex roles and societal expectations may strongly influence perceived control. Depression, one of the principle results of learned helplessness, seems to be more of a female phenomenon. Women are twice as likely as men to become depressed. Type A behavior, however, has been more common in men.

In contrast to the extremes discussed above, emotional health is perceiving oneself to have a moderate amount of control.

Ellis lists two irrational ideas that contribute to the perception of helplessness and emotional disorder. One of these is the idea that emotional misery comes from external pressures and people have little or no ability to control or change their feelings. (p. 138). The second is "the idea that one's past history is an all important determiner of one's present behavior and that because something once strongly affected one's life, it should indefinitely have a similar effect" (p. 168).

Self-control and self-mastery seem somehow incongruent with our understanding of Christianity. Deep inside, we feel that there is no place for self-mastery. Instead, true holiness is allowing one's life to be directed by God.

Christian women have felt this especially keenly as they have faced not only the demands of Christian behavior that they give up control, but also the demands of a society that has the expectation that they will be more self-denying and less self-determining than their male counterparts. For some, this has meant giving up their names, suppressing their own needs for the needs of their husbands, or passively assenting to all decisions. (See Propst, 1982, for a further discussion of this issue.) The recent research in psychopathology and psychotherapy thus presents a dilemma for women, attested to by their higher depression rates. In many cases, however, this dilemma is also shared by the Christian man who is torn between the supposed claims of Christian spirituality which call for passive resignation to the will of God, and the claims of mental health which call for self-efficacy.

The humanity of Jesus is the model. Jesus was the Man in charge. He made the decision to go to Jerusalem. He said to his accusers, "You would have no control over me, were it not given to you from above." As we noted in Chapter 3, his ultimate seizing of the direction of his life occurred in the statement, "No one takes it [my life] from me, but I lay it down of my own accord" (John 10:18). His decision for servanthood was just that, a decision. As Barth (1960) has said, true humanness is not merely desiring, it is also willing (p. 406ff.). To desire God is a passive activity; to will to surrender ourselves to God is an active choice. As we will, we become responsible for our desiring; the decision is ours. The Apostle Paul has said, "Work out your own salvation with fear and trembling, for God is at work in you, both to will and to work for his good pleasure" (Phil. 2:12–13).

Similar self-control themes are expressed elsewhere in scripture. The Apostle Paul lists the fruits of the Spirit as love, joy, peace, patience, kindness, goodness, faithfulness, gentleness and self-control (Gal. 5:22–23). The Greek word self-control is *egkpateria*. The stem *egkpat* denotes power or lordship, and means the dominion which one has over oneself or over something. The use of the word in the New Testament, however, is different from the classic Greek use. In the New Testament, self-control is not rated as a personal merit of the individual, but something practiced for the sake of a goal, for the sake of a solution, or for the sake of others (Grundmann, 1935/1964, pp. 339–342). In other words, self-control is not an end in itself, but merely something to aid us in the tasks of life.

In 2 Timothy 1:7, Timothy is advised to have self-control. The literal translation of self-control here is "sound mind" and means to have a mind-set that does not allow us to be afraid of the world. Instead we have a "spirit of adoption," which allows us to resist the control of the world and make our own God directed decisions (Luck, 1964/1971, p. 1104). We are free to go in our own directions. The Spirit has given us ourselves. Choosing to set our attention on one direction means other forces in other directions will be held more lightly. Focusing our attention on the Spirit draws us away from the pressures around us. When I am bound up with another's approval, I am controlled by it. Focusing on God allows more interior freedom.

The issue of control is particularly relevant to women. As we noted, they make up two-thirds of all cases of depression. Generally, these depressed women are a prime example of the learned helplessness that underlies depression. Indeed, the feminist theologian Judith Plaskow, in her book *Sex, Sin and Grace* (1980), contends that perhaps women express sin somewhat differently than men because of their socialization. Reinhold Niebuhr (1953) construed sin as the failure of the individual to admit his creatureliness. He prefers to see himself as the center of the universe, as the final arbiter of authority and responsibility. Man pretends he is not limited, by identifying himself with God. This behavior certainly fits the model of the attempted overcontrol of the Type A personality.

Plaskow asserts than women are more likely to abdicate responsibility than overclaim it. Women often fail to take advantage of the freedom that they are given. They will not take responsibility for change, but instead give all control of themselves to the environment. In other words, rather than claiming identity with the Deity, they completely deny any aspect of the *imago Dei* within themselves. They have failed to recognize that they even bear the image of God within themselves. Grace, for these women, is therefore taking responsibility for themselves, claiming the identity they do have. They need a greater identity with the personhood which Jesus claimed for himself.

One additional way we often feel out of control is by our use of what David Burns (1980) calls "emotional reasoning." We assume that our negative emotions necessarily reflect the way things really are: "I feel inadequate, therefore, I must be a worthless person," or "I feel overwhelmed and hopeless, therefore my problems must be impossible to solve." This attitude reflects a perception of too little control, because we have somehow given the world total responsibility for our feelings. Somehow we think that our feelings are a reflection of the true state of things, but our emotions are only a reflection of our thoughts and beliefs. The world does not always dictate our feelings, though we may think it does. Realizing this unnecessary helplessness can be a big step for individuals. The moods we experience are not always the prerogative of the forces around us. We can also make some choices.

Though much of our depression and stress comes from a perception of too little control, sometimes the opposite is true. We may think we have more control than we actually do. David Burns calls this personalization. We see ourselves as the cause of some negative external event, for which we are not, in fact, primarily responsible. This thought distortion frequently shows up in parents. They confuse influence for control. Whenever a child misbehaves, such a parent is apt to say, "I have failed as a parent. This child's misbehaving is all my fault."

The truth is, however, only God has complete control over the world. Not even Jesus had control over those he interacted with. In Matthew 23:37–39 we read that he wanted to gather the children of Jerusalem to himself as a hen gathers her chicks under her wings. However, they would not come to him. They continued on a negative course. It may actually be a useful therapeutic exercise for us to realize the frustration Jesus must have felt in that situation. One may either imagine oneself in that situation, or remind oneself of that situation when frustration occurs.

Too often, we assume that we are the cause of negative events. Elaine was a highly successful businesswoman who felt that her mother had always loved her brother more than her. She was able to provide some substantial evidence that, at least on the surface of it, showed her conjectures to be true. Her conclusion was that she was then a worthless person. After all, she must be the cause of her mother's attitude. She must have done something wrong.

We see this distortion very frequently in young children whose parents have decided to divorce. The children often feel guilty. They have caused the divorce either with their bad tempers or their misbehavior. As we noted previously, the world believes in absolute justice. We get what is coming to us. The victim deserves it. Indeed, it is only Jesus's victimship that allows us to step out of this trap. "For he who is noblest and worthiest was most completely reduced to nothingness, most foully condemned and utterly despised" (Juliana of Norwich, c. 1392/1977, p. 115). Jesus alone tells us that our rough treatment by the environment does not mean that we deserve it. He alone shows us that we do not cause all of the terrible things that happen to us.

Judy was a severely depressed twenty-nine-year-old woman. She had come from a strong Christian background, but now felt no comfort or relationship in that background. She very adroitly combined an example of personalization and emotional reasoning when she said, "I feel so far from the Lord, so there must be something wrong with me. I must really have blown it." God's acceptance, however, is dependent upon neither our behavior nor our feelings.

Rather, God's acceptance of us is assured in God's acceptance of

Jesus. Karl Barth repeatedly reminds us of this. Humanity and its value to God has gained a new value because of God's acceptance of Jesus's humanity (Barth, 1955/1958). We merely need to remind ourselves that we are accepted, and look to Jesus as that reminder.

Focus on the past versus focus on the future.   A. T. Beck (Beck, Rush, Shaw, & Emery, 1979) states that depressed and anxious individuals spend a great deal of time ruminating about past mistakes. These individuals also ruminate about the future, usually with negative expectations. Albert Ellis (Ellis & Harper, 1975) reminds us that that it can be detrimental to believe our past history is an all-important determiner of our present behavior. Likewise, David Burns's (1980) term "overgeneralization" refers to that tendency to see a negative event in the past as indicative of a never-ending pattern of defeat. A typical example of this type of thinking occurs in a shy young man who musters up his courage to ask a young woman for a date. When she refuses, he says to himself, "I am really a nerd and no one will ever want to go out with me. I'll never be able to get a date."

When our attention becomes fixated on our past, we can easily think too much of all the opportunities we wish we had taken advantage of, of all the people we said the wrong things to, or of the decisions we wish we had made differently. We continually find ourselves being angry either for doing or saying something in the past, or for not doing or saying something. Even a cursory survey of our past will bring up many of these situations. Another problem with focusing on the past is that we frequently become angrier at others. We remember the time a colleague may have taken advantage of us in dividing up a job, , or we remember the time someone else was given an advantage we were not. The evidence mounts up. Any good that may be happening in the present or has a potential for happening in the future is soon swallowed up by our preoccupations with unfortunate events.

A more extreme form of overgeneralization is called "labeling" by David Burns (1980). Instead of merely describing our error or another's error, we attach a negative label to it: "I'm a loser," "I'm a failure," or, "All men who work for that institution are irresponsible." Labels often become highly colored and emotionally loaded.

Josie was a thirty-five-year-old woman who had made substantial progress in recovering from depression. However, she was still troubled with what she had called her "bizarre images."

In one session she reported having been extremely depressed and agitated during the previous week. We focused on these agitated periods to help her clarify her thinking at that time. She reported images of bashing in her teeth, of stabbing herself, and of running the car off a cliff. The violence of the images frightened her and convinced her she was indeed troubled. As we continued to explore the thoughts behind the images she reported, "I'm no good, I didn't stay on my diet this week. I am a worthless person. I didn't straighten up the house. Worst of all, I didn't work out this week."

Part of Josie's problem was certainly her perfectionism. However, she was also overfocused on the past and her failures. As we continued our conversations, I asked her,

"Why are you so hard on yourself?"

"I feel like I have to atone for something. Maybe if I get my body in perfect shape it will be okay."

"What do you have to atone for?"

"I don't really know, but I keep thinking of the fact that when I was an adolescent, my dad's friends called me Joe's boy."

"Your dad and his friends saw you as a boy?"

"Yeah, he had always wanted a boy."

"So it is very difficult to think of yourself as being acceptable as a woman?"

"Yeah, that's why I try to work out five times a week. I remember that the way to be acceptable to my dad was to be physically strong. When I don't do that, I get really mad at myself."

"And those images of bashing yourself was your anger at yourself?"

"Yes!"

"Rather than allowing your dad's perception of you in the past to dictate your present attitudes about yourself, can you look at yourself realistically now in the present for what you do have to offer, and what your strengths really are?"

Josie then began to struggle to look at herself more realistically in the present and began to be more sensitive to how the past was dictating her behaviors.

If some people focus too much on the past, others focus exclusively on the future. They worry incessantly about what might happen or might not happen. Other "future" worriers are continually focusing on what they plan to do in time to come. As each present activity comes, they are thinking only of tomorrow. Consequently, they never really experience or enjoy the present. David Burns calls some of these distortions "fortune-telling." Often one of the major hurdles for de-pressed individuals in therapy is to counter the thought, "I will never get better. I will always be depressed. I will feel miserable forever."

Not only is focusing exclusively on the future dangerous for those who think the worst will happen, but it makes pressured individuals of us all.

John was a forty-year-old successful professional who was diag-nosed as having irritable bowel syndrome. His physician determined that stress was one of the primary contributors to this condition. Not only was John a perfectionist, he was just plain busy. He seemed utterly incapable of sitting on the deck and reading the paper on a Sunday afternoon, or of taking a walk, or even of "wasting" 3 hours in front of the TV. The prominent thought that kept creeping into John's thought-logs was:

"I am afraid that the future is going to be here too soon, and I won't have anything accomplished."

It was a great struggle for John to live in the present.

Certainly our past failures need not dictate our present behaviors, nor our future. In John 18:15–17, we read that Peter denied that he even knew Jesus. One might assume, with some justification, that per-haps Peter then saw himself as a failure as a friend, and really could never again consider himself to be a worthy friend of anyone, especially Jesus. In John 21:15–19, however, we find Jesus asking Peter if he loves him, and then being willing to trust Peter with a most important mission. We later see Peter in the entire book of Acts playing a very active leadership role in the early church. With this one masterful example, our Lord states very clearly that past failures do not doom us to be stuck forever in an unproductive existence. We are free to begin anew. What is needed, however, is a willingness on our part not to focus our attention on unfortunate past events. As Martin Luther said, our attention must be drawn away from thinking about certain things and focused on other concerns.

Neither do we need to dwell on the fears of the future. Obviously, no one can know the future. Jesus cautions, in Matthew 6:25–34, that focusing on the future will not improve it. It is often a good reminder to ask ourselves how much we actually know about the anticipated event, and to believe only what is absolutely certain. The remainder is mere conjecture and may be dismissed from our thoughts.

True mental health is living in the present. Authentic mental soundness is awareness of the sacrament of the present moment.

Wholeness of perspective and a sound mind can lead us to say, "This is God's moment, he made it, he sent it, he watches its effect" (Dorgan, 1984).

Denying the positives versus denying the negatives.   Ellis has noted that some individuals have the irrational idea that it is easier to avoid than to face certain of life's crises and responsibilities. They thus ignore and deny problems and troubling emotions. They hope that by such denial, disturbing emotions and events will go away. Problems avoided, however, only return, often in aggravated form.

The individual who blocks the distressing emotion, pretending it is not there, is only beset by even more agitation. Typically, his attitude towards such emotions is that they are *bad,* they indicate a defect in the personality, and they should not be dwelt on, nor even acknowledged. These individuals become trapped. Simply because they tell themselves that anger, fear, mistrust, or resentment are *bad,* they suffer much more from such emotions. Because they label negative emotions as catastrophic, those they feel then engender more depression-causing thoughts, which in turn lead to worse sense of despair. They refuse to accept the darkness that is part of any human life. Juliana of Norwich (c. 1392/1977) wrote, ". . . . It is profitable for some souls to experience these alterations of mood—sometimes to be comforted and sometimes to fail and to be left to themselves. God wills that we know that he keeps us ever equally safe, in woe as in well-being" (p. 107).

We can step back from the helplessness of thinking that our desolations and dark nights come only from our external circumstances. We can cease believing that we are helpless pawns in the hands of our emotions. Instead, we can reclaim our emotions by accepting them as a product of ourselves. In reclaiming our emotions, we can also cease believing that dark emotions must be avoided. For, indeed, it is only in facing them that we will change them. It is only in thinking differently about them, that they will cease to haunt us.

Our faith is really only faith when there is darkness. Juliana of Norwich has commented that our prayers are most precious to God when we feel nothing. It is only then that we have faith.

The Psalms are full of negative emotions, of pain. In Psalm 63, for example, the writer reports a general dissatisfaction, a dryness, and a longing for God. "My soul thirsts for thee; my flesh faints for thee, as in a dry and weary land where no water is." Later in the same Psalm, however, the psalmist rejoices in finding God, the living water.

Only the thirsty appreciate good water. Indeed, only the thirsty actually want water.

We can choose to take control of our worst emotions by choosing to think differently about them. The "dark nights" actually have value of their own.

> Divine light . . . acts upon the soul . . . in the same way as fire acts upon a log of wood in order to transform it into itself; for material fire, acting upon wood, begins to dry it, by driving out its moisture . . . Then it begins to make it black, dark and unsightly . . . and as it dries it little by little, it brings out and drives away all the dark . . . which is contrary to the nature of fire. And, finally, it begins to kindle it externally and give it heat, and at last transforms it into itself and makes it as beautiful as fire." *Dark Night of the Soul*, St. John of the Cross, p. 127

Just as a block of wood is charred on its way to becoming a fire, so do we struggle with pain for maturity. Often we wish to move from an everyday existence to a higher level of maturity with no pain or struggle, when in fact it is impossible. We can, however, cultivate the ability to look at our emotions differently. Beck has commented that we can teach depressed individuals to learn to tolerate sadness (Beck, Rush, Shaw, & Emery, 1979). The individual must realize that sadness is natural. Ultimately, control will only be gained over negative emotions when attempts to control or change these emotions are relinquished.

Additionally, we can, as Christians, actually have the self-control to reconsider our darknesses as dark nights of the soul, as a stage on the contemplative journey. Such a new way of looking means changing our minds about our emotional helplessness. We can have control, so to speak, even over the uncontrollable. This occurs when we cease avoiding the threatening aspects of our life, when we have embraced struggle as actually playing a constructive role in our existence. Indeed, recent studies on the emotion of exaltation (Kahn, 1984) have defined it as occurring only after a period of struggle within a doubtful situation. Positive emotions and positive situations are the outgrowth of previous negative ones.

Although we must learn to accept our darkness, focusing *only* on the negative aspects of life may result in a splintered existence. At present there is quite an extensive research literature suggesting that depressed individuals are more likely to focus exclusively on the negative aspects of their existence and deny the positive ones. Hollon and Beck (1979), in a review of that research literature, conclude that depressed individuals are less likely to expect any type of success or reinforcement. If a failure occurs, it is attributed to themselves, and a success is usually attributed to a random feature of the environment. Finally, depressed individuals are more likely to recall negative rather than positive information. Goldfried (1979) reports some of the same phenomena occurring in anxious individuals.

Ellis (1975) feels that individuals who fit this description believe that:

If something is or may be dangerous or fearsome, one should be terribly concerned about it and should keep dwelling on the possibility of its occurring (p. 145).

Likewise, Jesus described the futility of worrying:

Therefore do not be anxious about tomorrow, for tomorrow will be anxious for itself. Let the day's own trouble be sufficient for the day. (Matt. 6:34)

For David Burns, the chronic worrier disqualifies any positive event when it occurs by saying that such experiences "do not count." The individual is able to maintain a negative belief that is contradicted by his everyday experiences. These individuals do not just ignore positive experiences, they actually turn them into negatives. A friend sadly told me about his father. Before his father had committed suicide he had been a superb furniture-maker. His products were a remarkable example of hand-crafted furniture at its best. I marveled at the precise manner in which such a man had been able to integrate skillfully several different types of wood into one piece of furniture. My friend commented, however, that his father only reacted to such compliments with phrases such as, "You're only being nice to me."

If some individuals turn positives into negatives, others ignore positives altogether. Burns calls this technique "mental filter." Such individuals pick out a single negative detail and dwell on it exclusively.

A very depressed but successful salesman I once had as a patient, would become despondent over any missed sale. When I asked him how many successful sales calls he had had in a day, he would comment that they were all successful but one, and then proceed to express his fear that he was losing his knack because that one sale had fallen through. He completely ignored his successes.

Often, as Christian patients have lamented their failures, I have given them an assignment to list and think about some of their accomplishments. Sometimes I have used imagery and asked them to visualize that positive trait or behavior and then to visualize Christ's positive reaction to it.

Patricia was a young female pastor involved in some power struggles with the older senior pastor in her congregation. She often lamented her failures: "I have made no impact on the church, I have failed."

I straightened up in my chair and looked the slumped-over discouraged figure directly in the eye and said, "Simply being a woman pastor in the church today is a prophetic role."

She looked at me intently for a second.

I repeated my position with an equally intense gaze. "The church has imitated the world in its treatment of women as second-class citizens, and you are challenging that worldly behavior by your very existence."

She too straightened up in her chair. "I hadn't thought of that in that way."

Defeatism versus perfectionism.   The perfectionist believes in the dictum, "I must be thoroughly competent, adequate, and achieving in all possible respects if I am to consider myself worthwhile" (Albert Ellis 1975, p. 102). According to David Burns (1980), these same individuals are also guilty of all-or-nothing thinking. If their performance falls short of perfect, they see themselves as total failures. The trouble with such thinking is that such individuals fear any mistakes or imperfections because these are taken as an indication of their own worthlessness.

This way of looking at life is unrealistic. Rarely, does *everyone* like us, rarely do we *always perform perfectly,* and rarely do we *always* find the *perfect solution.* When such individuals are not perfect they often resort to intense diatribes against themselves, and carry the implications of any failure to extremes. Ellis calls this activity "catastrophizing," and Burns speaks of "magnifying the negative." A depressed housewife had some lumps in her gravy, and she remarked, "How *disgusting!* I'm a hopeless housewife and cook. I can't do the simplest thing right."

Rehm (1977) has found that depressed individuals often have deficits in their self-monitoring and self-evaluations. Not only do they attend selectively to detracting points, but they also set excessively stringent criteria for self-evaluation. They require themselves to perform at an extremely high level before they will reward themselves. Any failure on their part is treated with excessively self-punishing words to themselves.

Such perfectionistic individuals also frequently set themselves a lot of "shoulds," according to David Burns (1980). They often say to themselves, "I should clean my room," "I should do a better job at work," or "I should spend more time with my kids." Working mothers are especially guilty of "shoulds." They tell themselves, "I should clean the house more, do more on the job, and give more time to the kids." Such "shoulds," however, do *not* motivate people. When we say I *should* do something, we do not do it. It is only when we say, "I *want* to do something," that we follow through on it.

Scripture does not speak of our spirituality as necessarily based on perfection. St. Paul, in his Epistle to the Romans, for example, declares that all have sinned. We all fail in some ways. He then proceeds to use the entire book of Romans to say, in effect, that even though we are *not* okay, we *are* okay. In other words, we are accepted by God anyway, through his forgiveness (Rom. 3:23–34).

Juliana of Norwich (c. 1392/1977) presents the most beautiful image of God's continuing acceptance and pleasure with us, even though it is obvious that we have flaws. She portrays God as delighting to dwell within us:

> For it is his delight . . . to sit restfully in our soul, and to dwell·in our soul endlessly (p. 186). . . . The place that Jesus takes in our soul he shall never remove himself from. For in us is his most homelike home and his endless dwelling. This he showed in the delight he takes in the creation of man's soul . . . And what can make us rejoice in God more than to see in him that he rejoices in us, the noblest of his works? (p. 206)

Ultimately, it will be our acknowledgement and acceptance of our imperfections that free us to live a fuller life. Van Kaam (1976) has reminded us that we will never be perfect. We will always be striving. We can never *arrive*, because the Holy Spirit is continually inspiring *new* aspirations. This sense of imperfection should be taken as a merciful voice from God leading us in new directions. Joseph Metz in *Poverty of Spirit* (1968) observes that if we do not accept our innate poverty, we will become a *slave to anxiety*. We will constantly be striving for that perfection which does not exist.

Harriet was a bright young mother of two who suffered from

intermittent irritable bowel syndrome. Her physician had determined that stress was a major factor in her difficulty.

She appeared in the office as a perfectly dressed young woman with not a hair out of place. The most conspicuous aspect of her appearance was her constant smile. The smile remained even as she described her symptoms and her sleepless nights. It was almost as if a smile was defined as what the well-dressed young mother is wearing these days, so she was wearing it. She proceeded to describe her concerns and goals:

"What I want most is to be a good mother to my children and be available to them when they need me."

"What does that mean to you?"

"Well, it means what did *not* happen this morning. My four-year-old son was upset that I was coming here and had left him at a baby-sitter."

"What happened?"

"He demanded to know why I wasn't going to be with him this morning."

"What did you say?"

"Well, it was difficult to know what to say. I felt guilty, like I was failing him. So I said I had an appointment."

"What did he say?"

"He was upset and said that I shouldn't leave him alone. He didn't like to be left alone. A good mother would stay with him. He was angry with me."

"How did you react?"

"I really felt intimidated."

"Do things usually happen this way?"

"Yes, my son is fairly demanding of me and usually tells me if I have done something wrong."

Further discussions with Harriet revealed that her son's demands had obviously been learned from her husband's demands. She felt that to be a perfect mother, she should always be available, with no questions asked. Further inquiry revealed that her son, as a result of the family pattern, was becoming demanding and self-centered. She constantly reported being intimidated by her four-year-old son!

Harriet's task in therapy was to realize that a good mother is not necessarily always available to her children regardless of their demands. Her task, ultimately, was to realize that it is possible to be a good mother without always being perfect.

The other extreme of the perfectionist is the one who has given up. This is usually the end result for many individuals who have set up unattainable standards for themselves. Finally, they quit. The inherent danger of perfectionism, of course, is always that we will end up at this other extreme. Continued failure in not meeting our expectations of ourselves, because they are too high, leads to despair and giving up. Severely depressed individuals whom I encounter all have a history of perfectionism. They have never been able to meet their standards in the past so they have surrendered to despair.

In the final analysis, wholeness and good mental health means having a level of self-expectations that acknowledges our own poverty, yet realizes that some things can be achieved.

External focus versus internal focus.   Some individuals constantly take their cues for behavior from others as they strive for approval. Other individuals refuse to listen to anyone. They accept no feedback from anybody.

The young mother mentioned in the previous section suffered not only from perfectionism, but also from too much concern about what others would think. This is often the case with perfectionists. Their perfectionism is too often an attempt to have others' approval.

Albert Ellis (1975) proposes at least two irrational ideas that relate being overly concerned with others approval.

"It is a dire necessity for an adult human being to be loved and approved by virtually every significant other person in his community"; and, "One should be dependent on others all the time" (see p. 88).

David Burns (1980) describes this problem as the "approval addiction" (p. 250). We are convinced that we cannot exist unless we have another's approval. One of the symptomatic thought distortions of such an addicted individual is "mind reading." Such a person is so concerned with others' impressions of him that he often jumps to conclusions as to what the other person is actually thinking about him. If a friend says she does not have time to continue speaking with this individual on the telephone, he is apt to think, "She doesn't want to speak with me, because she doesn't like me, and she only wants an excuse to get away from me."

Assumptions about how another person perceives you are usually inaccurate. I treat such patients by giving them an assertive assignment to check out the other person's actual perceptions of them.

If we become overly concerned with others' expectations, we may become alienated from own true direction. On the other hand, living our life in Jesus does not result in a loss of self-direction. In fact, such living and participation in the life of Jesus should stir us to deeper self-knowledge and self-examination. As we live our life in this manner, we become faithful to our own God-given spiritual direction, rather than others' expectations. Ultimately our inner peace depends upon faithfulness to God, and not to others.

Listening to God means not only responding to God's directions as they are outlined in scripture, but also responding to the voice of God as we "hear it" in our own life. As A. W. Tozer (1948) has reminded us, "God is a present speaking voice." The fact that God is *here* and speaking *now* is what keeps our faith alive. God may speak to us in our present ongoing circumstances, in our present longings, or in our thoughts and experiences. Each daily life-situation can be a message from God. The message does not come from responding to others' demands, but from listening to God. Faith is ultimately this redirecting of our sight towards God. Only as we develop the habit of the "inward beholding of God" can we ultimately hope to lessen the noise of the demands of those around us.

Anxiety comes from the burden of always wanting others to think well of us. This burden can crush us. We have to make an impression on others. We constantly compare ourselves and get into further complications. We worry and ruminate that perhaps we have failed in their estimation. Sometimes, we are even afraid tthat people will see us for what we really are! What we long for is a rest from this burden. We long to be ourselves, but don't know how.

Responding to others' expectations can be especially discouraging for those who have made great strides and changes in counseling or psychotherapy. A number of theories of psychopathology and depression today (cf. Coyne, Aldwin, & Lazarus, 1981) assert that at least part of the individual's difficulty results from the behavior pattern that has been forced upon him by his environment. This was vividly demonstrated to me in the case of the depressed schoolteacher. Her activities during the previous few years of her depression were limited. They consisted in teaching sixth grade, teaching Sunday school, and baby-sitting her pastor's children. She was referred to me by her pastor because of her depression. As our work together progressed, she began to have new confidence in herself and tried new activities, especially more activities with other single adults. This meant less time for baby-sitting and Sunday school, and she gave up both. She came to one session in tears.

"My pastor is concerned. He wonders why I don't have time to baby-sit anymore. I told him that I needed to be involved in some social activities with adults, for my own sanity."

"What did he say?"

"He was concerned that I not neglect the church. He also felt that I must be angry at him and his wife. I tried to explain, and he could not seem to understand."

"Then what happened?"

"I got frustrated and started crying."

"What happened then?"

"He said it seemed that counseling was not doing me any good. Not only did I seem upset, but I no longer had time for my former friends, who were more than willing to listen to my problems."

Her assignments over the next several sessions were focused on how to communicate clearly her new direction to her former friends. Each attempt was only met with hostility. Finally, I said.

"Perhaps the piece doesn't fit anymore?"

"What do you mean?"

"You have changed. You have more confidence in yourself and you are exploring new directions for your life and are even starting to develop a few intimate friends. How do you feel about that?"

"I am very pleased. I was really depressed when I spent all my time with children and had no single friends."

"Your former friends are having difficulty accepting that change in you?"

"Yes, I guess so."

After some additional futile attempts to express her love and concern for her friends, and also the changed direction of her life, she began to realize that perhaps she would not get everyone's approval for her changes. Her friends meant well, but could not accept her new behavior. They expected her to continue the baby-sitting and Sunday school activities at the same level. She eventually found another church, and became involved with some adult ministries to balance out all the time she spent with children during the week. Her social life changed dramatically, and she is now pursuing a graduate degree.

In John 9 we read of Jesus healing a blind man. The Pharisees had difficulty accepting the man's former blindness and the circumstances of his healing. A positive change in this man's life so disturbed them that they excluded him from the synagogue. A dramatic change in another, whom we have known for a period of time, is difficult for all of us. Ultimately, the one undergoing the changes may have to realize this, and stop looking for approval from his environment. It will not come.

Paradoxically, self-forgetfulness can be a start in the direction of freeing ourselves from other's expectations. Researchers in anxiety (cf. Goldfried, 1979) have found that highly anxious individuals are full of thoughts about themselves and others' perceptions: "I wonder how I am performing at this task?" or "I don't think I am doing a very good job," or "The manager is probably not very pleased with me." Their heads are full of such thoughts. The less anxious individuals, however, usually have completely forgotten about themselves and others and are focusing on the task at hand. "Let's see, after I answer question 1, I can go on and answer question 3, because that will give me the answer to question 2." Paradoxically, our preoccupation with and absorption into the mind of Christ, rather than our own concerns and worries, may free us to listen to our own self-direction rather than the expectations of others.

Whenever we become overly concerned about others and their impressions of us, Jesus longs for us to focus on him. "I am what you desire. Seek to please only me." It often helps to visualize Jesus, when the internal voices and actions of others become too insistent, and once his image is present to us, to listen to Jesus's voice. What is the voice saying? Allow your whole being to become focused on the voice. As in any meditation, this does not come easily. The voices around us are too loud. Many of us require our little retreat into the desert of solitude before we can *hear* that liberating voice of Jesus.

If some individuals seem too concerned about others' approval, other persons have completely excluded the community from their existence. As we discussed in Chapter 3, a journey away from others to find our own God-given direction always ultimately leads back to the community. Just as we are not to allow ourselves to be possessed by others, so are we not to shut them out of our lives. Humanity represents the *imago Dei* as it is in community. True humanness is allowing ourselves to be known by others (cf. Karl Barth, 1948/1960, pp. 250ff.). We encounter the other with gladness and not from compulsion. True human encounter in the image of God occurs when each individual is *who* she is *gladly,* and not because of imposed external laws.

We cannot be intimidated by others' expectations. Neither can we back away from a true encounter with others. True holiness is authentic mutuality. Neither person is lost in the other's expectations nor seeks to control the other. (Barth, 1948/1960, pp. 269ff.) Healthiness is listening accurately to the other's feelings and words about us, and incorporating those words that make sense in our own experience into our definition of ourselves. When another person has given us some feedback or placed some expectations upon us, we must always ask ourselves: "Is this feedback accurate? Does it make sense in terms of what I know about myself and my life's direction? Do these expectations fit with my life's direction? Is there anything in this feedback that I should incorporate into my life? What aspects of this feedback do not seem accurate to me? What aspects should be discarded?"

Meaninglessness versus an airtight system.   Antonovsky (1979) presents an impressive body of evidence in his review of the stress literature which suggests that individuals need a "sense of coherence," a "generalized, long-lasting way of seeing the world and one's life in it" (p. 124). Such a sense of meaning leads to less vulnerability to stress. Woolfolk and Lehrer (1984, p. 352ff.) emphasize, however, that holding any set of beliefs or worldview simply because of its instrumental value is inherently self-limiting and self-defeating. Rather, alienation and defeat are only overcome through some passionate commitment to a direction in life. Woolfolk and Lehrer stress that such a passionate commitment, if it is to be healthy, should contain the following elements: 1) a recognition and acceptance of the inevitable misfortunes and difficulties of life; 2) tolerance for the imperfections of oneself and others; 3) involvement in the *process* of life rather than its results; 4) a commitment to something outside oneself; and 5) a balance between effortful striving and detached observation (p. 356).

Christianity can contribute to each of these elements of the healthy belief system. First, Christianity is the religion of the "crucified God"—the God who understands that life comprises pain, and has come to share that pain. Secondly, Christianity is the religion of the "forgiving God"—the God who understands and accepts our failures. Third, Christianity is the religion of the "God of the present moment." This is the God who calls us to enjoy his presence now. Salvation is by grace, not by works. For example, John Calvin (1559/1972) has declared that "the chief end of man is to glorify God and *enjoy* Him forever." Finally, Christianity is the religion of the "God who calls us both into self-examination and then back out into relationships with others." Health is always a circle. There is a time for contemplation and a time for action.

The sense of a meaningful belief system is important to health. However, some individuals may hold such a system in an unhealthy manner. The opposite of complete meaninglessness is a rigid adherence to an airtight system, a rigid adherence to one theological framework in which all elements are very carefully and specifically delineated for all time.

The adherent to such a system tends to suffer from perfectionism. Everything must have an explanation that is always understandable to the individual. When such an individual is confronted with the tragedies of life, a detailed explanation for such tragedies is always forthcoming. When these individuals comfort others, they are like Job's comforters. "If you set your heart aright, you will stretch out your hands toward Him," (Job 11:13) they told Job. "If iniquity is in your hand, put it far away, . . . you will forget your misery; you will remember it as waters that have passed away," (Job 11:16), they counseled. They had all the answers. Job had merely to repent of any wrongdoing, and his fortunes would be restored.

Job responds with a lament: "Behold I go forward, but He is not here; and backward, but I cannot perceive him; . . . for I am hemmed in by darkness, and thick darkness covers my face" (Job 23:8,17). Job had no answers for his tragedy. He did not understand "why *him*."

At the end of the Book of Job, however, God speaks to Job's conforters and says, "My wrath is kindled against you and against your two friends; for you have not spoken of me what is right, as my servant Job has" (Job 42:7). Apparently, Job's confusion regarding the causes of his misfortunes was acceptable to God.

Even within our Christian belief system, there are ambiguities. The healthy individual can recognize that tragedies in life may leave one with uncertainties. He understands that all ambiguities regarding God will not be clarified. Such an individual is ultimately less vulnerable to loss of faith, and accepts ambiguities as part of the "dark night of the soul." The individual who has a complete answer for every circumstance is in danger of losing his faith when the inevitable periods of darkness do come. This individual has not relied ultimately on faith, but on rationality.

How to Use this Chapter

The materials in this chapter are best used after one has gained some knowledge of one's thoughts. Each thought may then be examined in light of each of the polarities. This chapter is intended as a tool to allow the individual to take a more objective perspective on his or her thoughts. Not every polarity will be relevant for every thought. It is likely, however, that any one thought can probably be examined from the standpoint of at least several polarities.

For example, the thought "I will never be able to succeed in my chosen profession" is relevant to several categories. (See Figure 4-2 in Chapter 4). First, the individual may feel somewhat helpless to influence his life's direction. Secondly, the individual has focused his attention on the future and his fears of what may happen then, rather than on what is occurring now. The individual may also be denying any successes, in his exclusive focus on some failures. It is also conceivable that the individual may have an overly perfectionistic attitude regarding what may be considered success. On the other hand, the individual may have given up. Thus, this thought may be relevant to at least five of the six basic polarities.

A self-monitoring form, like Figures 4-1 and 4-2 in Chapter 4 provides a place where the polarities of each thought may be evaluated. The position of each thought on each polarity can be easily marked for comparison purposes. Extreme positions are a signal for thought-modification.

After placing a thought in its appropriate place on each of these polarities, it is then possible to ask oneself how the thought may be modified so that it is more centrally located on the polarity. Thus, for example, the thought mentioned above, "I will ultimately never be able to succeed in my chosen profession" must be modified in the following manner. First, the individual will need to ask himself in what way he can have more control over his circumstances. Then he should ask himself what positive aspects of the present circumstances have been ignored. Finally, he needs to ask himself in what ways he may be able to alter his standards of success.

Chapter 7

IMAGE TRANSFORMATIONS

Then shall we all come into our Lord, knowing ourselves clearly and possessing God most fully. We shall endlessly be completely possessed by God, seeing Him in truth, most fully feeling Him, spiritually hearing Him, delectably smelling Him, sweetly swallowing Him. Then shall we see Him face to face, familiarly and most fully.—Juliana of Norwich, c. 1392/1977, p. 151

Our minds are full of images. They run through like numerous little white mice scampering across a floor. Often they go so quickly that we don't see them clearly. We only know that they were briefly present. At other times, these images come back again and again to haunt us. These are the intense images, the very good ones and the very bad ones. We try to catch the good ones. We want to savor them more fully, or view them more clearly. We try to dispel the threatening ones. We want to eliminate them even as our minds almost compulsively are driven back to these same images, just as we find our eyes inevitably drifting back to the spot where we saw the mouse run under the bed. Our minds drift back to that spot almost as if we were waiting for the mouse to emerge once again.

Because intense and often emotion-laden images flood our conscious mind, they become apt subjects for psychotherapy. Indeed, sometimes the images are so intense that only *other* images can have any impact on them.

Images were familiar to the Hebrews and the early church. Indeed, most abstract lessons to be taught in both the Old and New Testament were taught by concrete examples and word pictures. Yahweh seems to be a God of visual illustrations; God is less of an abstract discourser. God's ultimate lesson, the nature of the divine, was taught by visual concrete example. "And the Word became flesh and dwelt among us, full of grace and truth: we have beheld his glory, glory as of the only Son from the Father" (John 1:14).

Psychological Theories of Imagery Use

Images play an important role in many theories of psychotherapy. This section will discuss briefly the role which images play in the psychoanalytic and cognitive approaches to therapy. Additionally, an approach will be presented that combines some of the features of both of these models.

Psychoanalytic theorists have traditionally seen images as examples of more primitive or primary-process thinking. Primary-process forms of thought are thought patterns developed earlier in childhood, according to the psychoanalytic point of view (Horowitz, 1978).

Even though images are often a result of past negative experiences, they may be reexpressed due to association with a specific present situation. They may also be due to a breakdown of conscious experiences. The individual's consciousness becomes preoccupied with these experiences from the past. According to Horowitz (1978), these images may continue until the person has mastered this experience from the past. Thus images are expressions of an unconscious conflict. Mastering an image, according to Horowitz, means translating that image into word representation, and processing it for memory storage by multiple-coding systems. For example, an individual may have a terrifying image continuously running through his mind until he is able to label it, until he is able to say, "That is only an example of such and such."

A traumatic event might overwhelm the individual at several different stages. First, too many images may be perceived. Secondly, there may be difficulty in giving a verbal label to these images, and finally there may be no coding system for storing either the images or the label. By a coding system, Horowitz means some type of overall conceptual framework that can be used to make sense of the event. Negative images just do not go away until they are dealt with, until they are reinterpreted into a different framework. Repression means a failure to deal with these images. An example of primary process thinking is the assault victim's continued reliving of the assault scene. The feelings associated with the scene are too intense to allow them to be assimilated into any current framework of the patient.

Paivio (1971) has concluded that images and verbal memory commonly interact, and that images play a particularly important role in matching current impressions with what has been stored from the past. Images may not necessarily always represent more primitive types of thinking, and may be useful in performing an integrative function for other thoughts. Horowitz also admits that sometimes images may have an adaptive function, as when an image of food motivates one to continue living in spite of hunger. Noy (1969) has argued that viewing images as more primitive was based upon a consideration of only those images in pathological states, such as psychotic images. Indeed, later dynamic theorists, like Jung, have seen a more positive role for images and primary process thinking.

Cognitive theorists also do not necessarily see images as more primitive. Instead, they consider them merely to be a different mode of processing information, and perhaps a mode·we used earlier in our lives, before speech was available.

Currently, imagery formation is seen as a concept-matching process. We match up new images with images stored in our mind. This is not too different from the verbal process, in which we take a new idea and try to make sense out of it, in terms of our larger conceptual framework, or the ideas we already understand. A thought won't fit, and will cause conflicts if we can't make sense out of it in terms of what is already familiar to us.

Likewise, an image that is not acceptable to our larger images of ourselves and our world will not be easily assimilated. It does not fit. It comes back to haunt us. The larger older image will have to change. We may need some new images of ourselves. For example, the abuse victim will ultimately have to modify her internal image of an abuse as being associated with helplessness, or terror. Somehow, new meaning must be given to that image. Each time that image is relived due to its association with another present, more positive experience, the original absolute negative meaning is challenged (Kosslyn, 1980). Lang (1977, 1979) also views images as visual thoughts. Images are not stimuli we are responding to; rather, they *are* our responses. He calls images "stored propositional constructs." He means by this that images are not merely pictures, but they are stored in our mind via a common underlying code, just as verbal thoughts are stored via a linguistic code. Troublesome images may have a negative meaning in terms of this code.

Importance of Images

Images are major therapeutic tools because they are immediate and direct and are less likely to be interpreted in terms of any pre-conceived ideas. This is because images bring us closer to experiencing certain emotions before we have had an opportunity to categorize them. Images are thus more likely to produce more intense emotions, and have a greater effect on physiology than words.

Images also seem to have a greater capacity than the linguistic mode for allowing us to keep a continuing focus on emotionally laden materials. It is easier to keep an image of an object in one's mind than it is to tell oneself continually that I must remember that object.

Images are also important because they can be great motivators. Individuals usually act more on the basis of imagined consequences of an action than on the probability that the consequences will actually occur.

Images may also give us access to preverbal memories, that is, memories that we held before we knew language and could label what we experienced or saw. This idea must be interpreted cautiously, however. Often we later put verbal labels on what we had experienced earlier. Finally, some individuals may be able to use images to fill in a situation or an idea that they cannot yet express verbally.

Meichenbaum (1973) likes images because he believes they help us to rehearse solutions and mentally rehearse alternative actions more effectively than words. Many athletes also use imagery rehearsal to perform their sports (Mahoney & Avener, 1977). One pole vaulter in the 1984 Olympics, for example, gained a certain notoriety by his imagery rehearsal of his jump beforehand. Television viewers were treated to a young man standing in front of the bar bobbing his head up and down as he visualized all of the steps involved in the actual vault.

Jung has long noted the adaptive values of images. He sees imaging as an internal dialogue with oneself (cited in Horowitz, 1978), and strongly believed that images had a life of their own. Images that came from the unconscious could not be easily modified or actively directed.

The humanistic psychologists have also valued imagery because they felt such imagery brought the individual into contact with different aspects of himself.

Though imagery use has a long history in psychotherapy, it has usually stayed on the fringes of acceptable methods, until the recent cognitive revolution.

Theological Reflections

The parables and images of Jesus and the Old Testament prophets vividly demonstrate many of the mysteries of the divine. In fact, at one point Jesus seems to have confined his teaching almost exclusively to parables: "with many such parables he spoke the word to them, . . . but he did not speak to them without a parable . . ." (Mark 4:33–34). The Hebrew God is a God of images, showing himself ultimately in the incarnation: "He is the image of the invisible God." (Col. 1:15).

Images are also part of much Christian devotional literature. Thomas Merton (1961), for example, used an image to demonstrate the image-making of God.

> As a magnifying glass concentrates the rays of the sun into a little burning knot of heat that can set fire to dry leaf or a piece of paper, so the mystery of Christ in the Gospel concentrates the rays of God's light and fire to a point that sets fire to the spirit of man. (p. 150)

Merton cautions, however, that the Christ of God is not always the Christ of our imagination or images. It is ultimately faith and not imagination that gives us life in Christ, according to Merton. Nevertheless, sometimes our imagination may serve to remind us of the Christ in whom we believe. Similarly, Brother Lawrence (c. 1700/1958) describes his way of practicing the presence of God:

> Sometimes I considered myself before Him as a poor criminal at the feet of his judge; at other times I beheld Him in my heart as my Father, as my God. I worshipped Him the oftenest [sic] that I could, keeping my mind in His holy presence, and recalling it as often as I found it wandered from Him. (p. 31)

Methods of Imagery Transformation: General Considerations

First, image formation is a process. This means that any image of a difficult subject or of a desired action may need to be approached in a step-by-step method. When helping another individual form an image, one must be careful to accept where the other is in the process. We then can use his present level of awareness to build on. Whatever the patient imagines is to be accepted. Whatever image he reports is to be complimented. Essentially we communicate, "What you are doing right now is exactly what will allow you eventually to imagine the desired image." After we accept the other's present image, we then encourage him to go one step further with a comment like, "Now, as you see yourself at home, what can you see around you?" A smooth rhythm of acceptance and encouragement of progress should be present. This process, not unlike empathy, has been called "pacing and leading" (cf. Zeig, 1982).

When you are attempting to image on your own, acceptance of whatever images you form initially is helpful. Some individuals become frustrated if they feel that their initial images are not vivid enough or involving enough. One patient reported, when asked to monitor her thoughts and images, that all she could get was the thought that, "I can't remember any of my thoughts," and an image of herself coming back and telling me she could not remember any thoughts or images. I remarked that those images were actually very important because they reflected her concerns about what I might think about her. Such images then became a basis for further images.

Secondly, care must be taken to maintain the individual's attention and absorption in the image. Often, anxious individuals have difficulty maintaining attention on anything. Having the eyes closed is a useful first step. It is also important to communicate with the patient regularly. "What are you seeing right now?" and "Good!" are helpful toward keeping another on target. We can best maintain our own attention if we start imagery alone and in a quiet environment.

Third, the ultimate focus in imagery should be on the desired response, not the precise imagery that is used to obtain the response. If one wants to relax, then it is possible to imagine any number of situations that allow relaxation. Each individual may find that she can come up with her own unique combinations. If the focus is on trying a new behavior, there may be many different situations that would lead to the same behavior. Allow the person involved to make the decision.

Some individuals may fear imagery. They fear a loss of control. These individuals have mistakenly believed that they do not control their images. Emphasizing that the individuals involved still makes the decisions increases their sense of control. The freedom to change one's images has always been a delightful discovery for my patients, who in the past have felt dictated to by such images.

A fourth factor that may aid imagery production is what Erickson (cf. Zeig, 1982) has called the "affect bridge." Usually, there has been a time in the past when we have had certain sensations or feelings that we desire to feel now. We may, for example, recall the pleasant, relaxing sensation of sitting beside a peaceful mountain stream in the warm sun. We may recall that not only were our muscles relaxed, but we had an emotion of exhilaration. If that emotion is desired in the present, it is possible to imagine that scene from the past. Likewise, if one feels depressed in the present and wonders what produces that depression, it may be possible to recall other scenes in which the same emotions are present.

Some patients may say that they already image positive images and it has not been helpful. These patients, however, do not use the positive imagery to *change the negative imagery* they already have. Instead, they attempt merely to push the negative imagery out of their minds without dealing with it. One must always confront what is already there.

It is also imperative that both the monitoring of images and the changing of images be completed immediately when the conflict is occurring. In my experience, the patients who have had the most success with these procedures have learned to apply them immediately when they are beset by bad images or thoughts.

Images can be profitably used by anyone using this book on their own. For deep past hurts, however, it is often good to have someone else present. This is especially important if there is a tendency to stay stuck in the hurtful images, rather than modifying those images.

Methods of Imagery Transformation: Specific Techniques

Often the true nature of what we can be is hidden from us. We become aware only of our failings, or our incapacities and limitations. We see no hope of any change. We have no *image* of any greater potential. Often, it is only when individuals do have a vision of what they can be, or what is possible, that they can begin to change. A good therapist will begin to provide those possibilities by example, suggestion, and the new respectful way she treats the patient.

According to Karl Barth (1948/1960, p. 41), the man Jesus is the source of our knowledge about the nature of humanness as created by God. We know ourselves as creatures loved when we know about Jesus. Even more than that, we know ourselves as we can begin to be when we know about Jesus. All human nature as it can be, can be seen in Jesus. We participate in that true nature of true humanity only because Jesus did so first and showed us the way. In him, human nature is not concealed, but revealed in its original form. We are invited to infer, from his human nature, the character of our own human nature; to really know ourselves in him, to gain a fuller insight into what we can be (". . . so also in Christ shall all be made alive" 1 Cor. 15:22).

Because the images of Jesus play such a central role in correcting our own self-definitions, visual images of Jesus and ourselves can also be used profitably within the psychotherapy process. At least four different types of relationships between ourselves and the image of Jesus are possible. (1) There is the image of surrender. Various images of giving oneself to Christ can be therapeutic. (2) There is the image of Christ's reaction to us. (3) There is the image of Christ with us as we engage in specific tasks, and finally, (4) there is the image of Christ within us.

Surrendering thoughts to Christ.   This type of image is the simplest and often the most used, especially for tension. Several different approaches are possible.

1. Active recollection has been defined as a process in which we collect our faculties and enter into ourselves to be with God (Dorgan, 1984). One way in which this process may be brought about is by holding in our mind one continuous image of Christ. Whenever any other images arise, they are surrendered to this image.

As noted in Chapter 6, this process has much in common with the relaxation response (Edmonston, 1981). According to Edmonston, the ingredients needed for a relaxation response are, first of all, a mental *device,* or an object to dwell upon. This should be a constant stimulus, on which the individual concentrates to the relative exclusion of all else. In concentrating on this mental device, a passive attitude should be maintained. If the individual becomes distracted, his attention should always be brought back to this object. Finally, it is important not to be concerned with performance, but just allow oneself to be part of the process.

St. Teresa of Avila, in *The Way of Perfection,* has observed, "When the intellect is bound, one proceeds peacefully" (cited in Dorgan, 1984). When our thoughts are not allowed to wander all over the place, we are generally more relaxed. The idea is to let go of all competing distractions until we are truly centered only on this image of Christ. This is an active surrender, an abandonment of oneself, one's thoughts, and one's cares to the Divine One. One must cultivate the attitude that nothing really matters, except attending to the Lord, via this image. Any thoughts either good or bad, are actively given to God. Our whole self is taken up with the center of our focus, God.

This process has sometimes been helpful for insomnia. The primary characteristic of insomnia is racing thoughts. Insomniacs often report that it seems that they have thought about everything that happened in the previous year, everything that might happen in the coming year, and conversations real and imagined with just about everyone they know, and all in one night! As the thoughts continue, the insomniac eventually becomes more aroused and wide awake. This process is further aggravated as he attempts to get back to sleep and becomes worried about the lack of sleep.

In recollection, one must determine to keep one's thoughts on an image of Christ. This focus on Christ must be *more important than sleep*, or any other thoughts that might intrude. At first, the process will be difficult as the thoughts intrude, but we must be determined to hang onto our image of Christ. Often it also helps to lie in one position so that this focus is not disturbed.

The particular image that may be used should always be selected by the individual. Each person has one image that for them is most helpful and most engaging. It is good to focus our attention on this image when we *are* relaxed, so that later, when we need to relax, the image will be associated with relaxation. We must learn to "cast all our anxieties on him, for he cares about you" (1 Peter 5:7). This ability comes only as we have cultivated the presence of Christ.

Images of surrender have also been used in the process of the healing of memories. Denis and Matthew Linn (1978) in their book, *Healing Life's Hurts,* state that when we want to repair ourselves, we have to ask ourselves how God meant us to be. They suggest looking at the parts of ourselves, including our memories, and attempting to understand how God has used them. This process means looking at the gifts we have been given and thanking God for each of those gifts. It is helpful to associate each gift with some visual image.

A number of cognitive psychologists (cf. Rehm, 1982) have included a procedure in their therapist manuals which they call focusing on the positives. Essentially the individual is asked to call to mind or list positive attributes and focus on that list for a period of time.

Frequently, with severely depressed patients, I will start our therapy together by asking them to focus on their strengths. After a discussion of possible strengths, I will ask them to go home and make a list of those attributes we discussed, as well as any more they may become aware of. This process can be intensified by imagining an image associated with each of those attributes.

Christ's reaction to us.   A second type of imagery is to imagine Christ's reaction to us. This process requires careful preparation before the image itself can be dealt with. There are two essential ingredients. The patient must first be able to image successfully a biblical scene in which a Bible character with a problem similar to the patient's is responded to by Christ. When a biblical scene has been imagined, then the individual can be led gently into his own painful image.

Examining Christ's reaction to us is not a new idea. Such exercises were part of the *Spiritual Exercises of St. Ignatius* (1548/1951). Frequently, St. Ignatius would ask the participant in his exercises to image the village where Christ preached, or imagine the Nativity. There are at least two important differences, however, between those exercises and the present ones. In the present case, I ask the participants to become even more intensely involved in the images, to the extent of feeling what the participants felt, and putting themselves in the place of the participants.

Additionally, the purpose of the present exercises is somewhat more positive. St. Ignatius often used his images to instigate recalling one's sins, or in preparation for offering oneself for a task. The purpose of the present exercises is to help the participants develop a more accepting view of their present thoughts, actions, and emotions.

If we imagine a biblical scene in which Christ accepted a troublesome emotion or thought, we have a cognitive basis for believing that the present negative emotion is acceptable. Intense images often provide the most persuasive arguments.

Frequently, we fail to see the relevance of Bible stories for our own present everyday life, since the stories were about people of another day and time. This failure to grasp the present relevance of scripture for our everyday emotions and struggles exists in all corners of Christendom, regardless of the doctrine of scripture held. Scripture cannot be viewed as relevant simply by asserting that it is. The stories and images of scripture must be experienced in our own ongoing stream of life. The pain, blood, sweat, and tears of the participants must be likened to our own. We must live and strive with the characters as they are confronted with the Christ. Only then will scripture be experienced as relevant to our own lives.

Kelley was a young professional woman who had been consulting me about how to handle a crisis at work. She then was notified by a surgeon that a lump was discovered in her breast and that she needed a biopsy. She came to my office the afternoon of the revelation quite distraught. Not only was she in tears, and anxious, but she was also angry at herself. She was angry at herself for being upset over the possibility of breast cancer. She felt desperate, and was also angry at herself for feeling that desperation. She felt that such desperation was unbecoming a Christian.

I suggested that the woman in Mark 5:25–34 with the issue of blood must have felt such desperation. She apparently pushed through the crowd with such urgency merely to touch the hem of Jesus's garment.

I helped Kelley develop an image of the scene, using some of the procedures of imagery development discussed above. It is important for the helper first to read the relevant story. The best procedure for then helping the patient develop an image of the scene is to ask her to start by imagining the most innocuous parts of the images and gradually move to the more emotionally intense parts.

"Try to image this crowd of people pushing around Jesus. What does the environment around the crowd look like?"

"It looks like dry desert and it is very dusty. There are a few scraggly trees beside the road."

"Good! As you see the trees and the dry surroundings, who are the people present, and what are they doing?"

"There is a large crowd of people pushing in around Jesus. There must be 200 people."

"What are they wearing?"

"They have typical garb of that time on, sandals, head-coverings, and long robes. There are only a few women in the crowd."

"Can you see the woman with the flow of blood?"

"Yes, she is pushing in behind Jesus."

"What is she wearing?"

"She is wearing a brown head-covering and a brown robe."

"Does she have sandals on?"

"Yes, but her feet are also dusty."

"What kind of body posture does she have?"

"She is bent over as she is using her head to butt her way towards the crowd. And as she is bent over, her hand is stretched downward to try to grab some of Jesus's clothes."

"What color is her hair, and what does her face look like?"

"Her hair is brown, and her eyes are brown. She has a fearful look on her face. Her eyes are red from crying, and she has a number of wrinkles around her face from worrying. She is gritting her teeth as she tries to grasp for Jesus."

"What must she feel inside?"

"She is anxious and has a knot in her stomach. She feels desperate. This is her last chance."

"Imagine now that she touches Jesus in her desperation and Jesus turns and looks at her. What is Jesus wearing and what color are his hair and eyes?"

"He has a long white robe on. His hair is also brown, and so are his eyes."

"Imagine that the woman is fearful and trembling about Jesus's reaction."

"I can see that. She is afraid he will disapprove. Everyone else disapproves of her problem."

"Imagine now that Jesus says to her, as it says in scripture, 'Daughter, your faith has made you well; go in peace, and be healed of your disease.' What type of expression does Jesus have on his face?"

"He has a very kind expression."

"How do you know that?"

"His eyes are very kind, and he has a smile on his face. He reaches out and takes her hand."

"Imagine now that you are that woman standing in front of Jesus. Tell him about your problem and your feelings of desperation, as the woman did."

"I can see myself doing that."

"Imagine now Jesus's reaction to you."

"He is looking at me with kindness. He tells me he understands that I must be scared, and that it is okay to be scared." (Kelley started crying at this point.) "I guess it is okay to feel desperate."

This process was important to Kelley. She had to allow herself to accept the feelings that were hers, rather than being so hard on herself.

In any image, the amount of time spent on imagining the surrounding environment versus the central characters depends upon the patient's feelings and abilities to get into the image. If the image is difficult for the patient, it is usually better to start slowly with the surrounding environment.

A second way in which biblical images may be helpful is in restructuring our thoughts and feelings about a past event. The recent blending of cognitive and psychoanalytic theories suggests that events of the past that still traumatize us do so because we still have the same perspective on them that existed when they occurred. We have not been able to allow these events to be exposed to the reality-oriented scrutiny that we currently hold in other areas. We have not brought these events out into the light so that they can be examined. Not only can such events be reanalyzed with thoughts, but images are also useful. In fact, if the original event was a traumatic one that has left a terrifying image, the image itself may need to be addressed and modified.

It is important for us to realize the relevance of scripture for our past as well as present experiences. Often we need to go back to those past events that haunt us, for which we feel unforgiven. We have to realize that even in those events we are totally loved by God. The relevance of God's love for these past events, however, cannot be merely an intellectual proposition. This relevance must be tested out in our own experience.

Jim and Paula were a middle-aged couple with marital difficulties. Paula had been depressed for about 3 years, and her depression had driven the couple further apart. Early in the course of marital therapy and individual therapy for Paula, it became apparent that the couple had practically no sexual relationship. Eventually Paula disclosed that she had been gang-raped 1 year previous to their marriage. (At the time of the counseling, they had been married about 15 years.) Paula found it very difficult to talk about the rape. She expressed a great deal of shame and guilt regarding it, feeling that she was somehow responsible. She also found it difficult to have any physical contact at all with her husband or any other male. She felt unclean and repelled by any idea of sex.

In order to change the intensity of her negative feelings and thoughts about the rape, she was helped to reexperience some of these feelings in the context of the story of the prostitute who washed Jesus' feet with her hair (Luke 7:36–50).

After an initial reading and discussion of the story, she was helped to imagine the scene surrounding the encounter between Jesus and the woman. A procedure similar to that discussed in the section above was used.

After a great deal of time had been spent on her imagining the surroundings, she imagined the woman approaching Jesus.

"The woman is scared and a bit intimidated by the fact that only men are in the room."

"How do you know she is scared?"

"Her hands are shaking and she has a knot in the pit of her stomach. She has a dread of going into that room with all of those men."

"Why does she persist and go ahead with it?"

"Somehow, she wants to get rid of all the guilt she bears and she feels that Jesus will forgive her. She feels that things will be all right after she does it."

"Imagine that she is washing Jesus's feet now. What is happening? What is Jesus's reaction to all of this?"

"He looks at her with a look of love in his eyes."

"What does she do?"

"She starts crying." (Paula starts crying even as she has her eyes closed imagining the scene.)

"What is Jesus' reaction?"

"He starts crying too. He is very moved."

"Imagine, now, Paula, that you are that woman kneeling at the feet of Jesus. Can you see yourself in that room?"

"Yes."

"Can you imagine yourself in front of Jesus?"

"Yes."

"What is his reaction to you?"

"He is very kind, and his eyes are very warm."

"Are you able to touch him?"

"No! I just can't do that!"

Paula had a great deal of difficulty touching Jesus, or allowing him to touch her. She felt that her difficulty in that imagery was a capsule summary of her current relationship with Christ and the church. She felt that there was a closed door and she was afraid to open it.

Prior to Paula's seeing me, she had been counseled rather harshly by a pastor who had told her that she was sinning by not having sex with her husband. Her reaction to his pronouncement was to attempt suicide by carbon monoxide poisoning.

For Paula, Christ's maleness and his divinity were inextricably intertwined. Because of her negative reaction to one (maleness) she had closed her emotions to Christ as divine. Consequently, her feelings of guilt were only further increased.

Gradually, as we worked with the image of Christ in a different setting, she was able to touch Christ and to experience some healing. The process was slow and painful, however.

The maleness of Christ can be a stumbling block for some individuals. The Christian woman whose devoutly Christian father had sexually molested her as a child will have a great deal of difficulty with images of God and Jesus as exclusively male.

Anderson, in *The Resurrection of Jesus as Hermeneutical Criterion* (1984), has provided an interesting alternative to viewing Jesus as exclusively male in all of our theological discussions. He states that it should be the risen Lord who is the criterion for all our understanding of Christ. The human category of male circumcised Jewishness died on the cross. The resurrected Jesus is beyond the distinction of male versus female, circumcised versus uncircumcised, and Jew versus Gentile. Just as Paul saw his contact with the risen Christ as his criterion for apostleship, so we must interpret our faith through the resurrected Christ. We still have the world, with its roles, structures, and relationships. However, they are raised with Christ. Yahweh is not just a set of propositions and theology, but a risen Being. One must ultimately understand how this risen Being would stand with those who are in pain in the world.

The importance of Jesus to the creeds has always been his humanness. His maleness while on earth was incidental. Christ's relationship to us at present is as the resurrected Lord who is beyond human categories of sex. Christ in our present experience is One who loves us as God, not as male or female. Demanding that one image be present at the cost of alienating those in pain from a Savior whom they desperately need is not a proper understanding of the care and love of Yahweh.

Juliana of Norwich, writing in the thirteenth century, has provided us with a lovely image of Jesus' motherly love. Such an image may bring healing where the male image will not.

> Our high God, the sovereign wisdom of all, arrayed himself in this low place and made himself entirely ready in our poor flesh in order to do the service and the office of motherhood himself in all things. . . .
>
> We realize that all our mothers bear us for pain and for dying. . . . But our true mother, Jesus-All love-alone bears us for joy and for endless living. Thus he sustains us within himself in love and hard labor, until the fullness of time. Then he willed to suffer the sharpest thorns and the most grievous pains there ever were or ever will be, and to die at the last. . . .
>
> Therefore it was necessary for him to feed us, for the most precious love of motherhood had made him a debtor to us. A mother can give her child her milk to such, but our precious mother, Jesus, can feed us with himself. . . . The mother can hold her child tenderly to her breast, but our tender mother, Jesus, can lead us in friendly fashion into his blessed breast by means

of his sweet open side and there show us something of the godhead and the joys of heaven with a spiritual assurance of endless bliss. (pp. 191–192)

In another place she writes:

But frequently when our failure and our wretchedness are shown to us, we are so terribly frightened, and so greatly ashamed of ourselves. . . . but then our courteous mother does not will that we flee away; for him nothing could be more loathsome. But he wills then that we act the way a child does. When a child is in discomfort and afraid, he runs hastily to his mother, and if he can do nothing more, he cries out to his mother for help with all his might. . . . Jesus wills that we act this way, saying like a meek child, "My natural mother, my gracious mother, my most precious mother, have mercy on me. I have made myself dirty and unlike you, and I may not and cannot make it better, except with your secret help and your grace." (p. 195)

Christ with us in a difficult situation.   The image of Christ with us can be helpful in at least two different ways.

A mental rehearsal of an anticipated event has been found to be a great aid in enabling an individual eventually to carry out that behavior. This rehearsal can be enhanced by imagining Christ with you in the situation, as you rehearse an anticipated conversation or action that you have found difficult in the past.

Imagery can be a useful method whereby we may experience more fully the truth of scripture that Christ has promised to be with us in all things.

A second method of imagining Christ with us is to visualize a difficult or painful past situation in which Christ is with us in that situation. When Christ is added to the painful traumatic event, the tone and flavor of such an image may be changed. Such a process is actually a cognitive restructuring of the image as we remember it. Often, such images are so intense and so painful, that only other equally intense images will be able to have impact on them.

For some patients, Christ will change the actual content of the image. For others, Christ's presence will give the original painful content new meaning. As with other situations, when extremely negative material is to be accessed, it is imperative to start with a healing base. Thus, the counselor should insure that patients has first been able to develop a relevant image of Christ, before going into their own pain. Some individuals find it difficult to escape from their negative traumatic images after they have been brought back to awareness. It is not easy to transform such loaded negative images into more relatively benign images. For these individuals, an equally intense image of Christ must be developed *first*. Such an image provides an intense positive image that can be returned to when the painful images occur.

Ann was a severely depressed, suicidal patient who had a long history of abuse as a child. Ann worked with me for several months before she was able to share her stories of abuse. She was quite embarrassed by them. In fact, she had been in therapy off and on for 10 years as an adult, and had never been able to tell another therapist her history.

As she told her recollections to me, she shook and trembled. She believed that my knowledge of the abuse would end our relationship. Not only had she been severely physically abused as a very young child by her real mother, but she was later sexually molested as a preadolescent by her foster father. Both experiences of molestation had left her with traumatic images which she regarded as a negative stigma signifying her worthlessness. She also had some scars which she regarded as proof that she was no good. Ann believed the cultural myth that victims are guilty.

Before allowing Ann to become completely involved with her images of abuse, I helped her develop an image of the healing Christ. We started by reading one of the stories of Jesus's trial and crucifixion.

"Ann, try to imagine an image of Jesus standing in front of you right now. What is he wearing?"

"He is wearing a white robe and has brown sandals on his feet."

"Good! And as you see his white robe and his brown sandals, what color are his hair and eyes?"

"His eyes are brown and his hair is brown."

"Imagine that this is after his crucifixion. As you see his brown eyes and hair, can you see his wounds? What do they look like?"

"He has deep cuts in his hands and feet and scars on his back and legs."

"What kind of facial expression does he have?"

"He is in pain."

"Is there any other expression?"

"His eyes still look warm."

"What lets you know he is in pain?"

"His eyes have some tears in them, and his mouth is tense."

"Now, Ann, I want you to switch to the image of you with your mother. Tell me what you see."

"I see myself sitting on the floor as a young child crying."

"As you are crying, what else is happening?"

"My mother is angry at me, and tells me to be quiet."

"Then what happened?"

"I continued crying, so my mother tied my shoestrings together and took me to the kitchen."

"What happened then?"

"She turned on the kitchen stove and held me down on the stove." (She started sobbing at this point.)

"Ann, imagine now that Christ, whom you saw earlier, comes into the kitchen now. What would he do?"

"He walks over to the stove and takes me off the stove."

"Then what happened?"

"He is telling me that he understands what I feel, he has lots of scars too."

"Ann, imagine what Jesus's eyes look like as he tells you that he understands."

"He has tears in his eyes, and they are very warm."

"Ann, just allow yourself to look at Jesus's eyes."

This is an abbreviated version of an exchange that took about one hour, and was repeated several times. I gained a new insight into the healing Christ through this event. There is no human hell that is so deep that Jesus has not already been there.

Christ within us.   Christ has promised that he would dwell within us, as we dwell within him. Barth notes that our reconciliation is completed by virtue of our inclusion in the humanity of Jesus. A power flows from Jesus's existence into our existence, which gives us a new direction (Barth, 1955/1958, pp. 180–181). Christ has graciously accepted us, and consented to dwell within us. We are therefore exalted, because Christ has been exalted.

Often, however, individuals with low self-esteem imagine that they have such loathsome elements in themselves that no one could ever like them if they knew about it. They fail to realize that they are accepted by God.

It is often a healing experience to become aware of that aspect of ourselves that we do not accept and to realize that Jesus still chooses to dwell within us as Christians, regardless of those unlikable aspects.

Such a realization means that perhaps our image of that unlikable aspect of ourselves may be modified.

As we have earlier quoted, Juliana of Norwich affirms that, "It is His delight to dwell in our soul endlessly. . . . For in us is his most homelike home and His endless dwelling" (p. 186).

One way in which we may experience more fully the phrase "Christ dwelling within us richly" is through our imagination. Most of us have never really stopped to think about what "Christ living in us" means. Because Christ has chosen to dwell within us, we can reflect upon what this means in our everyday lives by use of imagery. In becoming human, God became not only Jesus Christ and dwelt within Jesus Christ, but he became potentially every man and woman that existed. Paul's statement, "For me to live is Christ . . ." (Philippians 1:21) expresses this truth. The presence of God in the world and in us is dependent upon no one. However, as we become aware of his presence in our life, and live as if we *were* Christ, then the presence of Christ is felt more forcefully in the world.

I have often asked patients to reflect on Juliana's statements quoted above. As they reflect, I ask them to imagine just where Christ might dwell within them. While our understanding of this concept is limited, an image of Christ within us is certainly no more limited in its meaning than is the theoretical statement that "Christ dwells within us." Participants picture where that Christ might be, and what that Christ might look like. Some individuals react by saying they experience a certain warmth. Indeed, many great voices in the church have often told us of the fire within where Christ dwells.

After we have experienced Christ dwelling within us through imagery, we may then focus on our more loathsome aspects. I often ask individuals to show these characteristics to God in their mind's eye. I ask them to notice that Christ has promised that he will not leave, and indeed that he does not. For some individuals, such an experience provides the first real glimmer that God indeed does accept them. Often the self-esteem of those in mental anguish needs such assurance. Making that assurance more understandable and concrete via imagery completes the picture.

Once we can imagine that Christ dwells within us, and that we become one with Christ, it is often a short step to changing our actions. We can begin to act as Christ would act. Imagining ourselves as Christ in the world often results in a dramatic change of perspective. "For me to live is Christ." Such we may become and claim by the gracious grace of God.

Susan was a very timid woman who rarely spoke up to defend herself, or to take a stand on any issue. As she began to view herself as the dwelling-place of God, she began with the counselor's help, to believe that it was all right for her to speak out.

One final way in which our identification with Christ may prove therapeutic is through identification with the sufferings of Christ.

Often our negative emotions and disappointments become more than we can bear. We find it hard to identify with the Apostle Paul's statement, "I have been crucified with Christ." Perhaps this is because we have been taught that we are really only suffering with Christ when we suffer because of our faith. It is hard to see that in our other sorrows we can also feel the sorrow Christ has felt. Even though we may feel at that moment the desolation that Christ felt on the cross, we don't feel justified in claiming that identification. We feel blocked off from the very healing we need.

Christ, however, became human in order to identify with all our pains, not just those that seem obviously to come directly from our trials and tribulations as a Christian. In some of our darkest moments, we need desperately the love of Christ through identification with his suffering. We need to have that suffering redeemed. We need to re-structure our view of that suffering. Juliana reflects:

> I understood that what our Lord means is that we are now on his cross with him in our pains, and dying with him in our sufferings. If we deliberately stay on the same cross, with his help and his grace, up to the final point, suddenly he shall transform his coun-tenance for us and we shall be with him in heaven. (p. 116)

Most of us choose to run away from our negative emotions. We choose to deny them. We attempt to keep a stiff upper lip. Such denial, however, means that the pain is often not confronted. The painful emotion itself must be faced and experienced. And, just as we ex-perience the intensity of that pain, just as we are aware of our tight chest, the knot in our stomach, and the tears in our eyes, we can take comfort in the fact that we have chosen to stay on the cross with Christ. Suddenly, we can look at our pains in a new manner. We can see that through these pains we have gained an insight into Christ's pains. Actually, our pains have become a gift offering us that insight. Our pains become transformed.

Ann, the young woman who was abused by her mother and foster father, was able to come to this insight. After a number of images, she commented:

"I guess now I know what Christ must have felt when he was physically abused, and stripped bare."

"Yes, you know that in a way that most of us cannot understand. Your scars have given you that understanding."

"I guess I feel a bit closer to Christ because of that. I had not realized that Christ was such a victim."

"I guess you might say that your scars are even a gift of that understanding."

"Yes, I guess I don't have to be so ashamed of them."

Ann was able to restructure her thoughts about her traumatic past. Her identification with Christ began to help her understand her self and her past experiences in a more positive, and a more accepting manner.

The healing Christ has been an explicit theme in this chapter. Sometimes Christ heals by providing us a peaceful focus for our often tortured thoughts. Sometimes Christ heals by accepting us even when we cannot accept ourselves. Finally, Christ heals us by the divine presence in the midst of our pain.

Chapter 8

SPIRITUALITY OF ACTION

Anger and Assertion

> We cannot love God unless we love each other, and to love we
> must know each other. . . . Heaven is a banquet and life is a ban-
> quet, too, even with a crust, where there is companionship. . . .
> We have all known the long loneliness and we have learned that
> the only solution is love and that love comes with community.—
> Dorothy Day, 1952, pp. 285–286

A Spirituality of Action

True emotional health eventually shows itself in all of our affairs
and exchanges with our fellow human beings. Our changed minds
and repentance ultimately issue forth in changed behavior. "So faith
by itself, if it has no works, is dead" (James 2:17).

The initial steps of the healing process often require us to move
away from others in order to discover our true self, our inner thoughts,
or the inner voice with which God speaks directly to us. Ultimately,
however, we move in a circle. Our healing is only completed as we
move back into relationships with others and test the mettle of the
"new self." The final test of our wholeness is in our relationships with
others.

The importance of relationships is not only touted by those il-
lustrious extroverts among us who delight in constant interactions.

The deepest contemplatives also emphasize our changed relationships with others. Teresa of Avila (1577/1961) declared ". . . the important thing is not to think much, but to love much; do then, whatever most arouses you to love" (*The Interior Castle*, p. 76). Thomas Merton (1971) warns that we must all ". . . face the 'dread' that arises out of a serious confrontation with infidelity on a community level" (*Contemplative Prayer*, p. 106). Ultimately we are called back to deal with our associates.

Jurgen Moltmann (1974) also points out that even the mysticism of the cross means action. The wounds and suffering of Christ give new meaning to *our* wounds and suffering. That is, Christ's wounds mean that he was not afraid of suffering, he was not afraid of what was sick and ugly, but he accepted it unto himself and gave it new meaning. Jesus has identified with our suffering, and understands it. Likewise, we who suffer emotionally or physically understand Jesus.

Moltmann rightly warns us, however, that there is a danger in this position. The mysticism of suffering must not be perverted into a justification of suffering. Identification with Christ must be complete. Christ did not suffer passively. Rather, his sufferings come from his actions. Moltmann contends, "The poverty and sufferings of Christ are experienced and understood only by participating in his mission and in imitating the task he carried out" (p. 52). Thus, even the mysticism of the cross does not lead to passive resignation, but to action.

We have emphasized thus far that changed thinking is a crucial ingredient of healing. However, inadequate thinking often leads to inadequate behavior. This inadequate behavior, in turn, results in conflicts and barriers in interpersonal relationships, which then influence our perceptions and attitudes about ourselves. Thus, we become caught up in a vicious cycle. The behavior itself may need to be changed before our attitudes can be changed. Indeed, Aaron Beck (Beck, Rush, Shaw, & Emery, 1979) maintains that some of our outdated hypotheses about ourselves will only be changed or disproved by new behaviors.

The Final Link in the Circle of Health

Our acts of compassion do not begin our spiritual journey. That journey begins at the instigation of God, not ourselves. That journey begins as we cease to respond to the demands of others, and hear anew the voice of God. Our acts of compassion, however, are part of the spiritual journey. Ultimately, Jesus has said we arrive in his Father's Kingdom when we have fed the hungry, listened to the hurt, and visited those in difficulties (cf. Matt. 25:35–36). Our changed acts are a significant indicator and barometer of our progress in the spiritual journey.

Changes in our actions are also a significant barometer of our prayer life. Any real prayer begins to make demands in our life. Real prayer has a moral imperative associated with it. It calls us to make changes. In the light of our prayers and meditations we see ourselves and hear God's challenges to us. As we reflect on and become aware of who we are, we naturally begin to want to live out those changes, to take up the new challenges, or to live out the implications of this new self. New images and thoughts should move the soul to love, and to encounter others more freely. The kingdom of God means actions. The kingdom of God is not territory but relationships among people, how people act with each other, and how they influence each other. (cf. Barth 1948/1960).

Changes in our actions are also a significant barometer of the life of the *imago Dei* within us. According to Karl Barth, (1948/1960) the *imago Dei* is related to the kind of actions we take and to our relationships with others. When the "word became flesh," the body was given new meaning. The acts Jesus did in his physical body became as important as any spiritual concept. The acts were one manifestation of the spirit. The spirit and the body were no longer in opposition. The body worked for the spirit. As it was with Christ, so it is with us. Christ provided us the vision whereby our body and our acts became as important as our thoughts which arise from the soul. The spirit of Christ unites both our acts and our thoughts. Christ's activities declare that the acts carried out by the body are important and also holy (pp. 350ff.).

Thus, the older dualism, that saw a radical distinction between acts and thoughts, no longer applies. The Christian no longer thinks just of thoughts or his soul. His body is also important. True humanness not only thinks and desires, but it also chooses and wills (pp. 406ff). Wholeness is not merely thinking or feeling differently. Wholeness is also choosing, and acting on those choices. The biblical view, then, is neither spiritualistic nor materialistic, but *realistic* (p. 434). We must not only correctly understand reality, we must act in accord with reality. We are both soul and body crying out to God:

"My soul longs, yea, faints for the courts of the Lord;
My heart and flesh sing for joy to the living God" (Psalms 84:2).

In wholeness we act on our thoughts. The body, which is not to be confused with Paul's concept of the flesh, is given new importance. This action is not in a vacuum, however. It is in relation to others.

Indeed, it is only in this authentic encounter with others that the *imago Dei* is fulfilled. Just as Jesus's humanity was for others, so our self is finally authentic when we encounter others. We can not have an "I" if there is not a "thou" (Barth, 1948/1960, p. 244).

Psychological Value of Action

Advocates of Interpersonal Psychotherapy (Klerman, Rounsaville, Chevron, Neu, & Weissman, 1979) believe that problems such as depression, regardless of symptoms, severity, or presumed biological vulnerability, occur in an interpersonal and social context. They stress that understanding and changing that social context is important to the person's recovery and the prevention of further problems. There is a considerable body of research demonstrating the relationship between social events and depression and stress (e.g., Pearlin & Liberman, 1977). Similarly, Weissman and Paykel (1974) found the depressed woman was considerably more impaired in all areas of social functioning as a worker, wife, mother, family member, and friend. Indeed, Rounsaville, (Rounsaville, Prusoff, & Weissman, 1980) found that if interpersonal difficulties were not improved, depression was more likely to return after therapy. Finally, Coyne (1976) found that people just do not enjoy talking to depressed people.

Coates and Wortman (1980) believe that depression is one way some individuals have learned to recover some lost power in interpersonal relationships. Where before they were ignored by their environment, now their depression, or other affliction, affords them a more special place. Usually, depressed individuals express helplessness. They have not learned a healthy way to effect change in the environment. It is very hard for such individuals to be direct, for example, and being depressed may enable some of them to have some influence over others in their environment. They substitute covert influence techniques for overt ones.

The reality of this formulation has been vividly demonstrated to me while working with married couples, in which one of the spouses is depressed. In one case, the wife had suffered from a fairly severe intermittent depression for a number of years since their marriage. In observing their interactions, I noticed that he usually first ignored her suggestions, and offered his own. Her reaction to his suggestions was to withdraw and develop a sad, hurt expression in her voice and eyes. He reacted almost instantaneously. He usually went back to her original suggestion, which he had previously ignored.

When I pointed out this interaction pattern, they were quite surprised. She reported a long history of having been ignored in their marriage. This was coupled with her belief that she should not assert herself, as a woman, and not ask for more attention or a better relationship. Having refused to allow herself to speak the truth to him, she had resorted, almost unconsciously, to an indirect way to accomplish her purposes. Gradually, as she became more assertive, her depression became less necessary and she felt less helpless.

Bandura's (1977) concept of self-efficacy and Seligman's (1975) learned helplessness model are both relevant here. Self-efficacy refers to the individual's expectations that she has the competency to accomplish a certain necessary activity. Learned helplessness, on the other hand, refers to the notion that, regardless of the individual's competency or ability to execute a certain necessary task, no rewards will be forthcoming, even if the task is executed. Thus, individuals in this state give up trying. They give up, not because they may not be assured of their capabilities, but because they expect their efforts to produce no results in an environment. The individual who lacks self-efficacy gives up because he seriously doubts that he can do what is necessary to achieve his goals.

Individuals who have given up need to be helped to realize how others around them have put them in this helpless position. They need to go further than that, however. Most importantly, they need to begin to learn new skills to overcome this helplessness. Research suggests that some individuals are depressed and anxious about their surroundings, simply because they have not had the opportunity to learn proper skills to relate to that environment (e.g., Lewinsohn, 1974). These individuals need to be taught how to challenge others in their environment, how to confront others when that is necessary, and how to ask for what they want. These are assertion skills. These individuals also need to be taught how to communicate with others. In some cases they may need to learn more effective means for organizing and changing their lives. They need to learn to initiate actions to make their lives more positive. Sometimes they simply may need to be taught to relax. All of these skills are needed for health and are part of the spirituality of action.

Anger and Assertion: Psychological View

> Spew forth, oh noble Aetna, spew . . .
> Break forth, oh molten belly of the hill,
> Oh mountain, hot within and breaking forth.

Let all the primal rage and heat belch forth . . .
Let the fire burn and rip the mountain side.
                                    —Kelsey, 1976. p. 281.

Anger is a strong feeling, an ungentle emotion. When anger occurs, blood pressure increases, neck, face, and chest muscles tighten, and respiration increases. The stomach may also churn, and frown lines may appear on the face.

Though anger is never comfortable, anger itself is neither always healthy or unhealthy. That depends upon the external circumstances, the way the anger is expressed, and the individuals involved.

External circumstances certainly play a role in anger arousal. The individual who is continually passed over for a promotion, when that promotion is given to a less qualified individual, certainly has good reason to be angry. The wife who suffers either verbal or physical abuse also has reasons for such anger. The world is not always fair. When we or someone else are the victims of that unfairness, anger is only a natural result.

Anger is not always due to these external events. It is also due to our expectations and what we say to ourselves about the event. The individual who does not expect to get a promotion is usually not angry when another receives that promotion. The individual who feels that he is deserving of punishment or abuse is less likely to be overtly angry about such abuse. Ironically, it is only as an individual's expectations for positive events increase that he has to deal with the stress of anger. It is only as an individual's self-esteem increases, that she feel justified in protesting another's unfairness. Increased expectations mean more anger. Increased anger may thus be a sign of increased self-esteem. Perhaps this explains the increased anger of those individuals in the civil rights and women's movements. As blacks and women feel better about themselves, they feel they deserve more.

Clear statements of angry feelings and demands can cut through many indirect tangles of communication. Clear statements of anger usually involve "I" messages, and can be used to confront the other with his need to change insensitive or uncaring behavior. Continued denial means that the cause of the anger is not confronted, and a physiology of anger becomes long-term, often with devastating results, such as high blood pressure or headaches. Secondly, the cause of the anger is never corrected when anger is ignored. Most anger usually has a righteous component. That is, most anger is displeasure at injustice. All of us deplore injustice, whether it is directed at us or another, whether it is real or imagined. To be angry at injustice is not wrong. To express the anger in an ineffective and uninformed manner, however, results in increased conflict.

Many women who are dependent upon others for their self-definition will not speak out when that very self-definition is further taken from them by their environment. They will not reclaim the *imago Dei*, or their own ability to make their life's choices. As a result, they secretly resent what has been done to them, and often react with a passive resignation. Those individuals who have never learned to express any anger are lacking in a necessary skill of expression. They must learn not only the correct words, but a firm voice to go with the words. This may necessitate some practice sessions or catharsis in a safe atmosphere in which no one will be hurt.

The expression of anger may be a necessary skill for some to learn. Other individuals, however, who are quite aware of their anger, may need to learn anger control. While there are many situations in which becoming angry is justified and appropriate, sometimes anger occurs when it is neither necessary nor useful. Anger becomes a problem when distinctions are not made between the times when it is all right to be angry and when getting angry does not serve a purpose.

Getting too angry too often places stress on the body. Anger mobilizes our body's resources. But when it is too frequent and intense, it causes excessive wear and tear on the system (Novaco, 1979).

As with all types of stress, anger is partially determined by our perceptions; that is, by our expectations and appraisals of a situation.

When our experiences do not meet our expectations, arousal occurs (Novaco, 1979, p. 259). This arousal becomes anger when expected, desirable outcomes are perceived to be thwarted by someone in our environment. For example, the woman who sees her expected job promotion dissolve when she perceives that it is given to a less qualified man will become angry at the man and at her company. Her expectations are thwarted.

Anger can also occur when one anticipates that negative events will occur. If one expects a negative response to a request, that request itself may be made somewhat angrily.

Finally, one may become angry when one expects that anger will be helpful in achieving desired goals. The housewife may perceive that no one will listen to her quiet requests. She has discovered, however, that if she raises her voice, the children may be more likely to do their chores.

In all of the above cases, the individuals felt that they would not be able to cope adequately with the environment. They feared that they would not, or did not succeed in their anticipated task, so they become angry in order to obtain success.

David Burns (1980) points out several thought distortions that lead to anger. First, very angry people may be too quick to categorize or label others. When an individual is described as vicious, as out to get you, or as totally irresponsible, it is easier to be angry at him. This labeling ignores the idea that no one is totally bad.

Another type of distortion that Burns suggests may lead to intense anger is mind reading. Often, it is very easy to imagine the person we are angry at as plotting and thinking all sorts of evils, although we can never know what another is thinking.

Believing that the world should always be fair is also going to lead to anger. Rarely is the world fair. It was certainly not fair to Jesus. Avoiding anger when unfairness exists does not mean one should consent passively to injustice. It does mean that anger should be expressed in a way that will serve a purpose.

A. T. Beck (Beck & Emery, 1979) notes that anger also arises when we fear control by the other person. We fear that we will not have the strategies to withstand the other's control. This type of anger frequently occurs between parents and grown children. The children somehow still find their feelings and behaviors controlled by the parent. They resent this control, not realizing how they themselves have given up control. The solution in this case is first to become aware of the helplessness, and then to develop new ways of behaving when around the parent, so that one feels more freedom.

One final source of anger is the thought that *I must retaliate.* The belief that the matter is not closed until I have had the last word, or settled the score, will feed anger. Poisonous images of revenge and retaliation often lurk in the mind. Monitoring of those images is the first step to changing them.

Assertion would seem to be necessary for passive individuals, not angry individuals. However, there are cognitive similarities between nonassertive individuals and angry individuals. Both types may tell themselves that they do not have *control* in a situation. Both may tell themselves that they do not know what to do in a given circumstance. Simply teaching both types to make more hopeful statements to themselves has impact. Learning to cope assertively with a situation does not imply aggression. Assertion is an active, problem-solving orientation towards a situation.

Anger and Assertion: Theological View

"Resentment is the last-ditch stand of freedom in the midst of confusion," says Thomas Merton (1961, p. 108). We feel pushed and shoved on every side. We feel that forces lurk in every corner to steal our freedom. Newspapers and magazines tell us what to think; friends tell us what to feel; and institutions and economics tell us how to behave. There is no defense. We fear that there is no way to preserve a little island within ourselves that is not responding to someone else, yet we desperately try to hold on to such an island. Many of us stake out that little sanctuary of freedom through silent protest, through walls of negativism, through resentment. We may have to be pushed and shoved, but we do not have to like it.

Resentment is painful. It exacts a heavy price for its supposed gift of freedom. We soon find that the freedom has turned into a churning stomach, tight muscles, and elevated blood pressure. We discover, to our horror, that we no longer freely choose resentment as a path to freedom. Resentment chooses us. Resentment picks us up, grasps us, and proceeds to strangle us with its all-consuming possession. We suddenly find ourselves trapped. We feel, on the one hand, the ever-tightening clutches of resentment. On the other hand, we are afraid to give up the anger. We somehow think that without this anger, we will lose what little leverage we have.

Eventually, in one way or another, we have to face the truth. We cannot escape some sort of control. We always dance to some tune. Psychologically we are beings that respond to environmental stimuli. Scripture says we are either slaves of sin or slaves to righteousness. "When you were slaves of sin, you were free in regard to righteousness . . . but now that you have been set free from sin and have become slaves of God, the return you get is sanctification and its end, eternal life" (Rom. 6:20,22).

How is this scripture to be understood? It seems foreign to our experience. First, sin has many meanings. (cf. Stahlin & Grundmann, 1933/1964, pp. 267–316). One of the more common meanings of the word in ancient Greece and in the Old Testament was to be intellectually in error, to miss the point. In the New Testament, and especially in Romans, the meaning is invariably linked to the individual's asserting himself against God. The individual feels that he or she can live an independent life without God. Such individuals are wrapped up in themselves.

Because we have the ability to transcend ourselves, and step outside of our situation, we think we are no longer influenced by the situation. We want to deny the influence of those around us. Even as we think we are making the decision to be angry at someone, even as we think it is in freedom that we respond, it is not. We become anxious when we feel out of control (cf. Niebuhr, 1953, p. 183). So we delude ourselves into thinking we have full control. Indeed, psychological research shows that even those who do not actually have control in a situation will attempt to view it in a way that seemingly gives them control (Rothbaum, Weisz, & Snyder, 1982).

For example, Rothbaum et al. refer to one type of control as "illusory control." Persons sometimes will attempt to associate themselves with chance so as to share in the power of this larger force. Often these persons will speak of luck as an ally that they can "rely on," and of being "born lucky." Through various means, including superstitious behavior, people will attempt to believe that they have control, when in fact they do not.

In contrast to our own efforts to exercise freedom by denying any external control of ourselves, scripture says that freedom from the world that would control us comes only when we become a slave of righteousness. This also sounds foreign to us. However, the word righteousness (*diakosune*) is closely linked with justification. Justification is in turn linked with union with Christ in the sense of identification with his destiny and being (cf. 2 Cor. 5:21). One way of viewing this is to realize that as we begin to live as if we had an identity with Christ, as if we had the mind of Christ, we are able to step back and view our world more freely.

For example, Betty was a young black woman who felt an intense anger at the injustices that being black and female leveled against her. She resolved to work for justice. However, her anger became so intense that she developed chronic headaches. These headaches became so unbearable that she was forced to curtail her activities. She had only to recall certain incidents of the past and her stomach began to churn and her headaches returned. She felt trapped by these angry memories, but she was afraid to give them up for fear that she would again become a passive, silent victim. The people in her past continued to exert a powerful influence over her, thwarting her actions. She could certainly agree with Epictetus, the Stoic philosopher:

> If any person was intending to put your body in the power of any man whom you fell in with on the way, you would be vexed; but that you put your understanding in the power of any man

whom you meet, so that if he should revile you, it is disturbed and troubled, are you not ashamed at this?—Epictetus, the *Encheridion.*

Betty's identification with Christ and corresponding gradual freedom from her anger came in her realization of the abuses suffered by Christ, and her ability to see that anger was also a passion, a passion not unlike Christ's Passion. Whenever she felt the intensity of the anger she was able to visualize herself on the cross with Christ. Her anger was the nails that were crucifying her. Such a meditation begins to change the meaning of one's anger. A different cognitive label is put on the emotions. There is less need to be angry at those who have caused the anger. Such meditations can begin the process of freeing one up to take direct actions, rather than being incapacitated with anger.

Paradoxically, it is only our identification with Christ in his Passion and crucifixion that frees us from enslavement to the world around us. It is not necessary to allow ourselves to be controlled. It is important to step out from under the tyranny of another human, even if that tyranny is only one of emotions. We must make this active choice.

According to Karl Barth (1948/1960), our true humanity is experienced as we are in an authentic mutual relationship with others. Those characteristics about us that are most human are those that are expressed in relationship with others. Just as Jesus reflected his true meaning in relationship with others, so do we. This relationship must be mutual, however. Each individual must give and receive. Neither should lose oneself in the other. If one should control the other so that one loses his own life and responsibility, true humanness for both would be lost. If I am controlled by the other, not only do I lose my true humanness, but so does the other, because this other no longer has any genuine counterpart, a reflection of himself. Control results when there is either intimidated passivity or angry aggression.

Jesus is a model of faithful action in the manner in which he was direct with others. First, he was straightforward and quick to respond when there were questions needing his answer. When the rich young ruler and Jesus's disciples inquired about entrance into the kingdom of God, Jesus was uncompromising about what was required (Matt. 19:16–30). Jesus was also direct when others responded in hostility to him and rejected his credentials. He usually did two things. First, he gave an initial response to his critics. Secondly, if they did not accept this response, he moved into other relationships (Matt. 13:53–58; Luke 4:16–30).

People may need direct feedback about their initial hostility. If the environment remains hostile, however, the most productive action is sometimes to move to another more accepting environment. No one can relate to everyone. Often, as previously unassertive patients have begun to confront their environment, the environment and old friends have put up a roadblock and refused to give an inch. A certain amount of effort should be made to get through. On the other hand, there are so many people in the world and so much to do, that sometimes it is best to move away from those relationships that continue to react with hostility to us.

When Jesus's preaching was rejected in his hometown of Nazareth, he left the town and carried on his ministry elsewhere. Not even Jesus could work with all people. If the situation was important enough, however, Jesus did stay around a bit longer and actively confront hostility (Mark 11:15–19, John 10:22–41). He was willing actively to debate and challenge differences of opinion. If hostility continued, he would withdraw (John 11:54). He argued with the Pharisees about differences in the law. However, after a while, he "no longer went about openly among the Jews" (John 11:54).

When people were being hurt, he spoke up. For example, Matthew 23 reports an extended diatribe against the Pharisees: "But woe to you, scribes and Pharisees, hypocrites! because you shut the kingdom of heaven against men; for you neither enter yourselves, nor allow those who would enter to go in" (Matt. 23:13).

There are even occasions in scripture when Jesus allows his anger to escalate into a hostile confrontation. For example, he drove out the money-changers in the temple, and told them, "Is it not written, 'My house shall be called a house of prayer for all the nations?' but you have made it a den of robbers" (Mark 11:15–17).

Jesus not only provides a model of direct action, but he advocated it. "So if you are offering your gift at the altar, and there remember that your brother has something against you, leave your gift there, and go; first be reconciled to your brother" (Matt. 5:23–24). He also says, "If your brother sins against you go and tell him his fault. . . . If he refuses to listen, tell it to the church" (Matt. 18:15–18). Differences of opinion should be discussed and brought out in the open. If two individuals cannot do it adequately, then the community should become involved.

What is obvious from the above discussion is that conflict itself is neither good nor bad, it is how we handle the anger. The goal is not to explode, but to *change the situation.*

Methods of Assertion and Anger Control

The remainder of this chapter will focus on controlling destructive anger and expressing healthy anger in a healthy manner. The first two sections will review ways to control anger, while the third section will discuss constructive actions.

The suggestions in this section are very useful skills if you are reading this book on your own, without a guide or counselor. It is best to try these skills, however, after you have some facility with monitoring your own thoughts (Chapter 4).

Controlling anger by anticipation of anger.   Sometimes the best way to avoid an intense angry situation is to prepare oneself ahead of time. Novaco (1979, p. 269) suggests that several strategies are necessary. First, one must become aware of the situations and persons that precipitate anger. Do these anger situations involve frustration, annoyance, insult, inequity, or abuse? It may be useful to keep a diary on one's anger in order to gain some insight into the determinants of the anger. For some individuals, certain situations always arouse anger, regardless of who is involved. For others, the crucial ingredient may always be a certain person. In learning to cope with anger situations, some individuals may want to construct a hierarchy, so that situations provoking less anger are listed first, and more intense situations are listed last.

When an anger situation is identified, then several actions can be implemented. First, one must prepare oneself to deal with the provocation. Novaco (1979) suggests repeating to oneself one of the following statements:

"This could be a rough situation, but I can work out a plan to handle this." Or, "Remember to stick to the issues and don't take it personally."

One might also want to prepare comments to make to oneself about the specific person or situation such as, "The reason John insults me so much is that he is so insecure." Or, "I should see the sad side of this rather than be angry about it. Joe just does not know how to deal with differences of opinion. He prefers to ignore them." It is often helpful to tell ourselves that certain situations are not worth getting tension headaches or high blood pressure over. It may also help to ask oneself what the other person's viewpoint is of the situation at hand. He or she may be frustrated or anxious. He or she may have different expectations about the situations. Much anger is caused by misunderstanding and miscommunication. Some individuals have reported that picturing the individual in an image with Jesus has been helpful to them. Others try to imagine what Jesus's feelings might be in the situation. It is often helpful to write down some of these possibilities ahead of time, in order to prepare oneself adequately.

Burns (1980) advocates anticipating anger by making a list of the pros and cons of expressing anger in a given situation. Is the anger actually useful? Does it enable one to achieve desired goals, or is it merely getting in the way of one's goals?

In my own life, I have found it very useful to become aware ahead of time of those situations that "set me off", and then prepare some statements I can make to myself to keep my cool.

Controlling anger during the provocation.   Self-statements, those ideas we think and say to ourselves, can also be used to reduce anger during the experience itself. Novaco (1979, p. 269) has listed four phases of the anger experience that are self-statements that could be helpful for each of these phases:

1. *Impact and confrontation.* This is the immediate anger. This anger occurs when you recognize that you are indeed angry in the situation. Novaco suggests such statements as "Stay calm. Just continue to relax." Or, "There is no point in getting mad." For some Christians it helps to imagine the abuse they experience as analogous to the abuse of Christ. This may take the mind off the intensity of the moment and prevent an explosion.

2. *Coping with arousal.* This is the stage in which agitation and tension begin, if the anger management has not been successful. Novaco suggests such statements as "My muscles are getting tight. Relax and slow down." Or, "I am feeling angry. Time for problem solving." After the emotion of anger has been experienced, it may also be possible to restructure the meaning of that anger by means of religious imagery. One of my patients said anger is passion, and thus could be likened to the Passion of Christ. Each time you experience the emotion of anger, close your eyes and imagine that the pain of the anger is actually the pain of your crucifixion. This is particularly helpful for those individuals who deny their own anger even as others are aware of it. Allow yourself to stay with your anger for a minute or so. Imagine

that Christ is there with you. This changes the emotion of anger and paradoxically makes it more difficult to be angry over the anger.

3. *Reflecting on the provocation.* This is often a time when you remind yourself of past provocation. You may relive the experience. If the conflict is resolved, it is important to remind yourself that the situation has resolved itself, and praise yourself. Novaco suggests such statements as, "I handled that one pretty well." Or, "I could have gotten more upset than it was worth." One might also say, "This situation is concluded—time to go on to other things." Or, "I don't need to allow my emotions to continue to be controlled by a sistuation that is old business and irrelevant to my daily business." Sometimes when there is a tendency to ruminate continually over past hurts, even after they have been resolved, the sacrament of the present moment is needed (cf. Chapter 4). In times of anger we can say to ourselves, "This is God's moment. He made it, he sent it, he watches its effect. I will say to him, give me thy spirit."

Sometimes, when the past provocation remains unresolved, forgetting about it can be more difficult. Novaco suggests that the following self-statements may be helpful: "Forget about the aggravation. Thinking about it only makes you upset." Or, "Can you laugh about it, it's probably not so serious." Often we are afraid to face our anger because we fear that it will overwhelm us. We are afraid to face just how bad the evil or immorality is in the world. We are also afraid to face the evil in ourselves. We hope somehow that if we avoid thinking about what we are angry about it will go away; but the thoughts and images continue to lurk there in the background. At the opportune moment, they leap out to possess us again.

On the other hand, as we face the intensity of our anger, we can put it on the cross and stay with it until it is transformed, as we noted earlier. Juliana of Norwich has said that if we stay on the cross with Jesus in our pains and sufferings, they will eventually turn to joy. Rather than denying and turning aside from our anger, we must face it, until it is transformed, until we can somehow understand our passionate anger in the light of Christ's Passion. This must involve the realization that indeed anger is a painful passion. Unfortunately, most of us do not try to cope with anger, because we do not realize that it is a source of stress. Relaxation may also help the process. It is difficult to be angry and relaxed at the same time.

All of the above procedures will be more helpful if internal rules about anger are changed. Holding unrealistic expectations that people should always behave sanely will inevitably lead to frustration. The expectation that others should always respect us will lead to disappointment and eventually resentment. Just as we would wish that others not control us, so we cannot control others. Real human relationships of the type that reflect the *imago Dei* imply a mutuality. Our part in that mutuality may be sometimes to accept where the other is at the moment, and to attempt to understand why he is there. It does not help to say that this person should not be there, because he is.

John was a twenty-nine-year-old engineer who was mildly depressed because his father refused to acknowledge that John's differences of opinion in politics were legitimate. He repeatedly told John that his views were trivial. John's depression alternated with anger as he attempted to help his father understand that though they had differences of opinion, he wanted his own view to be respected and not merely dismissed as trivial. At times, his anger became so intense that he developed a headache. John eventually had to accept where his father stood, and realize that a change would not happen. His father saw a rejection of his own views as a rejection of him. Such acceptance of the situation may be necessary, when direct discussions of differences fail to lead to mutual respect.

We can basically see the world in two ways, and thus see the exact same behavior as meaning two different things. Thus, for example, we may see the other's lack of respect toward us as either due to innate malice or innate insecurity. The unhealthy person feels that others are out to "get him." The healthy individual realizes that hostility most often arises from insecurity and people's desperate attempt to defend their own turf. In the first stance, we tend to have our own fists up for self-defense. In the second stance we see the other's pain, the other's insecurity. We begin to see the world through Christ's eyes. People know they are finite and they are desperately trying to escape from that. They know they are temporary, and they want to cover that up. They refuse to accept the tragic element of life.

We, however, need not fear the tragic. We need not cover our eyes to the idea that events will not always turn out fairly. We don't have to believe that there is always a just world. We can see reality as it is. See it, and not be overcome by it, because darkness has been given new meaning. Pain has been transformed. We need not fear to go right into the core of the pain itself. We plunge ourself into the belly of the volcano because we know that it is there that we discover Christ. It is there that we are given the gift of identification with the sufferings of Christ. It is there that we glory in our crucifixion with Christ, we glory in our pains so that we may rise with him. And the resurrection is glorious. It is a resurrection to a renewed vision. Pain and passion are no longer to be feared. The resurrection is a resurrection to holy action, not passive resignation. Action is not possible, until we cease to fear our pains.

Active coping and looking.   The opposite danger of exploding is always "stuffing it." These individuals either deny that they have any anger at all, or they avoid all anger-inducing situations because they are afraid of losing control. The control loss can be one of two kinds. They may be afraid that they will be so intimidated by others that they will not know what to say. The other individual might control them. Some individuals also fear that they might lose control of their own emotions. Both types of individuals need some specific instructions as to what to say and do in a particular provocative situation. That is, sometimes they need some assertiveness training.

Some Christians protest against assertiveness training. They have the mistaken idea that Christianity implies passivity. However, as we have seen, Christ, the model of humanity, was frequently assertive. He was never intimidated by his environment. Even his ultimate sacrifice was a choice, and as we have noted, he saw it as that (John 10:18). One's objections to assertion and one's self-statements about it should always be addressed before any self-assertion is taught, otherwise the assertiveness training will not get off the ground (cf. Beck, Rush, Shaw, & Emery, 1979).

It is necessary, and very important, to make clear that assertion is superior to either aggression or passivity. Aggression is violating the image of God within the other. Passivity is violating the image of God within one's self. In both cases, the ideal of human mutuality as reflecting the image of God is violated. One should neither seek to control another nor allow another to control you. Assertion is taking adaptive action to solve a problem, so that no one's rights are violated. Assertive behavior is defined as an open, honest, direct, and appropriate expression of one's thoughts, wishes, feelings, or opinions that does not violate either one's own rights or the rights of anyone else (Bower & Bower, 1976). When true spirituality is defined as a circle involving first our integrity before God, and then our integrity with others, assertion becomes a necessary ingredient of any spirituality.

First steps: Active looking (eye contact).   Assertion is not merely speaking up when one's rights have been violated. Assertion is also being able to look directly at another person, to look them in the eye (cf. Barth, 1948/1960, p. 250). Assertion is also being able to initiate greetings and give positive compliments. For some very passive, depressed individuals, even this is very difficult. As a first stage in assertion training, for very passive patients, I give an assignment to look actively and directly at others. I am usually very specific with this assignment, both naming the others, and the times of the encounter. At first it is not necessary that the other person be aware of the process. Bower and Bower (1976) suggest that individuals write down what they see. After direct looking is accomplished, an assignment can be made to initiate conversations and to give compliments. In both cases, the exact transcript of what is to be said should be first written out and then practiced in the therapy session. Anyone who is unsure of this process should approach it slowly, in order to avoid failure.

If you often find yourself having difficulty looking directly at others, you may find it helpful to give yourself an assignment to look directly at a number of individuals, and write down what you see.

Dealing with conflicts.   After positive assertion, it is then easier to approach conflict. Some general rules must be observed when dealing with a difficult individual.

In the counseling session, there should first be a discussion of general rules of assertive body language and voice. The picture of Jesus in the New Testament may be a useful model. We often neglect the very concrete humanity of Jesus in our rush for the more abstract theological concepts of his divinity.

1. It is important to use the expression "I" when expressing a concern, or when responding to someone. Saying "I do not like this behavior" rather than "You should not behave like this" means we assume more responsibility, ownership, and directness for what we are saying. Such words are also less likely to put the other on the defensive. Jesus always assumed responsibility for his statements. For example, in Mark 3:13–15, he said, "I have chosen you," or in Mark 14:16–62, he was not afraid to admit who he was: "I am the Messiah."

2. It is good to make eye contact and use good, clear facial expressions. We certainly get this theme from Mark 10:20–22 in which we are told, "with love, Jesus looked at him." Good assertive body language means to avoid blinking rapidly, or looking away. A tight-lipped mouth, or clearing one's throat excessively is also not good practice. Finally, it is important not to cover one's mouth when speaking, to scratch one's head, preen, tinker with jewelry, or adjust clothing (cf. Bower & Bower, 1976).

3. Expressing one's feelings to another is an important part of assertion. We have several examples of Jesus expressing his feelings

when he is angry at others' intolerance of his healing (cf. Mark 3:1–6; 9:17–19; 10:13–15).

4. Finally, when disagreeing with someone, it is important to say that. Jesus certainly did just that when, for example, he defended his picking wheat on the Sabbath (Mark 2:23–17). Others told him that what he was doing was not lawful. He immediately referred them to an example in the Old Testament that showed that it was, and added, "The Sabbath was made for man, not man for the Sabbath."

In addition to a discussion of the general body language and demeanor required in assertion, it is also important to use the counseling session to write out a script of what is to be said. If you are doing this exercise on your own, be sure and write out the following information before attempting the assertive behavior.

There are basic components that should be in any assertive message. (See Bower & Bower, 1976, for further detail).

First, it is important to be direct with the other individual about the particular behavior you are concerned about or find bothersome. Use simple, concrete terms to describe the behavior. It is important not to accuse, but merely to describe the behavior. Some examples may be: "You leave your clothes lying on the bathroom and bedroom floors after you take a shower." Or, "You usually watch TV when we are eating dinner and don't talk to me." (You can always ease into the above lines with "I would like to discuss something with you.")

It is also important to express what you are feeling about the particular matter at hand. This is not to be a hostile attack, but rather an honest communication of how you are actually feeling. Some examples may be (for the corresponding situations listed above): "I am annoyed when you leave your clothes lying on the bathroom and bedroom floors." Or, "I feel hurt when you don't talk to me during dinner; it makes me feel that you are unconcerned about our relationship."

Third, it is always most helpful to ask explicitly for a different, specified behavior. Such requests are more likely to be complied with if they are very specific and very brief. Some individuals are confused and do not know what to expect. It is important to ask for only one thing at a time. Essentially you ask, "Please stop doing _____, and start doing _____," instead. The request should be reasonable and possible for the other person to do. Some examples might be (corresponding again to the above examples): "I would like you to put your clothes in the clothes hamper when you take them off." Or, "I would like you to have a conversation with me and look at me while we are eating."

Finally, it is important to end a request on a positive note. One should specify the positive consequences that will occur if the other person complies with your request. Initially, it is usually best to list only positive consequences. Negative consequences should be mentioned later if repeated attempts at communication have resulted in failure. Some examples may be (for the corresponding situations described above): "If you put your clothes in the clothes hamper, I will feel that you also care about the inside of the house, and would be more willing to do more outdoor activities with you that you like." Or, "If we talk more during dinner, I will feel really good about our eating dinner together, and I am sure that will have a positive effect on our relationship."

Some negative consequences might be: "If you don't pick up your clothes, I will begin to think you don't care about how bad the house looks and I will probably begin to resent it." Or, "If you do not talk to me during our dinner times, I am afraid we will grow further and further apart, and there will be no intimacy left." Finally, one might say, "If you don't pick up your clothes, there will be no skiing tomorrow."

When the script has been completed, it is important to role-play the script, either with the therapist, or in front of a mirror if you are doing this on your own. I often first play the patient's role and have her play the role of the other person. This provides good modeling, which research has shown is one of the most crucial ingredients in learning new behavior. After the patient has seen my example, she then plays herself, using the script. This back and forth sequence is repeated until the person feels comfortable with the script.

The next phase of preparing for assertion involves covert rehearsal. Research shows that if an individual rehearses a behavior covertly, she is more likely actually to execute the behavior when the time comes. I guide the person in an imagery rehearsal of the situation, with one big difference. I also include some religious imagery if it seems appropriate. The sequence is as follows:

1. I guide them in an imagery of Jesus in a similar situation. For example, we might use one of the images of Jesus confronting the Pharisees. I am careful to focus on what Jesus's facial expression, body language, and voice tone might have been like. We use the procedures of Chapter 7 to set up the imagery.

2. The image is then switched to the situation in which the assertion will occur. The vividness of the situation is enhanced again using the imagery procedures of Chapter 7. The individual is then

asked to imagine Jesus there with her in the situation. Again the vividness of Jesus is enhanced, using the same procedures.

3. At the moment of confrontation in the image, it is important to ask the individual what her feelings are. This is a very important part of the imagery. If the individual reports some anxiety, this is good, because it suggests that the present image is real enough to be worthwhile practice. Also, these same feelings will be present later during the actual situation. At that point, because of the prior association, the feelings will serve as a cue to actually carrying out the assertion.

In any assertion assignment, it is always important to have an agreed-upon time and place for the assertion. Otherwise, it is too easy for it to be postponed. Also, when any assertion has been assigned, it is important to discuss the outcome of the assignment at the next session, as would be the case with any homework.

An assertion script can be written for small problems as well as big problems. Often the seemingly small problems may contribute as much to a perception of helplessness as a big problem. For example, Cindy felt frustrated because her children ignored her instructions regarding care of the house. She and I put together the following script to use when her children refused to put the dishes in the dishwasher as she wanted them to. Note how the script follows exactly the format set out above.

> Johnny, you continually put your dirty dishes on the counter or leave them in the living room. That behavior makes me feel frustrated. I would like for you to put all your dirty dishes directly into the dishwasher when you finish with them. If you do this, I'll feel less hassled and probably will be able to take you skiing more often.

Chapter 9

SPIRITUALITY OF ACTION

Necessary Living Skills

> The time of business does not with me differ from the time of prayer; and in the noise and clatter of my kitchen. . . . I possess God in as great tranquility as if I were upon my knees at the blessed Sacrament.—Brother Lawrence, c.1700/1958, p. 29

Christianity is not just a religion of the soul. We have already noted that true Christian spirituality also concerns the body. Jesus, the model of whole humanity, gave not only his soul, but his body. He taught not only about the spirit, but he acted with the body. These acts were not merely incidental but acts of the spirit (Barth, 1948/1960).

We also serve God with our bodies in those acts we do for ourselves and others. In the last chapter we focused on those occasions in which there is a disruption between "our body and others' bodies," in which there is anger. In this chapter we will focus on those behaviors that are necessary for healthy living with our bodies. Not only must we learn to take care of bodies physically by relaxing them, but we must also learn to balance our lives by doing a variety of activities, not just work. We must also learn to set goals for ourselves, and structure our lives around those goals. Finally, because we live and experience the world as a whole human being, we encounter others as both soul and body. We must communicate with others on many levels. The development of effective communication skills results in a greater harmony within such relationships.

The notion of biblical wholeness often gets lost in the guise of "caring for souls." From time to time there are prophets that remind us that "We cannot merely tell a soul to be warmed and filled and go away." We must change the world of bodies by social or political reform. Most often, however, these prophets are not pastoral counselors. Pastoral care and counseling has been remiss in its concern for the body. It has been called the "care of souls." The soul to be healed must, however, relate not only to its own body, but to the bodies around it.

Relaxation Skills

Psychological aspects. Relaxation skills are generally concerned with teaching the individual to control and relax his skeletal musculature, and hence the rest of the body. Generally one must first become aware of and sensitive to the tension as it actually exists in the body. Then, for control, one learns to focus on an alternative sensation. In the past 15 years, clinical research has indicated that various stress reduction methods are effective. A recent volume on *Principles and Practice of Stress Management* by Woolfolk and Lehrer (1984) for example, lists at least seven different types of stress reduction methods that have received considerable research support as effective stress reduction procedures. Three of these methods, progressive muscle relaxation, hypnosis, and meditation (discussed in Chapter 5) will serve as a basis for some of the relaxation procedures presented here.

In progressive muscle relaxation, one learns to become aware of the tension in various parts of the body. Sometimes this tension is made obvious by tightening the muscles in question. At other times, the individual is instructed merely to become aware of the tension. In the second phase, one attempts to relax the muscles by letting go, or imagining some sensation that would allow that particular muscle in question to relax. Progressive muscle relaxation has been used successfully alone or in combination with other methods to deal with a wide range of behavior problems. These include general anxiety and tension, phobias, insomnia, headaches, and even hypertension.

Generally, muscle relaxation instructions communicated directly to the patient face to face seem to be more effective than listening to a tape. However, after a tape is made for and geared to the patient, it is useful to have her practice the tape at home. Any tape made for yourself should be geared to your own particular areas of tension. Feel free to emphasize those areas in the tape. Progressive relaxation alone appears to be as effective as that done with biofeedback (Wool-folk & Lehrer, 1984). Some type of focus on body relaxation is very necessary for stress reduction when an individual's anxiety level is high. Cognitive techniques alone are often less effective for these higher anxiety levels.

Hypnosis, our second technique of interest, has been defined by Barber (1984) as suggestions for deep relaxation (p. 142). Barber suggests that hypnosis is effective because individuals are encouraged not to evaluate critically every idea that is given to them, but instead focus on the idea. This stance reminds us of Tozer's (1948, p. 43) comment, "We are today overrun with orthodox scribes. . . . but the Church waits for the tender voice of the saint who has penetrated the veil and has gazed with inward eye upon the Wonder that is God." Ultimately, we become affected by an idea when we cease analyzing it, and allow it to influence us. Having an intellectual understanding of relaxation is useless. Ultimately, we must let go and relax. For some individuals this is a difficult skill to master. Hypnosis may aid the process.

In hypnosis, imagining and fantasizing are acceptable. In hypnosis we ultimately adopt a passive attitude and shift our attachment from the external environment to the internal world (Benson, 1975). Hypnosis has procedural similarities to meditation. It is a cognitive technique in which the focus of attention is narrowed to one idea. When an individual's attention is focused on one idea, he ceases to ruminate about other concerns. Hypnotic trances range from the light trance of being involved in reading a book to a deeper state in which the individual is unaware of bodily sensations. In all cases, the individual has developed the skill to focus his attention in one direction. Contrary to many popular myths about the hypnotic process, hypnosis is a skill that must be cultivated and learned. Those individuals who are more skilled at focusing their attention will profit the most from hypnosis.

Research has shown that hypnosis is effective for general relaxation and headaches, especially those headaches associated with resentment or anger. Additionally, the physiological changes accompanying hypnosis appear to be similar to the relaxation response described by Benson (Benson, Arns, & Hoffman, 1981).

Both hypnosis and meditation are distinct from progressive muscle relaxation in one important way. They are cognitive activities. That is, a greater emphasis in these techniques is put on helping the individual change the way he thinks about things. The important goal is not "muscle relaxation" per se, but peace of mind and calmness in the face of stressful situations, and a reduction in anxiety, anger, and other negative emotions. Barber (1984) suggests that the ultimate efficacy of these procedures may result from the fact that they actually change the person's philosophical approach to life (p. 162). These procedures are different from straight cognitive procedures. They also use a relaxed state of the body to demonstrate experientially to the individual that it is possible and indeed desirable to live one's life in a more relaxed manner. We always remember more effectively those events we have actually experienced than we do those events that others have told us about. Thus, we understand relaxation better when we have experienced it.

Progressive muscle relaxation, meditation, and hypnosis have some features in common. First, they set up expectations that something beneficial will occur. This has been called suggestion, and is an important ingredient in both physical and emotional healing. The more one believes that something positive will occur, the more one will cooperate to bring about that change. All of these techniques also train the individual to focus his attention in one direction, and away from chaotic rumination. In progressive muscle relaxation, the individual focuses on his muscles. In meditation one focuses on a constant stimulus, and in hypnosis one focuses both on a constant stimulus (such as a dot on the wall) and feelings of relaxation.

All of these techniques help take the individual's mind off his worries and tension. The final point that all of these techniques share in common is their encouragement of trust or surrender in the individual. In all cases, an individual who is accustomed to being extremely tight or restless is encouraged to "let go." Anyone who typically feels that he has to supervise everything is encouraged to allow another to direct his relaxation. For most tense individuals, this is a new and difficult experience. They have never learned to "let go."

Theological aspects.   Each of the three characteristics of these relaxation procedures has its counterpart in spiritual exercises. First, hope and expectations are an important ingredient in our prayers. In the Old Testament there is no neutral concept of expectation. An expectation is either good or bad and therefore it is either hope or fear. To have hope, to have a future, is a sign that things are well. This hope, of course, is naturally directed to God (Bultmann, 1935/ 1964, p. 522 ff.). "Blessed is the man who trusts (hopes) in the Lord" (Jer. 17:7). Positive expectations and hope are even more closely linked to God in the New Testament, where hope or trust are paradoxical. That is, they are given to something that cannot be controlled or seen. "For in this hope we were saved. Now hope that is seen is not hope. For who hopes for what he sees?" (Rom. 8:24). In the New Testament hope is placed in the actions of God. Positive expectations for change are focused on God.

Secondly, spiritual exercises are also concerned with the direction of one's attention. Here too, as in the relaxation exercises, one's attention must be focused away from one's own concerns and onto God. It is difficult, however, for us to turn our inward eyes upon God. True spirituality means developing the inward *habit* of beholding God, as Tozer has so skillfully reminded us.

As we develop the inward habit of gazing on God, we soon find that spiritual exercises have a third factor in common with the relaxation response. As we gaze upon God, we surrender to God. We become less interested in the esteem of others. Our definition comes from God. As we surrender ourselves to God, we accept ourselves. We accept who we are, who God has made us. Finally, we enter into the rest [and relaxation] of God. (Heb. 4:9–10).

The *rest of God* means a hope in the goodness of God that results both in a shift of our attention to God, and a surrender and trusting of ourselves to the love of God. All of these techniques can be that process for the Christian. Regardless of who is directing the process, the surrender is always to God.

Methods. I have used at least three different procedures for teaching relaxation within the context of spirituality. Often these methods are tied together into one relaxation transcript. For purposes of presentation, however, I have introduced each of them separately here, and then combined them into one transcript.

All of these exercises are useful for individuals reading this book on their own. It is important, however, to make yourself a tape in a slow, relaxed voice, using the transcripts given below. Remember that the goal of these exercises is to slow down, not to complete them as rapidly as possible. If you find yourself getting impatient with the pace of the tape, perhaps that is a good sign. Concentrate on what is being said at the present moment on the tape, rather than allowing your mind to wonder ahead.

Tension-relaxation induction. This is the familiar procedure in which individuals are first asked to tighten a muscle, study that tension, and then slowly to let go of the tension, becoming aware of the relaxation, and of the differences between relaxation and tension. Adding tension before relaxation is most useful in those cases of high tension levels. Some of these individuals are less aware of the tension they do have, and the differences between tension and relaxation. Learning to distinguish the difference is necessary for them. I always include a few examples of this type of induction in most transcripts. The muscles I focus most on are the chest muscles.

In starting less anxious patients on this procedure, it is important to move fairly rapidly to the next procedure (after 1 or 2 weeks of home practice). The procedure itself is actually very flexible. I usually ask patients to tighten and relax muscles in the following sequence: hands (fists); forearms; upper arms; shoulders (shrug); face, including eyes (squint), lips (tighten), jaws, and forehead (wrinkle); neck (bending forward or backward); chest (holding breath); stomach; thighs; calves; shins and toes. It is possible to do all of these or some of them. Gear the length of the session to the needs of the patient. There are no hard-and-fast rules.

Letting go only.   These procedures follow the same sequence as the tension-relaxation induction, and the same muscle groups may be used. The difference, however, is that the individual is not asked to tighten his muscles before he relaxes them. The individual is merely told to "let go" of the tension. One example might be, "Focus in on the feelings in your right hand and let go of whatever tensions might be there. . . . Just relax. . . . Relax the muscles to the best of your ability."

Both tension-relation induction and "letting go only" focus on the muscles, and give the person some basic sensory awareness training as he begins to become aware of just actually what relaxation is. Additionally, in the relaxation phase this is a surrender. Both of these relaxation procedures can easily become a Christian meditation exercise by defining the surrender and the relaxation of one's muscles as a surrender to divine providence or to the divine presence. For example, one may phrase the tension-relaxation induction in the following manner:

> As you are seated in the chair, become aware of the presence of Christ with you. This may be an image of Christ, or a thought, or a prayer . . . whatever process for you reminds you that Christ is present with you . . . [pause]. . . . After you have done that, take a deep breath, and hold it. Then let it out slowly, allowing yourself to sink down into the chair. Do that once again . . . take a deep breath and hold it. As you let the breath out, allow yourself to sink more comfortably into the presence of Christ.

Now focus your attention on your left arm, your left hand in particular. Clench your left fist. Clench it tightly and study the tension in the hand and forearm. Study those sensations of tension. And now let go of the tension slowly. As you relax the left hand, allow it and the rest of your body to relax in the presence of Christ. Allow yourself to trust. Study the contrast between that trust and the previous tension. . . . [pause].

Once again, now, clench your left hand into a fist, tightly, noticing the tensions in the hand and in the forearm. Study those tensions, and now let go slowly, again allowing your body to express this trust in God. Let your fingers spread out, relaxed, and note the difference once again between muscular tension and muscular relaxation. Just allow your arm and hand and the rest of your body to rest there in the warmth of God's presence [pause].

Now let's do the same with the right hand. . . . .

The above sequence can be repeated for all of the muscle groups mentioned in the tension-relaxation section above. A relaxation-only procedure uses the same muscle groups. However, only the relaxation part of the transcript is read for this procedure.

Recollection.   This procedure is similar to the methods of meditation discussed in Chapter 5. The emphasis here, however, is on the role of the body in this process. The idea is to let go of all competing distractions or ideas until we are focused on one thing, or "centered," on the Quakers call it (Foster, 1983). The object is to focus our attention on God's presence. This may be done by focusing on an image of Christ; by merely having a sense of his presence (cf. Brother Lawrence, quoted above), or by repeating a prayer. If any frustrations or distractions arise, they are given to God, and one's attention is gently brought right back to God. In this centering process there is a releasing or a giving away of the body, an active surrendering to the divine presence.

Transcript.   The following is one possible transcript of how the three procedures listed above may be combined. Note that such an exercise should be done in a quiet environment, and in a very comfortable position, either sitting or lying down. If there is a tendency to fall asleep during such exercises, it is better to sit up. At least initially, it is important to follow the transcript closely. The goals of these exercises are twofold: to give the individual an object to dwell upon, and to encourage in him a passive attitude. Anxious individuals are those who have minds that are flitting to and fro, ruminating on a hundred worries at one time. They need to learn the lesson which

A. W. Tozer (1948) advocates: "Our strength and safety lies not in noise but in silence. . . . It is important that we get still to wait on God" (p. 80).

> As you get comfortable in the chair, take three deep breaths, holding each breath for the count of four, opening the eyes wide when inhaling and closing them when exhaling. Allow your eyes to remain closed after exhaling for the third time.
>
> As you allow yourself to relax in the chair, place yourself in the presence of God . . . so that you have some reminder of the presence of God. ..do this in whatever way seems comfortable to you. Some people like to visualize Christ's presence. Others merely say a silent prayer. If you are visualizing Christ, pick whatever image is most comforting to you.
>
> After you have become aware of God's presence with you, allow yourself to focus on that presence for the remainder of the exercise. As you focus on the presence of Christ, or the image of Christ, take a deep breath and hold it. Now as you let it out slowly, allow yourself to sink down slowly into the chair. Allow yourself to trust in that presence of Christ.
>
> Now take a second breath and hold it. As you let it out, notice the relaxation that begins to develop.
>
> As you follow my instructions, also allow yourself to remain in the presence of Christ. Sometimes you may find that you allow that presence to fade, or your attention wanders from the image, or presence. If this happens, merely bring your attention gently back to that presence or image.
>
> Even as you enjoy the presence of Christ, you can allow your body to express the trust you feel by allowing it to relax.
>
> As you visualize the presence of Christ, allow the muscles of your feet and ankles to relax . . . allow them to go limp. As you allow your feet and ankles to relax, you can also allow the muscles of your calves to relax . . . let them go limp. Then allow your thigh muscles to go limp. As you allow all these muscles to relax, you can begin to feel a pleasant feeling of heaviness in your legs . . . your legs are beginning to feel as heavy as lead. Just allow your legs to relax. Allow that portion of your body to surrender to the divine presence.
>
> As you allow your legs to relax more completely, you can feel more and more at peace. Your mind can become more and more calm and contented with the presence of Christ. You may begin to enjoy this very pleasant relaxed feeling. You may even begin to notice something very unusual. These feelings of relaxation are beginning to spread upwards over your whole body.
>
> As you begin to focus on these feelings, you can allow the

muscles of your stomach to relax, allow them to go limp. Then let go of any tightness in your chest . . . your upper back. . . . and your lower back. .let all of the muscles in your chest and back go limp . . . allow them to relax completely.

As you allow your muscles in your chest and back to relax, just continue your focus on the presence or image of Jesus. Just allow yourself to rest comfortably in his presence. You need not do anything or worry about anything. Just allow your mind to be in retreat, to enjoy this presence.

As you allow your muscles in your chest and back to go limp, you can feel a comfortable feeling of heaviness in your whole body . . . as if your body wants to sink down . . . deeper and deeper in to the chair or the bed. This can be a very comfortable feeling of trust.

As you feel the chair or bed supporting your body, you can again focus on the support of the divine presence. It is not necessary to strive or try, just allow yourself to relax in that presence. Just allow yourself to surrender to the divine presence.

As you allow yourself to surrender to the divine presence, you can feel warm and comfortable in this presence . . . completely at peace . . . a pleasant feeling of relaxation is spreading into your neck . . . and into your shoulders . . . and your arms. Allow your neck muscles to relax. .allow them to go limp. As you allow your neck muscles to relax, allow the muscles of your shoulders to relax, allow the muscles in your arms to relax . . . let them go limp . . . and feel a feeling of heaviness in your arms . . . as if your arms are heavy as lead.

As you continue to allow your muscles to relax, also gently remind yourself to stay in God's presence. If your mind should wander, that is okay. You can bring it gently back. As you continue in this presence . . . let all of your facial muscles relax . . . let go of any tightness in the corners of your mouth . . . allow your lips to part slightly . . . and allow your chin to sag and to feel plesantly heavy and relaxed.

As all of the muscles of your body relax, you can just lie there for one minute enjoying this pleasant experience of relaxing in the warmth of this divine presence . . . and as you enjoy this relaxation, your breathing can continue regularly and deeply. . deeply and regularly within your self, relinquish any tension or cares unto Christ . . . [Pause 1 minute].

Now that the minute is up, you can wake up whenever you like. All you have to say is "Now I am going to wake up," and count to three. When you do wake up you can take with you this very pleasant sense of relaxation and the warmth of the divine presence into your daily activities.

When reciting this transcript, it is important to pause sufficiently after each phrase, and to use a quiet, relaxed voice. Breaks in the phrasing within sentences indicate a pause should occur at that point.

Goal Setting

Time management, or organizing and planning one's activities, has received much attention in the literature (e.g., Lakein, 1973; Wheeler & Janis, 1980). Such skills are doubly important for those individuals who have difficulty with stress or depression, and are related to the ability to relax.

Psychological aspects.   As we have noted, the experience of helplessness is a crucial ingredient of both stress and depression (Seligman, 1975). The depressed individual feels he is helpless to bring about any changes in his environment. He has learned to believe that the outcome of any circumstance is out of his control. There appear to be at least three problems in learned helplessness. First, there is a cognitive deficit: the individual does not *expect* positive results in an endeavor. There is also a motivational deficit. The depressed individual does not even attempt many activities that might bring him some positive benefits. Finally, there is an emotional and physiological deficit. Negative moods interfere with any attempts at action.

Learned helplessness is also an ingredient in stress and anxiety. Most definitions of stress have focused on whether individuals perceived themselves to have control. Bandura (1977), for example, stated that efficacy expectations determine the initiation, degree, and persistence of coping efforts. If one expects oneself to have some effective control, one will try harder. Individuals who feel overwhelmed by their environment do not try. One way to increase feelings of control is to help individuals learn to organize their environment and the tasks demanded of them.

Theological aspects.   The actual task of organizing one's life may play a role in reducing the ambiguity and immensity of the task. One's attitude towards the task plays an equally crucial role. Often, depressed and anxious individuals will not attempt a task or a goal because they are sure they will fail. Their orientation toward any task is always in the future. They will not allow themselves to focus on the actual doing of the task itself. Instead, like most of us, they focus on the accomplishment of the task. Unlike most of us, however, their expectations of actually successfully accomplishing the task are much lower. Thomas Merton (1955) has stated that there are two possible Christian attitudes toward tasks or actions, right intentions and simple intentions. In right intentions we seek to do God's will. We hope to please God. In doing this, however, we still consider the work and ourselves apart from God and outside him. Our intention is directed chiefly upon the accomplishment of the work to be done.

A simple intention, however, is less occupied with the thing to be done. Merton says of the individual with this intention: "His spiritual reserves are not all poured out into his work, but stored where they belong, in the depths of his being, with his God. He is detached from his work and from its results" (p. 72). Our attitude toward the task is more important than the task itself. Our resources are kept within. Our growth and wholeness are not dependent upon the success of the task itself. A divestiture of one's wholeness and identity from one's task allows for more risk. The process itself becomes important. This is the message needed by those individuals who fear to undertake such tasks. Their roots must be put back within themselves and in the divine presence.

One way to shift the focus is to see new tasks as hypothesis testing as Beck has done (Beck, Rush, Shaw, & Emery, 1979). In this mindset, the individual is taught to see any new task he may attempt as merely an opportunity to gather data for himself. He gains information on how likely he is to succeed. Thus, rather than placing a demand upon oneself for success, one adopts a "wait and see" attitude. Merely gathering the information is more important than doing the task itself.

Another way to view tasks is to see them as spiritual exercises— exercises in which we learn to live in Christ. Removing one's roots from a task or job and putting them back within oneself is an attitude that is cultivated with time. It often helps to talk continually to oneself. Cultivating the sense of the presence of God in meditation may be helpful here. Imagery may also help.

Method.   There are three important steps in goal setting or problem solving. One must first develop a clear statement of the goal or problem. Secondly, the problem or goal must be broken into small enough steps so that it does not seem overwhelming. Finally, one must learn to reward oneself upon the successful completion of each step.

Problem or goal definition.   Setting goals or solving problems first means setting some priorities. Chapter 5 discusses a problem-solving attitude (pp. 90–92) which should first be cultivated before proceeding with the steps in the present process.

Division of project into steps.   The next step is to divide the project or goal into three to ten steps, depending upon the complexity of the project and the motivation level of the individual concerned. More difficult tasks for less motivated persons need more steps. One should indicate specifically what will be done in each step. It is useful to write these steps down.

The crucial point here is the number of steps. For some individuals one must go very slowly. For example, one very shy woman was merely asked to find some telephone numbers of some singles' groups as a first step towards meeting more people. Do not run ahead of the person's motivation level. This will only overwhelm him and lead to failure. If one step was not done successfully, that step should be made smaller and reassigned, in a slightly altered format. It is been my experience that a task is usually not done because it was too overwhelming.

Develop rewards.   It is important to develop rewards for yourself when you have completed each step. These serve as motivators before we receive the larger reward of having completed the project. The rewards should be chosen by the individual solving the problem. Some depressed individuals have difficulty giving themselves any positive rewards. The reward process will add an additional therapeutic element to problem solving for them. Formulating rewards may take more time with these individuals. If you are one of them, remember that just devising a reward that you enjoy will be therapeutic in itself. You need to reward yourself more.

Many depressed individuals have been so hard on themselves that they have no concept of personal reward. One severely depressed individual proposed that she would reward herself by washing her roommate's dishes. When asked if this was enjoyable to her, she said no. She was so accustomed to self-punishment rather than self-reward that she was unable to think of anything pleasurable. The size of the rewards should be appropriate to the size of the task completed. For example, if you divided cleaning the garage into five steps to be done in five afternoons, and you had specified just exactly what would be cleaned out each afternoon, you can set up a reward system to go along with the steps. Thus, if you had sorted through all of the paper boxes on your first afternoon, you might reward yourself by having coffee with a friend when you are finished.

In all of the steps above, it is important to discuss doubts about abilities to complete these steps with the therapist if you are in counseling. One should also be careful not to belittle any progress that has been made. Evaluate your progress realistically.

Adding Activities

Lewinsohn (Lewinsohn & Graf, 1973) has found that our mood is related to our activities. Individuals who have more positive activities in their lives have a better mood. While the exact direction of causality is not clear, it is clear that most of us feel better when we do things we enjoy. We read in the Gospels that even Jesus spent time alone with his disciples, away from demands. While some of this time was spent in teaching, it is very probable that other events occurred. If Jesus is the model of perfect humanness, and humanness involves the body as well as the soul, then it makes sense that Jesus enjoyed activites that refreshed his body. Jesus probably enjoyed conversation with his disciples when they were alone. Since they were outdoors they may have enjoyed swimming, or hiking, or simply watching the birds. Some people may find these suggestions comical. However, I think that is because we forget the human part of Jesus. If recreation, pleasure, or the sense of accomplishment are not a part of one's life, one is more at risk for depression.

Below is one procedure for adding pleasure to one's life. Additional references on this subject are available from Beck (Beck, Rush, Shaw, & Emery, 1979) and Lewinsohn (1974).

Follow these instructions in setting up some additional activities in your life.

1. Make a list of all possible activities that you enjoy or have enjoyed in the past. Also make a list of activities that you have never tried, but which other individuals seem to enjoy. Include some brief activities in your list, and some longer activities. You may feel that this step is not necessary because you are aware of many pleasurable activities. However, since you are not doing those activities, apparently they are not pleasurable enough. You need to look at some alternatives. Be sure to include activities that are affordable for your budget. This listing is important and should be given considerable attention and thought, before moving on to the next step.

2. Initially, pick one or two of those activities that can be done easily and in a short period of time, say an hour or so. Schedule that activity for a *definite time period* on a *definite date*. Definite scheduling means the activity is more likely to get done.

3. If you have enjoyed some of the briefer activities, try some of the longer activities. Again, it is important that the activity is scheduled for a *definite time period* on a *definite date*.

4. Follow the same sequence of steps one, two, and three above for activities that give you a sense of mastery or accomplishment.

Communication Skills

Necessary living skills not only involve caring for our own bodies, but also communicating with others. Good communication skills are a necessary part of wholeness. Unfortunately, many individuals who suffer from problems of stress and depression do not have such skills. Many individuals who suffer from loneliness, for example, feel helpless to avail themselves of relief from that loneliness by cultivating relationships with others. They have had little practice. I have had a number of lonely depressed single individuals in my practice who are lacking in social skills. Giving these individuals assignments that encourage them to form relationships with others is an important part of their treatment.

Psychological aspects.   As we have noted, some depressed individuals may lack the requisite social skills to obtain from the environment the needed support vital to good mental health. These individuals just do not know what to say, and when to say it. The development of these social skills may have been retarded originally by their low self-esteem and their statements to themselves about their undesirability. However, as time progresses and they do not practice these skills, the actual skills themselves are retarded. Social skills can be considered a coping resource that the individual can use to obtain other needed resources such as social supports.

Theological aspects.   It has been repeatedly stressed that the *imago Dei* is reflected in our relationships to each other. Humanity is beings in covenant with each other. As we relate in wholeness to each other, and allow ourselves to be known as we know, we reflect the image of God that was manifested in Jesus. Barth has said that this encounter must be mutual and it must be done gladly (Barth, 1948/1960, p. 265). Ultimately, then, we are a product of the accumulations of our relationships and exchanges with others. If these encounters are whole, we will be whole. If these encounters are fractured, ineffective, or artificial, the image of God within ourselves becomes marred. Spirituality can only become whole when relationships are whole. True spirituality is a healthy spirituality that allows for free and open communication between individuals.

Method.   In previous research by the author on the treatment of depression (Propst, Ostrom, Watkins, & Morris, 1984), individuals were given an assignment to renew some old relationships and make some new relationships as part of the therapy process. Below is a transcript of most of the information they were given. Some of the information in step three is derived from Bower and Bower (1980). This information may be given directly to individuals in order to encourage them and instruct them in developing more effective communication skills.

Step 1: Learning how and where to meet new people. Often many people who lack friendships do not go to the settings likely to provide them with friends. It is, therefore, important for them to seek out such settings, or to find out about such settings. Jesus actually sought out some of his disciples by going to the settings where he knew them to be, such as the seashore. There are several pointers that may prove helpful:

a. It is important to think about what one's interests are, and perhaps to make a list of those interests.

b. It is necessary to determine where in the local area people might be found who share our interests. For example, if one has an interest in outdoor activities, or hiking, one might inquire at a local outdoor-equipment store about the existence of such groups or look in the phone book under the appropriate headings. It is usually good to inquire about a number of options, because some groups will be more appropriate than others.

c. Decide to follow up on one or two of these groups by checking out the specific time and date of the next meeting and going to that meeting.

Step 2: Nonverbal skills. Sometimes we can attract people or put them off, merely by our body language before we have even talked to them. We should appear sure of ourselves, but friendly. It is usually good to make eye contact, stand up straight, and smile. It is interesting to note in the Gospels that Jesus usually looked at people when he talked with them (e.g., Mark 10:20–22). Sometimes people who have trouble making friends find direct eye contact difficult. The following are some helpful exercises to use.

a. Practice an assertive, friendly, confident body language and facial expression in front of a mirror until you feel comfortable with it.

b. When you are out in public, practice looking at people in order to gain more information about what is actually happening with them. Decide ahead of time what types of information you wish to obtain.

c. Practice a new, more assertive, friendly manner in public, without saying anything.

Step 3: Basic Conversation Components: The third set of skills important for building friendships are the basic components of conversation. Practice each of the following components with your therapist or in front of a mirror before attempting them the first time. It is usually best to write down a script beforehand.

a. *Openers.* The first step in any conversation is obviously to make an opening remark. This does not have to be profound. The sole purpose of this remark is to draw attention to yourself, in order to provide an opportunity for later conversation. In the conversation with the woman at the well (John 4), Jesus started a conversation with the woman by asking her for a drink of water. Some typical examples of conversational openers may be the following: "How does one get to the _____ building from here?" or "You're new around here, aren't you?", "How do you like the great sunset?", "How do you like the music (movie, etc.)?" or "How do you like living in this city?"

b. *Following up on openers.* It is also usually good to have two or three additional remarks planned in advance. Some of the following may be useful. "Is the fishing good in the state?", "How are the traffic sounds from where you live?" Or, "what are the winters like around here?" The point is to search for a topic of conversation, so that the two of you can start a conversation. You can always estimate how much the other person wants to converse with you by how much additional information they give about themselves beyond what you ask. For example, the Samaritan woman engaged in a conversation with Jesus volunteered more conversation by saying, "How is it that you, a Jew, ask a drink of me, a woman of Samaria?" Jesus then added some additional information to attract her interest and maintain the conversation (John 4:7–26).

c. *Keeping conversation going.* One can keep a conversation going by encouraging or prompting the other person to talk about himself while you interject frequent remarks about yourself. Listen for additional information about the individual, so that you can add similar information about yourself, or ask them more about what they have already said. There are three types of questions to match differing intimacy levels of a conversation. First, one can ask factual questions about external events. Examples would be,

"How did the baseball team do yesterday?" Or, "how much snow is there in the mountains?"

The second type of question is both factual and slightly personal. Examples of this type would be "What type of work do you do?" Or, "where are you from?"

Finally, there are the more personal questions that one asks after having known the individual a little longer. These are questions about personal feelings, reasons, motives, and emotions. Examples would be, "How do you feel about your work?" (or any other subject), or "What motivates you to do what you do?" In the conversation with the woman at the well, Jesus volunteers some additional information about himself as to who he might be. This encourages the woman to continue the conversation and become more personal (John 4:10).

d. *Open and closed questions.* Open questions require the other person to describe a situation in detail. These will keep the conversation running longer. For example, instead of asking an individual if she liked skiing, you could ask her what types of winter sports she liked and why.

e. *Sharing through self-disclosure.* People build friendships for intimacy. Therefore, sharing personal information about oneself is appreciated as the relationship progresses. You can share your opinions about your family, your upbringing, your life-style, your views on marriage, your hates, your view of God, death, or your failures and triumphs. Obviously, the longer you know someone, the more you share. Jesus certainly shared information about himself when he commented that he was the Living Water to the woman of Samaria.

f. *Dead ends.* When the conversation stops, it is helpful to have a few stock phrases to restart the conversation. One example is: "Let's forget about that heavy subject, and talk about a light topic. I was wondering what you think about (skiing, hiking, particular types of food, etc., etc.). One might also merely ask the individual what he thinks about a particular subject that he may have mentioned earlier. Use your imagination and plan some of these ahead of time!

g. *Listening.* Several pointers are important. Show that you are listening with your body language by attending fully to the speaker. Also, try to show pleasure at what he is saying, and certainly do not interrupt the speaker.

h. *Closers.* When you have to go, you can indicate this by standing up or by summarizing the conversation. You can also merely say, "I have enjoyed our conversation, but I must go now. I would enjoy talking to you again."

Some may regard the above instructions as too explicit or too simplified. Such instructions have been very beneficial for my depressed patients, however. These get to the problems of which depression is made.

Practicing friendship skills should be done in two stages. First, one should recontact old acquaintances. Secondly, one can then try out the skills with new friends. For individuals who feel particularly shy, substantial pre-meeting practice is important. After the initial meeting is set up, one should write out at least two topics or phrases to meet the requirements of each category of step three above. These phrases should be practiced in front of a mirror or with one's therapist. After the meeting with the friends, it is important to evaluate the conversation. One should ask oneself the following: What two or three things did I do well? What two or three things do I need more work on?

Judy was a third-grade teacher, who you first met in Chapter 3. Her main activities consisted of teaching school and baby-sitting for her neighbors. She was quite depressed and had no social life. She was in her late thirties and had never had a date with a man. She felt extremely lonely and helpless to change the situation.

Almost immediately in therapy, I began to give Judy social assignments. Her first assignment was to list activities she liked to do. She reported that she liked crafts and outdoors activities, and that she would like to follow up on the outdoors activities. She started this process by finding phone numbers of three outdoor recreation groups in the area and bringing them to the next session. I proceeded rather slowly with Judy, to give her a chance to get used to the idea of more social activities. She was quite timid and quite depressed. Her next assignment was to call two of the organizations and find out the time, date, and location of their next meeting. She then chose one of the meetings to attend. Her first assignment was merely to attend one of the meetings. I did not ask her to say anything. After the first meeting, she went hiking with the group. (Sports activities often provide a better setting for shy people to acquire social skills, because they are more informal. They are also very good for women who may never have developed the physical activity side of themselves.) During her first hike with the group, she was given the assignment to give casual greetings to three different people, either male or female. She reported that she felt awkward after the casual greetings.

While Judy was getting acquainted with the group, she also continued, as part of the assignment, to monitor her thoughts. Additionally, we worked on conversation skills as outlined in step three above. During the therapy session, she was required to carry on a conversation with me, the therapist, about various topics. Gradually, I became a more difficult conversation partner, requiring her to carry more and more of the ball. We also role-played potential conversations she could use on her hikes. It was important that her first attempts at extended conversations be successful.

Gradually she began to engage more and more members of the hiking group in conversations, beginning first with females and progressing to males. A strong expectation was expressed by me that each assignment was to be completed before progressing to another assignment. If she found one assignment too difficult, during the next session I simplified the assignment into another format. She said at the termination of our therapy together: "You would never let me off the hook, and I needed that." My firmness, of course, was always presented in a lighthearted manner.

Her realization that she must complete each assignment resulted in some real growth for her, and even a few somewhat funny situations. She would often go out of her way to find people to talk to. Once she missed a rendezvous with her hiking group. As the intended hiking area was well traveled, she decided to hike by herself and see who she could meet because, as she later said, "I better do this assignment."

This solo hike soon became a duet. During the hike, she met a man about her age. She started a conversation so as to complete her assignment. The two of them eventually ate lunch together and spent the remainder of the hike together.

Judy's social life changed, and so did her feelings about herself. Renewed relationships with others are integral to emotional growth.

Appropriate assertion, relaxation, communication with others, active problem solving, and recreation and accomplishment are some of the more important activities that complete our wholeness. Ultimately, any spiritual journey must include these.

We are both body and soul. As we explore our inner selves, and our souls, we discover that we have a passive vague awareness of ourselves, our thoughts, and moods. We also discover, however, that we have an active as well as a passive relationship with what we perceive. We can choose to view ourselves differently. As we explore our bodies, we become aware of desires. We discover that we not only have passive desires, but we can actively will. We can act and choose (Barth, 1948/1960).

Chapter 10

STEPS IN THE COUNSELING PROCESS

I began to think of the soul as if it were a castle made of a single diamond or of very clear crystal, in which there are many rooms.—
St. Teresa of Avila, 1577/1961, p. 28

Structure and Rationale of Chapter

We are very complicated beings. Not only are we complex physical beings, but we are even more complex emotional beings. Healing such a complex emotional being can be itself a mysterious and complicated process. One of the goals of science, however, has always been to illuminate and explain the mysterious, and the science of psychotherapy is no exception. The past decades have seen numerous attempts to understand more simply and succinctly those processes that may contribute to emotional problems.

The science of cognitive psychology and psychotherapy provides one relatively successful explanation for the causes of emotional disorders. Research in this area has focused on how individuals perceive and think about their environment. It has focused on how they organize the information they gain about the environment. Finally, it has looked at how such thoughts and assumptions, and indeed information-processing about the environment could be changed (e.g., Anderson, 1980).

Quite early in the process, cognitive and cognitive-behavior therapists began to write therapist manuals in which the steps and procedures deemed to be part of the change process were clearly specified. The result has been an entire new generation of psychotherapy textbooks (for example, Beck, Rush, Shaw, & Emery, 1979, or Woolfolk & Lehrer, 1984) in which the therapist is now given clearer instructions regarding what should happen in the therapy session. This has resulted in more effective therapy training and better therapy outcomes.

The purpose of this chapter is to provide a step-by-step description of cognitive therapy as it might be done within the context of an individual's Christian spirituality.

I suggest that the counselor who is new to either cognitive-behavioral therapy or to the inclusion of Christian spirituality in the counseling context follow rather closely the sequence of steps which is outlined. As you become more comfortable with the sequencing as it is presented, it is then possible to be more spontaneous with your counseling.

Each step of the counseling sequence will consist of two parts. First, there will be a brief description of that step. Then the reader will be referred to sections in the book where specific procedures for handling that step can be found.

Finally, each step will present some criteria for determining when the patient has sufficiently mastered the actions associated with each step and is thus ready to proceed to the next step.

Steps in the Counseling Process

Step 1: Preliminary concerns and relationship building.   There are basic ingredients of any counseling which must always be present in cognitive therapy, regardless of other steps used. These ingredients are warmth, accurate empathy, genuineness, basic trust, and rapport (cf Beck, Rush, Shaw, & Emery, 1979). The good counselor is able to listen, and indicate in a very caring manner that the individual in front of her is very important. (Barth, 1948/1960, pp. 246–259) suggests that it is only when we regard the other as a "thou" that we actually have an authentic image of God present. (Chapter 3, especially pp. 28–39 discusses the sacredness of the counseling relationship.)

Listening and relationship building are the backbone of any counseling. Accurate listening appears so simple that students of counseling often are eager to get on to bigger and better things. A wise counselor realizes, however, that increasing her listening skills is a lifelong task. I would always recommend training in this skill with the opportunity for direct feedback. Merely reading about this process is as inadequate as reading about hearing music. Not only must the counselor hear the content of the other's statements, but she also must hear the other's feelings and underlying thoughts. "You are feeling _____, because _____," is a good model for responses.

Hearing and understanding the other person's problems is a necessary prerequisite to any further counseling steps. Individuals must feel *heard* before they are ready to *listen* to directions for change. It is not inappropriate to ask the individual in front of you if he feels that you have heard and understood him. It is also very important to remember that the individual in front of us is the correct judge of whether or not he has been understood, not the counselor.

Thus, an important step in good counseling is helping an individual feel comfortable and valuable by good listening. Carkhuff (1980) provides a good model.

In addition to including empathetic nondirective listening, cognitive therapy also needs to be *structured,* because it is primarily educational. The therapist must communicate information, and the structure dictates what types of materials the patient must learn, and the sequencing of those materials.

Beck (Beck, Rush, Shaw, & Emery, 1979) is careful to emphasize that this communication of information is not one-way. Like any good educational enterprise, the information exchange must be two-way. The therapist should structure the therapy, but the patient should also make many of the important decisions. The therapist should be careful, for example, to check with the patient to see if the patient himself feels a particular assignment is appropriate. The patient is also the one who actually changes his own thoughts. He collects the information and decides whether the original thought was distorted. The therapist may coach the process, but the patient must ultimately execute it.

Step 2: Diagnosis. Before proceeding in counseling, it is imperative to determine whether or not the individual sitting in front of you has a problem that will respond to cognitive therapy. Thus far, cognitive therapy has only been tested for some types of depression and some anxiety disorders. If the individual does not fit that classification, perhaps another approach—medication or referral—may be appropriate. The depressive disorders for which cognitive therapy is appropriate include the unipolar depressions. These are distinguished from the bipolar depressions in which the depressed individual may also have cycles of hyperexcitability.

There are four categories of symptoms in unipolar depression:

1. *Mood.* Individual must report sadness, gloominess, or tearfulness.

2. *Biological Symptoms.* These symptoms include either poor appetite and weight loss or increased appetite and weight gain. Depressed individuals also report changes in sleeping habits. They may have difficulty falling asleep, wake up in the middle of the night, or wake up too early in the morning. Some depressed individuals may sleep longer than usual. Finally, depressed individuals may also report a loss of energy, fatigability, or tiredness.

3. *Cognitive Symptoms.* Depressed individuals report a changed attitude towards several areas of their life. They report a loss of interest or pleasure in usual activities or sex. They also report increased guilt and excessive self-blame. Thirdly, they report a lessened ability to concentrate or to make decisions. Fourth, they report a pessimistic attitude toward the future. Finally, depressed individuals are preoccupied with thoughts of inadequacy and failure.

Cognitive therapy has also been found to be effective for anxiety syndromes. Phobias, panic disorders, and generalized anxiety disorders have all been found to respond to this treatment. Obsessive-compulsive disorders and posttraumatic stress disorder will also respond. Other disorders, however, are less responsive to cognitive therapy. (See the *Diagnostic and Statistical Manual of Mental Disorders* (American Psychiatric Association, 1980) for a description of these disorders.)

In addition to ruling out other diagnosis, at least two other questions must be dealt with in cases of depression. First, is the individual suicidal? Suicidal cases require professional help. Also, in cases of depression, the counselor must also rule out potential marital problems before using cognitive therapy. Weissman (Weissman & Paykel, 1974) has found that marital difficulties may often be a chief underlying cause of depression, especially in women. Unless the marital relationship is dealt with, the depression will not be alleviated by cognitive therapy.

Step 3: Presentation of rationale.   Because cognitive therapy is both an educational and a collaborative enterprise, it is essential that the patient understand something of the rationale behind the procedure. Presentation of the rationale is best done after the patient has shared his problems with the counselor. A summary of the patient's problems should then include the statement that he is telling himself certain things. Possible examples of these "automatic thoughts" can be shared with him. If he agrees that these thoughts may be present, then the rationale can be presented. The rationale then becomes part of his experiences rather than an academic monologue.

An essential cognitive-behavioral rationale will include five ingredients:

1. The idea that thoughts strongly influence feelings.
2. An example of the above from the patient's own experiences.
3. A diagram demonstrating how one's thoughts effect one's feelings and one's behaviors, which, in turn, further effect one's environment and thoughts. A cyclic process should be demonstrated. (See Figure 2-1 in Chapter 2, p. 19).
4. The idea that the individual must change his feelings by changing his thoughts and assumptions.
5. A rationale from the individual's spirituality for the above.

A more detailed rationale for cognitive behavioral therapy is presented in Chapter 3, pp. 39–41, 47–48. It is usually best for the counselor to summarize the main points of that information in her own words when presenting it to the patient.

One may proceed with the next phase of counseling when the patient agrees that the rationale may be possible and is able to summarize the model for the counselor, using examples from his own life. The individual in front of us will usually not be entirely convinced of the model. That is not necessary. Such belief comes only as the patient has opportunity to test the model in his own life.

Step 4: Self-awareness and self-examination.   There are two parts to self-awareness in cognitive-behavioral therapy. First there must be awareness of feelings and then there must be awareness of thoughts.

Awareness of feelings are necessary because the patient must learn to use this awareness as a cue to examine what he is saying to himself at the moment he feels anxious or depressed.

Procedures for the self-examination of one's thoughts and images are found in Chapter 4.

Total awareness of thoughts is not necessary before proceeding to cognitive restructuring. Clinicians differ in emphasis here. Some clinicians encourage restructuring of thoughts almost immediately (cf. Beck, Rush, Shaw, & Emery, 1979). Other clinicians (Meichenbaum, 1973) feel that some facility must first be gained in thought-monitoring. The present work takes the later stance. In my clinical experience I have found that both active thought-monitoring and active thought-changing are new skills for most individuals. The procedures for both skills are confusing in the beginning. Sticking with thought-monitoring until an individual knows what a thought is gives the patient a better chance to grasp the process. This step-by-step process is also consistent with the philosophy of cognitive behavior therapy. That is, approaching the learning of a new skill in small steps usually means more possibility of success.

After a patient has been able to capture thoughts successfully on paper right at the moment they occur, then the changing of those thoughts can begin. For some individuals this may come after only one week.

Step 5: Cognitive restructuring.   Cognitive restructuring means the transformation of those negative thoughts that haunt us into either positive or neutral thoughts. We actually think or process information in two different modes, a verbal mode and a visual mode.

Thoughts in a verbal mode are the actual words an individual may say to himself. For example, I may think to myself that telling a woman friend that she should refer to herself as a "woman" and not a "girl" may have been too forward. I may further castigate myself and say I should not make others feel defensive. "Why can't I say the right thing?" Restructuring or changing these thoughts would mean evaluating them logically. One procedure may be to decide what types of distorted thoughts or illogical assumptions are present. In the example quoted above, the individual is saying some version of the following to herself: "I should always be perfect and say the right thing all the time." If this is logically evaluated, however, we realize that no one always says the right words all the time. Also, the individual in the example above is mind reading. It is difficult if not impossible to know what the other is thinking. Besides, there are also times to be straightforward with others.

Procedure for restructuring verbal thoughts are found in Chapters 5 and 6.

The second type of thoughts to be changed are internal images. These images are actual thoughts, in a visual mode. For example, one woman suffering from a panic reaction continually had images of driving her car off a cliff, or of lying in a hospital bed and dying. She was instructed to change the ending on these images and make them positive. The discovery that she had control over her images gradually alleviated her panic reactions.

Procedures for modifying troublesome images are found in Chapter 7.

Since cognitive restructuring is the central portion of the treatment, it should be given the most emphasis. Some individuals may need extensive coaching. It may be necessary to try alternative procedures. It is important to continue with these procedures, however, until the individual has some success in reducing her anxiety and depression. She should no longer feel tossed about by the intensity of her thoughts or feelings. Instead, such individuals should feel that they are the ones who can toss their feelings and thoughts into a safe place. For those individuals who require little counseling, this phase may only last a few weeks.

When someone has had some success in teaching himself to think differently and thus alleviate some of his negative emotions, it is appropriate to go on to the behavioral portion of the treatment. It is not necessary to gain complete facility in cognitive restructuring before continuing, for several reasons. First, the ultimate test of change is in behavior. It is important to encourage the individual to test out his new attitudes, or ways of thinking. Secondly, it may ultimately take some behavior change actually to change some thoughts. For example, the thought that I can not accomplish anything needs contrary evidence. Finally, cognitive restructuring can also continue along with behavioral assignments.

From this point on, it may not be necessary to use all of the following steps with each individual. The counselor may branch out in a number of directions, depending on the needs of the patient.

Step 6: Dealing with anger and passivity.   Not all individuals will need help in the area of passivity or anger control. However, all *depressed* individuals will need such help. Women, who comprise a large percentage of the depressed population, are especially vulnerable to the passivity that engenders depression. Women have been encouraged to be passive, and sometimes even helpless. Learned helplessness is one of the most important current models for depression. Seligman (1975) has found that depressed individuals learn to think that they have no control over their environment, or even their own life. They must ask others to exert control for them. Many women have been culturally conditioned to behave similarly. Thus, depression will not be alleviated until these woman are able to take some control of their life. This is especially the case with some more traditional women, who mistakenly think that Christianity does not permit them to be an active assertive woman. For these women, assertion training must always include a rationale for such assertion derived directly from their own Christian beliefs. Chapter 8 discusses one possible rationale.

Any thought or imagery content that hints of helplessness or a trapped feeling suggests that assertiveness training should be used. It is important in assertiveness training to start with simple tasks, and assign gradually more difficult ones. It is not necessary, however, to coach the individual through all of the assertive tasks she or he ultimately needs to accomplish. After the counselor has coached the individual through a number of success experiences, it is permissible to leave her or him on their own with the instruction to continue living life in this fuller, more active and direct style. It may also be necessary, at times, to come back to assertion or anger control if difficult issues arise.

Anger control is also a part of this step. It has been my clinical experience that many passive individuals have a great deal of anger that they have not admitted to themselves. Chapter 4, on cognitive awareness, provides some procedures that may begin to bring that anger into awareness. However, awareness is not sufficient. The anger must be channeled constructively. The admonition in scripture to "be angry and sin not" is actually a healthy track to follow. Chapter 8 (pp. 142ff) contains not only some assertiveness procedures, but also some procedures for dealing with one's anger both cognitively and behaviorally (pp. 146–162).

Step 7: Relaxation skills.   Relaxation tactics vary. The focus in Chapter 9 is primarily on specific tactics that involve the body directly. Some additional exercises that focus on relaxing by changing one's thoughts are included in the cognitive restructuring chapters (Chapters 5–7).

Relaxation training of some type should start as soon as an individual has been determined to have some type of anxiety problem. An immediate start is recommended because relaxation is a learned response that must be gradually strengthened and developed. Strong effects only come with practice. Ultimately, the strong effects come as the person learns to live her life differently. Life must be changed from a hectic on-edge existence to a more settled surrendered approach to existence. This new existence is an active surrendering, a self-abandonment that follows a basic trust not only in oneself, but in divine providence. There are, fortunately, however, small effects from this new process that begin almost immediately: We begin to pay attention to our bodies and senses in a new manner; and we lessen our focus on those frustrations or distractions that tend to grind us down. Relaxation skills are found on pp. 164–172.

When an individual reports that he is less tense, it is possible to suggest that he reduce his number of practice sessions. However, if this new less hectic life is to become permanent, some less structured forms of relaxation must be made a regular part of life. These forms may include simple things, such as increased exercise or quiet times of just sitting, or lazy hot baths.

Step 8: Communication skills.   Communication skills are the ability to feel comfortable around people and develop friendships. Depressed individuals often lack either the motivation or the ability to build relationships that provide them emotional sustenance. Often one with low self-esteem (a primary ingredient of depression) has not had the confidence to nurture and develop such intimacy.

Communication skills also refer to the ability to negotiate and discuss differences of opinion, and to come to a resolution. These problem-solving skills are a necessary part of successful marital, work, and friendship relationships.

Chapter 9, pp. 176–181 discusses communication skills.

As with the other behavioral skills, it is not necessary to work with the person until he has learned everything perfectly. Often, all that is necessary is some very thorough coaching on a few occasions. It is necessary, however, to start with easier situations and gradually progress to more difficult ones. Early success experiences are imperative. After the first few tentative successes at relationships, most of us feel much more confident in risking ourselves for significant relationships. The other's positive reciprocity is usually enough to carry us on to a deeper commitment in these relationships.

Step 9: Organizing one's life.   Quite often, depressed or anxious individuals report being overwhelmed by either their work requirements or their household tasks. They have no time for friendships. This submersion in work may result from perfectionistic attitude towards work. It may also result from poor planning. This section presents some guidelines for planning a more realistic and flexible schedule. Planning guidelines are discussed in Chapter 9, p. 172.

Successful completion of this step occurs when an individual reports more free time. All persons do not necessarily follow the schedule worked out with the counselor. Often, however, many persons use some of the principles presented to develop their own schedule.

Step 10: Adding positive activities.   Depressed persons usually curtail most recreational activities. Consequently, they receive very little positive reinforcement from their environment. The research suggests, however (Lewinsohn, 1974), that mood is improved by such positive activities. Often a successful beginning strategy is to encourage the depressed or anxious individual to have fun. For some individuals, the suggestions should be structured and simple. Chapter 9, pp. 175–176 describes procedures for encouraging an individual to add positive activities to his life.

Successful completion of this step occurs when the patient spontaneously begins to add positive fun activities to his or her life.

CONCLUDING NOTE

The system of interrelationships suggested between the emotional and spiritual aspects of our existence in this book is tentative. Any suggested relationship between these two dimensions of our existence depends upon our scientific understanding of the psychotherapy change process, and our understanding of the Christian tradition. Both understandings are continuously in flux. Yet we may hope that the next two decades of psychotherapy research will be as productive as the previous two. New effective change techniques will become available. Regardless of the changes that occur, however, or the revised methods of explanation, it is probable that the emotional healing process will always involve some type of personal reexamination and transformation of ourselves, and a transformation of our relationships with others. Some type of objective transcendent perspective or vantage point from which to evaluate this process will always be necessary. Jesus the Christ, the model of fulfilled humanity, and the "One for others" is such a vantage point for the Christian.

REFERENCES

Anderson, J. (1980). *Cognitive psychology and its implications.* San Francisco: W. H. Freeman & Co.

Anderson, R. (1984, March). *The resurrection of Jesus as hermeneutical criterion: A case for sexual parity in pastoral ministry.* Paper presented at the meeting of the American Academy of Religion, Western Region, San Francisco, CA.

Antonovsky, A. (1979). *Health, stress and coping.* San Francisco: Jossey-Bass.

Bandura, A. (1977). Self-efficacy: Toward a unifying theory of behavioral change. *Psychological Review, 84,* 191–215.

Bandura, A. & Walters, R. (1963). *Social learning and personality development.* New York: Holt, Rinehart & Winston.

Barber, T. X. (1984). Hypnosis, deep relaxation, and active relaxation: Data, theory, and clinical applications. In R. Woolfolk & P. Lehrer (Eds.), *Principles and practice of stress management.* New York: Guilford.

Barth, K. (1960). *Church dogmatics: The doctrine of creation* (Vol. 3, Part 2), (H. Knight, G. W. Bromily, J. Reid, & R. Fuller, trans.). Edinburgh: T. & T. Clark. (Originally published, 1948.)

Barth, K. (1958). *Church dogmatics: The doctrine of reconciliation* (Vol. 4, part 2). (H. Knight, G. W. Bromily, J. Reid, & R. Fuller, trans.). Edinburgh: T. & T. Clark (Originally published, 1955.)

Barton, A. (1974). *Three worlds of therapy: An existential-phenomenological study of the therapies of Freud, Jung, and Rogers.* Palo Alto, CA: Mayfield.

Batson, C., & Ventis, (1982). *The religious experience.* New York: Oxford University Press.

Beck, A. T., & Emery, G. (1979). *Cognitive therapy of anxiety and phobic disorders.* Philadelphia: Center for Cognitive Therapy.

Beck, A. T., Rush, J., Shaw, B., & Emery, G. (1979). *Cognitive therapy of depression.* New York: Guilford.

Bedrosian, R., & Beck, A. T. (1980). Principles of cognitive therapy. In M. J. Mahoney (Ed.), *Psychotherapy process: Current issues and future directions* (pp. 127–152). New York: Plenum.

Behm, J. (1967). *Parakletos.* In G. Kittel & G. Friedrich (Eds.), *Theological dictionary of the New Testament* (Vol. 5, pp. 800–814), (G. Bromiley, trans.). Grand Rapids: W. B. Eerdmans. (Originally published, 1954.)

Benson, H. (1975). *The relaxation response.* New York: Morrow.

Benson, H., Arns, P., & Hoffman, J. (1981). The relaxation response and hypnosis. *The International Journal of Clinical and Experimental Hypnosis, 29*(3), 259–270.

Bergin, A. (1983) Religiosity and mental health: A critical reevaluation and meta-analysis. *Professional Psychology: Research and Practice, 14*(2), 170–184.

Bonhoeffer, D. (1954). *Life together* (J. Doberstein, trans.). New York: Harper & Row. (Originally published, 1938.)

Bower, S. A., & Bower, G. (1976). *Asserting yourself: A practical guide for positive change.* Reading, MA: Adsdison-Wesley.

Bowers, K. S. (1973). Situationism in psychology: An analysis and a critique. *Psychological Review, 80,* 307–336.

Brianchaninov, I. (1952). *On the prayer of Jesus* (A. Lazarus, Trans.). London: John M. Watkins. (Originally published, 1860.)

Brunner, E. (1939). *Man in revolt* (O. Wyon, trans.). Philadelphia: Westminster. (Originally published, 1937.)

Brunner, E. (1964). *The word of God and modern man.* (David Cairs, trans.). Richmond, Virginia: John Knox Press. (Originally published, 1947.)

Buber, M. (1958). *I and Thou.* Edinburgh: T. & T. Clark. (Written 1937.)

Bultmann, R. (1964). *Elipis.* In G. Kittel & G. Friedrich (Eds.), *Theological dictionary of the New Testament* (Vol. 2, 517–523, 529–535), (G. Bromiley, Trans.). Grand Rapids: W. B. Eerdmans. (Originally published, 1935.)

Bunyan, J. (1911). *The pilgrim's progress.* New York: Henry Holt & Company. (Written 1678.)

Burns, D. (1980). *Feeling good: The new mood therapy.* New York: Morrow.

Calestro, K. (1972). Psychotherapy, faith healing, and suggestion. *International Journal of Psychiatry, 90* (2), 83–113.

Calvin, J. (1972). *Institutes of the Christian religion* (H. Beveridge, Trans.). Grand Rapids: Eerdmans. (Originally published, 1559.)

Carkhuff, R. (1980). *The art of helping IV* (4th ed.). Amherst, MA: Human Resource Development Press.

Carrington, P. (1984). Modern forms of meditation. In R. Woolfolk, & P. Lehrer (Eds.), *Principles and practice of stress management.* New York: Guilford.

Coates, D., & Wortman, C. B. (1980). Depression maintenance and interpersonal control. In A. Baum & S. Singer (Eds.), *Advances in environmental psychology* (Vol. 2, pp. 149–182). Hillsdale, NJ: Lawrence Erlbaum.

Coyne, J. (1976). Depression and the response of others. *Journal of Abnormal Psychology, 85,* 186–193.

Coyne, J., C. Aldwin, & Lazarus, R. (1981). Depression and coping in stressful episodes. *Journal of Abnormal Psychology, 90,* 439–447.

Curtis, J., & Detert, R. (1981). *How to Relax.* Palo Alto, CA: Mayfield Publishing.

Day, D. (1952). *The long loneliness.* New York: Harper & Row.

Delmonte, M. (1984). Meditation: similarities with hypnoidal states and hypnosis. *International Journal of Psychosomatics, 31*(3), 24–34.

Delmonte, M., & Kenny, V. (1985). Models of meditation. *British Journal of Psychotherapy, 1*(3), 197–212. *Diagnostic and statistical manual of mental disorders.* (3rd. ed.). (1980) Washington, DC: American Psychiatric Association.

Dittes, J. E. (1969). Psychology and religion. In G. Lindzey & E. Aronson (Eds.), *The handbook of social psychology Vol. 5.* (2nd ed.). (pp. 602–659). Reading, Mass.: Addison-Wesley.

Dorgan, M. (Speaker). (1984). *The way to divine union: Self-direction for stages of prayer* (Credence Cassettes). Kansas City, MO: National Catholic Reporter Publishing.

Edmonston, W. (1981). *Hypnosis and relaxation.* New York: John Wiley & Sons.

Ellis, A., & Harper, R. (1975). *A new guide to rational living.* North Hollywood, CA: Wilshire Books.

Epictetus. (N. D.) The Encheridion, or manual. In G. Long (Ed. and Trans.), *The discourses of Epictetus with the Encheiridion and fragments.* New York: The Chesterfield Society.

Fairbairn, W. (1952). *An object relations theory of personality.* New York: Basic Books.

Foster, R. (1983). *Meditative prayer.* Downers Grove, IL: Inter-Varsity Press.

Fowler, J. W. (1981). *Stages of faith: The psychology of human development and the quest for meaning.* San Francisco: Harper & Row.

Franks, J. D. (1982). The present status of outcome research. In M. R. Goldfried (Ed.), *Converging themes in psychotherapy* (pp. 281–290). New York: Springer.

Frankl, V. (1959). The spiritual dimension in existential analysis and logo-therapy. *Journal of Individual Psychology, 15,* 157–165.

Freud, S. (1958). Formulations on the two principles of mental functioning. In J. Strachey (Ed. & trans.), *The standard edition of the complete psychological works of Sigmund Freud* (Vol. 12, pp. 215–226). London: Hogarth Press. (Originally published, 1911.)

Freud, S. (1959). Obsessive acts and religious practices. In J. Strachey (Ed. & trans.), *The standard edition of the complete psychological works of Sigmund Freud* (Vol. 9, pp. 115–127). London: Hogarth Press. (Originally published, 1907.)

Freud, S. (1961). The ego and the id. In J. Strachey (Ed. & trans.), *The standard edition of the complete psychological works of Sigmund Freud* (Vol. 19, pp. 3–66). London: Hogarth Press. (Originally published, 1923.)

Freud, S. (1964). Moses and monotheism: Three essays. In J. Strachey (Ed. & trans.), *The standard edition of the complete psychological works of Sigmund Freud* (Vol. 23, pp. 7–137). London: Hogarth Press. (Originally published, 1939.)

Gallup, G. (1979). *Religion in America: 1979–1980.* Princeton, NJ: Princeton Religious Research Center.

Garfield, S., & Bergen, A. (Eds.). (1978). *Handbook of psychotherapy and behavior change* (2nd ed.). New York: John Wiley & Sons.

Gay, V. (1979). *Freud on ritual: Reconstruction and critique.* Missoula, MT: Scholars Press.

Gergen, K. (1971). *The concept of self.* New York: Holt, Rinehart & Winston.

Goldfried, M. (1979). Anxiety reduction through cognitive-behavioral intervention. In P. Kendall & S. Hollon (Eds.) *Cognitive-behavioral interventions* (pp. 117–152). New York: Academic Press.

Goldfried, M. R. (1982). Cognition and experience. In M. R. Goldfried (Ed.), *Converging themes in psychotherapy: Trends in psychodynamic, humanistic, and behavioral practice.* (pp. 365–373). New York: Springer.

Grahame, K. (1965). *The wind in the willows.* New York: Avon Books.

Grundmann, W. (1964). *Egkpateria.* In G. Kittel & G. Friedrich (Eds.), *Theological dictionary of the New Testament* (Vol. 2, pp. 339–342), (G. Bromiley, trans.), Grand Rapids: W. B. Eerdmans. (Originally published, 1935.)

Hollon, S., & Beck, A. T. (1979). Cognitive therapy of depression. In P. Kendall & S. Hollon (Eds.) *Cognitive-behavioral interventions* (pp. 153–204). New York: Academic Press.

Hood, R., & Morris, R. (1981). Knowledge and experience criteria in the report of mystical experience. *Review of Religious Research. 23,* 76–84.

Horowitz, M. (1978). *Image formation and cognition* (2nd ed.). New York: Appleton-Century-Crofts.

Hurnard, H. (1977). *Hinds' feet on high places.* Wheaton, IL: Tyndale House.

Jaeckle, C., & Clebsch, W. (1964). *Pastoral care in historical perspective.* New York: Jason Aronson.

Jencks, B. (1974). *Respiration for relaxation, invigoration, and special accomplishments.* Salt Lake City: Privately printed.

Jocabi, J. (1973). *The Psychology of C. G. Jung* (8th ed.). New Haven: Yale University Press.

Juliana of Norwich. (1977). *Revelations of divine love.* (M. L. del Mastro, Trans.). New York: Doubleday. (Written ca. 1392.)

Jung, C. (1959). The archetypes and the collective unconscious. In H. Read, M. Fordham, & G. Adler (Eds.), *The collected works of Carl G. Jung* (Vol. 9, Part 1, pp. 3–53), (2nd ed.), (R. F. C. Hull, Trans.). Princeton, NJ: Princeton University Press. (Originally published, 1954.)

Jung, C. (1970). The undiscovered self: Present and future. In H. Read, M. Fordham, & G. Adler (Eds.), *The collected works of Carl G. Jung* (Vol. 10, pp. 247–306, (2nd ed.), (R. F. C. Hull, Trans.). Princeton, NJ: Princeton University Press. (Originally published, 1957.)

Jung, C. (1972). Two essays on analytical psychology. In H. Read, M. Fordham, & G. Adler (Eds.), *The collected works of Carl G. Jung* (Vol. 7), (2nd ed.), (R. F. C. Hull, Trans.). Princeton, NJ: Princeton University Press. (Originally published, 1928 & 1943.)

Kahn, W. (1984). The structure of exaltation. *American Behavioral Scientist, 27*(6), 705–722.

Kaseman, C., & Anderson, R. G. (1977). Clergy consultation as a community mental health program. *Community Mental Health Journal, 13,* 84–91.

Kazdin, A. (1978). Nonspecific treatment factors in psychotherapy outcome research. *Journal of Consulting and Clinical Psychology, 47,* 846–851.

Kelley, T. (1941). *A testament of devotion.* New York: Harper & Row.

Kelsey, M. (1976). *The other side of silence.* New York: Paulist.

Klerman, G. L., Rounsaville, B. J., Chevron, E., Neu, C., & Weissman, M. (1979). *Manual for short-term interpersonal psychotherapy (IPT) of depression.* Unpublished manuscript, Yale University, Department of Psychiatry, New Haven-Boston Collaborative Depression Project, New Haven.

Kobasa, S. C., Maddi, S. R., & Courington, S. (1981) Personality and constitution as mediators in the stress-illness relationship. *Journal of Health and Social Behavior, 22,* 368–378.

Kosslyn, S. M. (1980). *Image and mind.* Cambridge, MA: Harvard University Press.

Kovacs, M., & Beck, A. T. (1978). Maladaptive cognitive structures in depression. *American Journal of Psychiatry, 135,* 525–533.

Lakein, A. (1973). *How to get control of your time and your life.* New York: Wyden.

Lang, P. (1979). A bio-informational theory of emotional arousal. *Psychophysiology*, 16, 495–512.

Lang, P. (1977). Imagery in therapy: An information processing analysis of fear. *Behavior Therapy*, 8, 862–886.

Lawrence, B. (1958). *The practice of the presence of God.* (Trans. from the French.). Old Tappan, NJ: Fleming H. Revell. (Original work written ca. 1700.)

Lewinsohn, P. M., & Graf, M. (1973). Pleasant activities and depression. *Journal of Consulting and Clinical Psychology, 41*, 261–268.

Lewinsohn, P. (1974). A behavioral approach to depression. In R. M. Friedman & M. M. Katz (Eds.), *The psychology of depression: Contemporary theory and research.* Washington, DC: Winston/Wiley.

Lewis, C. S. (1947). *Miracles.* New York: Macmillan.

Linn, D., & Linn, M. (1978). *Healing life's hurts.* New York: Paulist Press.

Luck, U. (1971). *Sophronismos.* In G. Kittel & G. Friedrich (Eds.), *Theological dictionary of the New Testament* (Vol. 7, p. 1104), (G. Bromiley, trans.), Grand Rapids: W. B. Eerdmans. (Originally published, 1964.)

Mahoney, M. (Ed.). (1980). *Psychotherapy process.* New York: Plenum.

Mahoney, M. M., & Arnkoff, D. (1978). Cognitive and self-control therapies. In S. Garfield & A. Bergin (Eds.), *Handbook of psychotherapy and behavior change* (pp. 689–722). (2nd ed.). New York: John Wiley & Sons.

Mahoney, M. J., & Avener, M. (1977). Psychology of the elite athlete: An exploratory study. *Cognitive therapy and research, 1*, 130–141.

Mallory, M. (1977). *Christian mysticism: Transcendence techniques.* Amsterdam: Van Gorcum Assen.

Matthews, K. A., Glass, D. C., Rosenman, R. H., & Bortner, R. W. (1977). Competitive drive, pattern A, and coronary heart disease: A further analysis of some data for the Western Collaborative Group Study. *Journal of Chronic Diseases, 300*, 489–498.

May, R. (1958). Contributions of existential psychotherapy. In R. May, E. Angel, & H. Ellenberger (Eds.), *Existence: A new dimension in psychiatry and psychology* (pp. 37–91), New York: Basic Books.

Mead, G. H. (1934). *Mind, self and society.* Chicago: University of Chicago Press.

Meadow, M. J., & Kahoe, R. (1984). *Psychology of religion.* New York: Harper & Row.

Meichenbaum, D. (1973). *Therapist manual for cognitive behavior modification.* Unpublished manuscript, University of Waterloo, Department of psychology, Waterloo, Ontario, Canada.

Meichenbaum, D., & Cameron, R. (1973). *Stress inoculation: A skills training approach to anxiety management.* Unpublished manuscript, University of Waterloo.

Merton, T. (1955). *No man is an island.* New York: Harcourt Brace Jovanovich.

Merton, T. (1961). *New seeds of contemplation.* New York: New Directions.

Merton, T. (1971). *Contemplative prayer.* New York: Doubleday & Company.

Metz, J. B. (1968). *Poverty of spirit.* (J. Drury, Trans.). New York: Paulist.

Michel, O. (1967). *Metamelogomai.* In G. Kittel & G. Friedrich (Eds.), *Theological dictionary of the New Testament* (Vol. 4, pp. 626–629), (G. Bromiley, Trans.). Grand Rapids: W. B. Eerdmans. (originally published, 1942.)

Miller, N., & Dollard, J. (1941). *Social learning and imitation.* New Haven: Yale University Press.

Moltmann, J. (1974). *The crucified God.* (R. Wilson & J. Bowden, trans.). New York: Harper & Row. (Originally published, 1973.)

Monte, C. (1980). *Beneath the mask: An introduction to theories of personality.* New York: Holt, Rinehart & Winston.

Niebuhr, R. (1953). *The nature and destiny of man: A Christian interpretation: Vol. 1, Human Nature.* New York: Charles Scribner's Sons.

Niebuhr, R. (1955). *The self and the dramas of history.* New York: Charles Scribner's Sons.

Novaco, R. (1979). The cognitive regulation of anger and stress. In P. Kendall & S. Hollon (Eds.) *Cognitive-behavioral interventions* (pp. 241–286). New York: Academic Press.

Noy, P. (1969). A revision of the psychoanalytic theory of the primary process. *International Journal of Psychoanalysis, 50,* 155–178.

O'Hara, E. (1984). Thomas Merton as spiritual guide. *Contemplative Review, 17* (4), 13–25.

Oden, T. (1967). *Contemporary theology and psychotherapy.* Philadelphia: Westminster.

Paivio, A. (1971). *Imagery and verbal processes.* New York: Holt.

Pearlin, L. I., & Liberman, M. A. (1977). Social sources of emotional distress. In R. Simmons (Eds.), *Research in community and mental health.* Greenwich, CT: JAI Press.

Peck, M. S. (1978). *The road less traveled.* New York: Simon & Schuster.

Plaskow, J. (1980). *Sex, sin and grace.* Washington, DC: University press of America.

Prince, R. (1973). Mystical experience and the certainty of belonging: An alternative to insight and suggestion in psychotherapy. In R. Cox (Ed.), *Religious systems and psychotherapy.* Springfield, IL: Charles C. Thomas.

Prioleau, L. Murdock, M. & Brody, N. (1983). An analysis of psychotherapy versus placebo studies. *The Behavioral and Brain Sciences, 6,* 275–310.

Propst, L. R. (1980). The comparative efficacy of religious and non-religious imagery for the treatment of mild depression in religious individuals. *Cognitive Therapy and Research, 4,* 167–178.

Propst, L. R. (1982) Servanthood redefined: Coping mechanisms for women within Protestant Christianity. *Journal of Pastoral Counseling, 17*(1), 14–18.

Propst, L. R., Ostrom, R., Watkins, P., & Morris, M. (1984, June). *Preliminary report of the comparative efficacy of religious and non-religious cognitive-behavioral therapy for the treatment of clinical depression in religious individuals.* Paper presented at the meeting of the society for Psychotherapy Research, Banff, Canada.

Rehm, L. P. (1977). A self-control model of depression. *Behavior Therapy, 8,* 787–804.

Rehm, L. P. (1982). *Self-control Manual-VIIa: Treatment for depression with combined behavioral and cognitive targets.* Unpublished manuscript, University of Houston, Department of Psychology, Houston.

Rogers, C. (1961). *On becoming a person.* Boston: Houghton Mifflin.

Ross, M., & Olson, J. (1981). An expectancy-attribution model of the effects of placebos. *Psychological Review, 88* (5), 408–437.

Rothbaum, F., Weisz, J., & Snyder, S. (1982). Changing the world and changing the self: A two-process model of perceived control. *Journal of Personality and Social Psychology, 42,* 5–37.

Rounsaville, B. J., Prusoff, B., & Weissman, M. (1980). The course of marital disputes in depressed women: A 48-month follow-up study. *Comprehensive Psychiatry, 21,* 111–118.

St. Augustine. (1963). *The confessions of St. Augustine* (R. Warner, Trans.). New York: New American Library. (Written ca. 401.)

St. Ignatius (1951). *The spiritual exercises of St. Ignatius.* (Louis J. Puhl, S. J., trans.). Chicago: Loyola University Press. (Originally published, 1548.)

St. John of the Cross. (1959). *Dark night of the soul.* (E. A. Peers, Trans.). New York: Doubleday. (Written, 1577.)

Sahakian, W. (1974). *Psychology of personality: Readings in Theory* (2nd ed.). Chicago: Rand McNally.

Schrenk, G. (1964). *Dikaiosune.* In G. Kittel & G. Friedrich (Eds.), *Theological dictionary of the New Testament* (Vol. 2, 192–210), (G. Bromiley, Trans.). Grand Rapids: W. B. Eerdmans. (Originally published, 1935.)

Seligman, M. (1975). *Helplessness: On depression, development, and death.* San Francisco: W. H. Freeman & Co.

Shapiro, D. (1980). *Meditation: Self regulation strategy and altered state of consciousness.* Chicago: Aldine.

Shapiro, D. H., & Zifferblatt, S. (1976). Zen meditation and behavioral self-control: Similarities, differences, and clinical applications. *American Psychologist, 31,* 519–532.

Shore, J. H., & Manson, S. (1981). Cross-cultural studies of depression among American Indians and Alaskan natives. *White Cloud Journal, 2,* 5–11.

Spilka, B., Hood, R., & Gorsuch, R. (1985). *The psychology of religion: An empirical approach.* Englewood Cliffs, NJ: Prentice-Hall.

Stahlin, G., & Grundmann, W. (1964). *Harmartia.* In G. Kittel & G. Friedrich (Eds.), *Theological dictionary of the New Testament* (Vol. 1, pp. 267–316), (G. Bromiley, trans.). Grand Rapids: W. B. Eerdmans. (Originally published, 1933.)

Teresa of Avila, (1961). *Interior Castle* (E. A. Peers, Trans.). New York: Doubleday. (Originally published, 1577.)

Tozer, A. W. (1948). *The pursuit of God.* Harrisburg, PA: Christian Publications.

Underhill, E. (1930). *Mysticism* (12th ed.). New York: New American Library.

Van Kaam, A. (1976). *The dynamics of spiritual self-direction.* Denville, NJ: Dimension Books.

Wachtel, P. (1977). *Psychoanalysis and behavior therapy: Toward an integration.* New York: Basic Books.

Walsh, R. (1983). Meditation practice and research. *Journal of Humanistic Psychology, 23*(1), 18–50.

Weissman, M., & Paykel, E. (1974). *The depressed woman: A study of social relationships.* Chicago: University of Chicago Press.

Wells, B. W. (1980). *Personality and heredity.* London: Longman.

Wheeler, D., & Janis, I. (1980) *A practical guide for making decisions.* New York: Free Press.

White, S. (1984). Imago Dei and object relations theory: Implications for a model of human development. *Journal of Psychology and Theology, 12,* 286–293.

Wilkins, W. (1979). Expectancies in therapy research: Discriminating among heterogeneous nonspecifics. *Journal of Consulting and Clinical Psychology, 47,* 837–845.

Wilkins, W. (1983). Failure of placebo groups to control for non-specific events in therapy outcome reseach. *Psychotherapy: Theory, Research and Practice, 20* (1), 31–37.

Willams, M. (1981). *The Velveteen Rabbit.* Philadelphia: Running Press.

Woolfolk, R., & Lehrer, P. (Eds.). (1984). *Principles and practice of stress management.* New York: Guilford.

Woolfolk, R. L., & Richardson, F. (1978). *Stress, sanity and survival.* New York: Sovereign Books.

Zeig, J. (1982). *Ericksonian approaches to hypnosis and psychotherapy.* New York: Brunner/Mazel.

Zuroff, D. C., & Schwartz, J. C. (1978) Effects of Transcendental Meditation and muscle relaxation on trait anxiety, maladjustment, locus of control, and drug use. *Journal of Consulting and Clinical Psychology, 46,* 264–271.

FOOTNOTES

Chapter 2. Beyond Counseling

1. Gay (1979), however, contends that Freud's earliest view of ritual and religion in his 1907 essay, "Obsessive Acts and Religious Practices" saw ritual and religion not as repression but as suppression. And ritualistic suppression, Gay contends, is not necessarily neurotic in Freud's model, but rather a typical action of the ego as it controls biological impulses to enable the individual to adapt to his world. Thus, one is not necessarily unconsciously denying certain aspects of oneself as in repression. Rather, in suppression, the individual chooses not to express certain impulses for a particular reason. According to Gay, Freud felt the ego often used rituals to accomplish this suppression. Repetitious reenactment of specific behaviors allows the individual to function smoothly. Religion, therefore, could be a coping tool for the ego.

Chapter 4. Self-Knowledge

1. These themes or archetypes are considered by Jung to be the cumulative effect of perpetually repeated experiences on the human nervous system's development. It is the subjective emotional reaction to the event that is impressed on human unconscious mental processes, and it is this emotional reaction that is inherited (Jung, 1928/1972). The major difficulty among contemporary thinkers with Jung's view of archetypes is their genetic impossibility.

Jung has done a heroic job of attempting to reconcile biology and psychology. However, he has rejected current scientific thinking in genetics. Essentially, his theory of archetypes contends that the psychological features characteristic of the mental content and processes of all human beings may be transmitted from generation to generation much as anatomy is inherited. This requires a Lamarchian genetics rather than the more accepted Mendelian genetics. Lamarck had contended that characteristics acquired during one's lifetime, due to extensive use, could be inherited. Thus, this theory would contend that giraffes gradually acquired longer necks because they stretched them during their lifetime to reach food in the trees. These acquired characteristics were then passed on to the next generation. Similarly, Jung's view of archetypes contends that ideas important to one generation are passed onto the next generation (cf. Wells, 1980).

CHAPTER 5. TRANSFORMATION

1. The Oxford English Dictionary defines rationalism as "the principle of regarding reason as the chief or only guide in matters of religion."

INDEX